JEWISH HISTORY
and
YOU

VOLUME 2

from the Renaissance to the 21st. Century

with Documents and Texts

ישראל

by Sol Scharfstein

This book
is lovingly dedicated
to my parents
Asher and Feiga
of
blessed memory
They are my History

Copyright 2003
KTAV Publishing House, Inc.

Library of Congress Cataloging-in-Publication Data

Scharfstein, Sol. 1921-
 Jewish History and You II / Sol Scharfstein; design & graphics by Oscar Rijo

 ISBN 0-88125-806-7

1. Jewish–History–Juvenile Literature

96-11250
CIP

Printed in Hong kong

Numerous multitalented people have worked hard to bring Jewish History and You to life. They believed in the project and labored long and arduosly, critiquing, editing, updating, and researching.

I wish to thank the following for their expert assistance. It is their, sensibility, sensitivity, and scholarship that have shaped the text.

Robert Milch
Bernard Scharfstein
Robert Shappiro
Adam Bengal

The final responsability for any omissions, errors and mistakes is my own

Table of Contents

Introduction

Jewish history is unique. Great ancient civilizations such as the Babylonians, Greeks, and Romans have risen and fallen, but the tiny Jewish nation, despite deportations, persecutions, and holocausts, has miraculously survived. The Jewish people is special, not only because it has existed so long with its unique religion, culture, and heritage; it is also unique because of the conditions under which it has survived. From the very beginning, the Jews came into close contact with other peoples, nations and civilizations. Throughout its history, the Jewish people has always been a minority in its political, religious, economic, and cultural environments. Yet, it did not disappear under the impact of powerful antagonistic governments.

Jewish History and You is about the people and events that molded Jewish history. It goes far beyond that! *Jewish History and You* is about all the many places where Jewish history took place: the ancient Kingdom of Israel, Babylonia, Africa, Europe, America, and wherever the Wandering Jew settled. In addition to facts and figures, people, places, and events, the book chronicles the story of the giants of the spirit, communal leaders, scholars, and military heroes who have earned eternity for their courage, tenacity, vitality, and dedication to the preservation of Jewish peoplehood. It is the story of their unbelievable strength in the face of the dangers and hardships and tragic events in which they often met their death. It also is the story of the miraculous rebirth of the State of Israel.

Jewish History and You is about your ancestors. I hope that it will help you relive that unbelievable 4,000-year journey from the fields of the Fertile Crescent to the miraculous establishment of the State of Israel and beyond.

It is a saga that will make you proud of your heritage and, I hope, inspire you to continue your Jewish history studies.

Sol Scharfstein

About the Text

Jewish History and You II offers concise information about events, people, religious movements, and heroes from the Middle Ages to the present time. *Jewish History and You II* consists of 42 profusely illustrated four–page narrative units. Each of the narrative units consists of a three–page article and a one–page historical document. Each document is preceded by a short introduction and ends with a series of questions related to the historical narrative, the source document, and you.

The source documents will involve students in an open inquiry and provide "free play" for historical and document analysis. The document analysis will train students to evaluate modern political events and movements in the light of the Jewish historical experience.

The Ghetto

The Franciscan priest Giovanni da Capistrano preaching one of his many anti-Semitic sermons. ca. 1430. Capistrano conducted constant anti-Jewish campaigns. He was an inquisitor and instrumental in imposing anti-Jewish restrictions in Germany, Italy, and Poland. For his good deeds, he was canonized in 1690.

After the Black Death epidemic in about 1350, Jews were allowed to live only in specific designated neighborhoods of a city. In time, this quarter was enclosed by walls and towers. The street or quarter where the Jews lived was called the ghetto.

The first ghetto was established in Venice. It was next to a cannon factory and was designated with the Italian word for "foundry," *getto*. Some, however, believe that ghetto comes from the Hebrew word *get*, meaning "divorce," indicating that ghettoization separated and divorced the Jews from the general population.

The ghetto was a crowded section with housing almost always inadequate. The houses had to be built high and close together in order to accommodate as many people as possible. The ghetto was enclosed in the oldest part of the cities, so that the Jews had to live away from the woods, the fields, and fresh, clean air.

Jews had to return to the ghetto at a certain hour and were not free to leave it at night. On Sundays and Christian holidays, they were not allowed to leave the ghetto at all.

The ghettos were surrounded by a wall and gates, guarded by non-Jewish watchmen who controlled the entry and exit of those imprisoned inside. Outside of the ghetto, Jews had to wear yellow badges and specially designed hats. These opened them to ridicule and attack.

Jews as Object Lessons

The position of the Jew is only one example that shows how little human life and dignity counted in medieval Europe, but it is one of the most glaring and disgraceful of examples. In medieval society, everyone was expected to remain in his own station in life. Everyone had to hold to the beliefs and practice the way of life acceptable to the king and the church or suffer the consequences. Those who did not would find themselves excluded from a guild, or if they were a town burgher, from the merchant's league.

Jews had to live in oppression and poverty as a penalty for rejecting Jesus, but they also had to survive as witnesses to Jesus's life. The Jews were intended to serve as an object lesson, an example of how people would suffer if they decided to live independently of the church and outside Christian society. Like the Jews, those who did so would be treated as despised outcasts.

Pope Paul IV

Paul IV argued that it was foolish for Christians to be friendly to a people that had not accepted Christ as their savior. In a papal bull, he decreed that Jews living in areas controlled by the church were to be confined in ghettos. They would be permitted to leave the ghetto in daytime to go to work, but forbidden to be outside at other times. The ghetto gates were to be closed at night and on Christian holidays. The pope also decreed that Jews were to wear yellow stars and pointed hats for quick identification. In a short time, these practices spread from Italy to the rest of Europe.

Blood Purity

The archbishop of Toledo, in Spain, in 1547, issued the Statute of Toledo called *limpieza de sangre* or "blood purity." According to this statute, no one of Jewish blood could hold a religious office in the church. In a short time, the Inquisition extended such *limpieza* statutes to other institutions: universities, guilds, and political jobs.

In 1555, Pope Paul IV adopted the *limpieza* and forbade Jews to possess any religious books except the Bible. To enforce the prohibition, he abolished Hebrew printing in Rome. *The limpieza* regulations remained on the books of Catholic religious orders until the 20th century. The statutes were the ancestors of the Nazi Nuremberg Laws.

Economic Restrictions

Economic regulations reduced the ability of Jews to earn a livelihood. Restrictions on commerce and banking deprived them of the ability to compete. Only two occupations were unrestricted: trade in second-hand

In 1417, the Jews of Constance, Germany, offered a Torah scroll to Pope Martin V, with a request that their privilege be restored. He replied, "You have the law but do not understand it. The old has passed away and the new has been found."

Jews were accused of using Christian blood for making matzot. This anti-Semitic picture shows Jews drawing blood from their victims.

Medieval painting of a Hebrew teacher and his young pupil. Note the whip and hourglass. Germany, 13th cent.

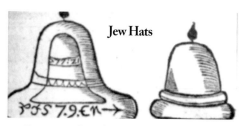

Jew Hats

Jews were forced to wear yellow stars and pointed hats for quick idenification.

A street in the Jewish ghetto in Venice.

merchandise and pawnbroking. People who for one reason or another needed a small loan brought something to sell or to leave in pawn. Poor people were thankful for a chance to buy good second-hand clothing cheaply. However, the Christian merchants who sold expensive new clothing objected to the competition.

The Communal Structure

Ghetto communities were usually governed by a council elected by the residents. The council was responsible for the ghetto's relations with the city government, and, in particular, was charged with collecting whatever taxes the government levied on the Jews. In addition, it supervised the ghetto's synagogue, schools, courts, charities, and other communal institutions.

Life in the Ghetto

Despite all the restrictions and humiliating laws, a vigorous Jewish life unfolded inside the ghetto walls. Occasional plunderers and aggressors might enter the ghetto from outside, but the rules of life that guided the community and the synagogue remained intact.

The medieval Jews cherished their heritage. The rabbi and merchants who were scholars usually were the leaders of the community. They led the people in prayer and communal affairs and organized the schools.

The heart of life for medieval Jews was the home. In the home, the father, the mother, and their children celebrated Sabbaths and holidays. The Jewish family worked together to uphold the traditions of Judaism.

Beginning at the age of five, Jewish boys started the study of Hebrew, then went on to the study of the Torah, the Prophets, and other books of the Bible, the Talmud, and the great works of the later scholars. The girls were instructed at home to become good Jewish women, to uphold the Jewish traditions, and to keep the home pleasant and neat. Some girls were also taught at home by their mothers to read and write.

THE FIRST GHETTO

The Jews in Italy and Germany were subjected to degrading laws, and the boundaries of their lives became narrowed and limited. The church, for thousands of years, used its power to preach contempt of the Jews and to have little to do with them. The expulsion from Spain spread the idea that the Jews were social lepers and were not fit to live in Christian society. Martin Luther, the founder of the Protestant Movement, advised the extermination of the Jews. In addition to religious opposition, the Christian merchants also wanted to rid themselves of Jewish competition. However, the Christian kings who ruled some of the important cities needed the income, which Jews poured into their treasuries. The rulers compromised by building ghettos for their Jewish subjects. One of the first ghettos was established in 1516 by the Senate in Venice.

. . . all Jews who at present are found residing in the various streets of this our city, as well as those who might come from elsewhere, shall, until it will be differently decided in accordance with the exigencies of the time, be obligated to proceed to dwell together in the kind of houses located in the ghetto next to the Church of St. Jerome.

The Jews of Venice: Cecil Roth

WHAT DO YOU THINK?

1. *Why did the Christian merchants want to rid themselves of the Jews?*
2. *Why did the rulers wish to hold on to the Jews?*
3. *What was the purpose of making Jews into object lessons?*
4. *What was the* limpieza de sangre*?*
5. *Pope Paul IV decreed that the Jews had to wear yellow stars. What other country forced Jews to wear yellow stars?*
6. *Why were Jews forced to practice pawnbroking?*
7. *How has this profession been a disaster for the Jews?*
8. *Can you think of other instances of making individuals or groups into "object lessons"?*

Religious Intolerance

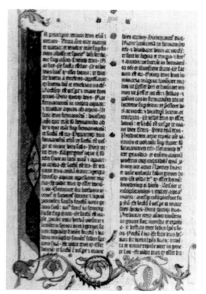

An illuminated page from Gutenberg's Bible.

Emblem of the Venetian printer Marco Antonio Giustinani.

Martin Luther, as depicted by the artist Lucas Cranach.

The Coming of a New Age

The 15th and 16th centuries–the period during which the tragic expulsion of the Jews from Spain and Portugal took place–witnessed many great social, technical, and religious changes.

New inventions radically transformed life everywhere. One of these was the printing press. As a result of the increased availability of books, people became more interested in learning and many were eager to read the Bible. Indeed, the Bible (in Latin) was the first book to be printed.

Martin Luther

In Germany, the new learning gave rise to a religious movement known as the Reformation. Martin Luther, the first to translate the Bible into German, opposed the power of the Catholic Church and strove to replace it with a reformed Christianity.

Martin Luther was in close contact with Jews, from whom he learned the Hebrew language in order to be able to translate the Bible into German. Until that time, the Bible had existed only in the original Hebrew and in the Latin and Greek versions, which could be read only by the educated and the clergy. By translating it into a modern language, Luther wanted to make it possible for each and every person to read the Bible.

Luther was anxious to convert the Jews to his new way of Christianity. When he realized that the Jews refused his new approach to Christianity just as firmly as they had refused the older church, he was greatly disappointed. Once friendly toward the Jews, he now became their enemy, expressing his hostile attitude in articles and speeches. His followers soon adopted the same attitude toward the Jews of Germany as that held by their Catholic opponents. The German Jews were bitterly disappointed, for they had hoped that the rise of the new Chrisianity would bring about an improvement in their position.

Four hundred and fifty-five years later, the Lutheran bishop of Thuringia, Martin Sasse, exulted, "On November 10, 1938, on Luther's birthday, the synagogues are burning in Germany." The bishop was referring, of course, to Kristallnacht. His joy was expressed in the foreword to his collection of Luther's anti-Jewish diatribes. He prayed that people would take to heart the words, as he put it, "of the greatest anti–Semite of his time, the warner of his people against the Jews."

The Apology

After 600 years, and tens of millions of murders, tortures, fires, drownings, hangings, and a Holocaust, one of the Lutheran branches issued an apology. In 1994, the Evangelical Lutheran Church in America issued a declaration repenting "Luther's anti-Judaic diatribes and violent recommendations against the Jews." Just one tiny branch from a deeply rooted, poisoned tree nurtured by Catholic, Prostestant, and Muslim hierarchies has fallen.

Protestants and Catholics

The new Protestant denominations that came to life in the Reformation and separated themselves from the Roman Catholic Church represented a grave threat to its unity. As a result, the church adopted stern measures to guard against the spread of Reformation influences. Protestants and Catholics became involved in a bitter struggle, each faction bent on proving itself more truly Christian than the other and vying with the other in performing pious acts. Both Catholic and Protestant rulers persecuted heretics and imposed new restrictions on the Jews.

Wherever Jews were permitted to live in Western and Central Europe, except in the tolerant Netherlands, there were ghettos. Jews were set apart and crowded into these confined residential areas, their freedom restricted. Of course, the bait of conver-

Painting by Hieronymus Hess, in the art museum of Basel, Switzerland. The Jews were forced to attend conversion sermons by Catholic priests. Note the priest slapping a Jew for snickering or for falling asleep.

Gate of the Jewish ghetto in Vienna.

A Jewish physician checks a Hebrew medical manuscript.

Italy was home to numerous Jewish physicians. Jacobo Mantino was the personal physician of Pope Paul III. Amatus Lusitanus returned to Judaism in Italy and made many contributions to medical research.

The logo of the printer and publisher Gershon Soncino. The book is called *Sefer Kol Bo,* and was printed in Rimini, Italy, in 1536. The Soncino firm was famous for the quality of its publications.

Entrance to the old ghetto in Rome.

sion was always held out to anyone who would accept it. But nearly all Jews disregarded this alternative and steadfastly clung to the heritage of their ancestors.

The Communal Structure

Ghetto communities were usually governed by a council elected by the residents. The council was responsible for the ghetto's relations with the city government, and, in particular, was charged with collecting whatever taxes the government levied on the Jews. In addition it supervised the ghetto's synagogue, schools, courts, charities, and other communal institutions.

The Jews of Italy

Although ghetto walls had been erected in Italy, the Italian Jews lived under far better conditions than their brethren in the rest of Europe. Sometimes, they became traders or bankers, although their commercial activities were restricted, as was true all over Europe,

Italy attracted persecuted Jews from both Spain and Germany. Spanish Jewish merchants, seafarers, mapmakers, doctors, bankers, and scholars all settled in Italy. Jewish printers from Germany settled in northern Italy, where they produced editions of the Talmud, the Bible, and the prayerbook. The most famous of these printers was the Soncino family, whose name was revived by a group of Jewish bibliophiles in Germany before World War II, and adopted by a London publishing house that still prints Jewish books, including an English translation of the entire Talmud.

Watercolor of the synagogue on the Piazza delle Scuole in Rome in 1837. Its two wings served the five main congregations of the Roman Jews after the papal edict of 1555, limiting each ghetto to only one synagogue. The synagogue was in continous use for 350 years. It was torn down in 1893 after a disastrous fire.

MARTIN LUTHER, ENEMY OF THE JEWS

Luther hated Jews because they refused to convert to Christianity. His hate and anti–Semitic diatribes have been the cause of pogroms, expulsions, and tens of millions of murders.
Here are Luther's ideas for dealing with the Jews.

First, their synagogues or churches should be set on fire, and whatever does not burn up should be covered or spread over with dirt so that no one may ever be able to see a cinder or stone of it. Secondly, their homes should likewise be broken down and destroyed.

Thirdly, they should be deprived of their prayerbooks and Talmuds in which such idolatry, lies, cursing, and blasphemy are taught.

Fourthly, their rabbis must be forbidden under threat of death to teach anymore.

Fifthly, passport and traveling privileges should be absolutely forbidden to the Jews . . .

Sixthly, they ought to be stopped from usury. All their cash and valuables of silver and gold ought to be taken from them and put aside for safekeeping. Seventhly, let the young and strong Jews and Jewesses be given the flail, the ax, the hoe, the spade, the distaff, and spindle, and let them earn their bread by the sweat of their noses as is enjoined upon Adam's children . Let us drive them out of the country for all time. For, as has been said, God's rage is so great against them that they only become worse and worse through mild mercy, and not much better through severe mercy. Therefore away with them . . .

If this does not help, we must drive them out like mad dogs, so that we do not become partakers of their abominable blasphemy and all their other vices and thus merit God's wrath and be damned with them. I have done my duty. Now let everyone see to his. I am exonerated.

Finally I wish to say this for myself: If God were to give me no other Messiah than such as the Jews wish and hope for, I would much, much rather be a pig than a human being.

About the Jews and Their Lies, 1543.

WHAT DO YOU THINK

1. **Why did Martin Luther hate the Jews?**
2. **What branch of Christianity did Martin Luther detest?**
   Why did he hate them?
3. **The Protestant Reformation taught that every individual could find his way to God without the help of intermediaries.**
   Were Luther's views on Judaism and Catholicism in tune with the spirit of the Reformation?
4. **Luther says that he would rather be a pig than a Jew. Do you think he was a bigot?**
5. **How have Luther ideas provided a framework for anti-Semitism?**
6. **How did Luther's ideas lead to the Holocaust?**

The Shtadlanim

Joseph Suess Oppenheimer
(1698–1738)

The tax position of Jews was unenviable. Taxes were imposed upon Jewish communities as a whole, and it was the responsibility of their own councils to see that the taxes were paid. Some taxes were levied on consumer goods, particularly slaughtered animals, others directly on income. These collection boxes *(right)*, built for safety in the gallery of the Old-New Synagogue in Prague, are from the 17th century.

The Shtadlan

The Jews of the Middle Ages managed to develop a well-organized system of internal self-government, much the same as the Jewish communities of ancient Babylonia. Rabbis, scholars and *dayanim* (rabbinical judges) were the leaders of the communities.

Grievances and legal cases of all kinds were taken to the Jewish court of law, the Bet-Din or, in a small town, to the rabbi. Often, all the communities of a realm or a land would choose one learned and righteous man to represent them at the court of the prince; or when the cities grew more powerful, before the city council. Such a representative was called a *shtadlan*.

The rulers of Europe in the 17th and 18th centuries needed people who were loyal and had the skills to supply their financial needs. They also needed people to represent them on confidential diplomatic missions, provide military supplies, and supply difficult-to-locate luxury items. This delicate and difficult role was often filled by court Jews or *shtadlanim*, who were dependent upon the monarch for protection and remained neutral in the power struggles raging between the clergy, nobles, and rising expectations of the general populace. The presence of a shtadlan at a royal court helped the Jews return to cities and countries from which they had been expelled.

Shtadlanim were the spokesmen for the Jewish community in dealings with town councils and governments. The shtadlanim sought to prevent persecution and defended the interests of the Jewish community. Some were rabbis, others were linguists, and some had widespread business connections and diplomatic skills.

Some of the shtadlanim used their skills and connections to establish banks and trading companies. A great many had far-flung financial connections with Jewish and non-Jewish commercial and industrial trading houses.

16

Joseph Suess Oppenheimer

Court Jews faced great opportunities and great dangers. Samuel Oppenheimer (1630–1703) loyally served Emperor Leopold I of Austria for 30 years, yet died penniless. Joseph Suess Oppenheimer (1698–1738) was shtadlan for Duke Charles I Alexander of Wuerttemberg, managing his estates and business enterprises. After the duke's death, Jude Suess, as he was called, was imprisoned and hanged in a public ceremony. Oppenheimer refused the offers of the clergy to save his life on the condition that he convert to Christianity. He is said to have died reciting the Shema Yisrael.

Samuel Oppenheimer, (1630-1703), Austrian court Jew.

Yosel of Rosheim

The outstanding shtadlan of 16th-century German Jewry was Yosel (Josel or Joselmann) of Rosheim, a town in Alsace (1480–1554). When still a young boy, he had seen all the members of his family perish as martyrs. Yosel traveled throughout Germany to carry out the task entrusted to him—the defense of the Jewish communities against attack.

Yosel was an active and talented financier, with an excellent background of Jewish learning. In addition to his practical work on behalf of his people, he managed to write two scholarly works, and in the course of his many diplomatic missions he engaged in debate with princes and priests who attacked the Talmud and other Jewish writings.

During the reign of Charles V, ruler of the Holy Roman Empire, when the Jewish communities were threatened with persecution and expulsion by both the

Anti-Semitic picture of Yosel of Rosheim, the Court Jew of Emperor Charles V. In one hand is a Hebrew Bible, in the other, a bag of money.

The public hanging of Joseph Suess Oppenheimer, whose corpse was then displayed in an iron cage. The anti-Semites used accusations against Oppenheimer to spread their message of hate.

Catholics and the Protestants, Yosel traveled hundreds of miles on diplomatic missions. He was not always successful, but many communities owed their peace and, indeed, their very lives to his efforts. The great community of Prague, in Bohemia, was saved from expulsion by Yosel. He kept a diary in which he recorded many of his experiences during his 40 years as shtadlan of the Jews of Germany. These notes have been preserved to this day.

The lives of Yosel of Rosheim, the Jewish shtadlan, and Martin Luther, the leader of the German Protestant Reformation, covered almost the same span: Luther's from 1483 to 1546 and Yosel's from 1480 to 1554.

Jost Liebmann

Jost Liebmann was a shtadlan in the court of King Frederick William I of Prussia. When he died, his wife, Esther, inherited the position and became the shatadlan-it. However, after the death of her benefactor, King Frederick William, she was imprisoned and fined for accumulating excessive profits.

Samsom Wertheimer (1658-1724)

Samson Wertheimer was a scholar, shtadlan, and a philanthropist. He married the widow of Nathan Oppenheimer. Through her family's influence he was introduced to Emperor Leopold I and became the chief administrator of his financial affairs. The emperor had great confidence in Wertheimer and entrusted him with numerous diplomatic missions. He was known by the title *Judenkaiser* (Jewish Emperor) and his home was guarded by imperial soldiers. Wertheimer successfully intervened on behalf of Jewish communities in the empire that were ravaged by war and anti-Semitism. Samson was a scholar and financed the printing of the Babylonian Talmud. He built several large synagogues and was in charge of the transfer of money collected throughout Europe for the Holy Land. In his old age, Wertheimer retired and his son Wolf succeeded him. His son was also active on behalf of Jewish communities in the empire.

Samsom Wertheimer

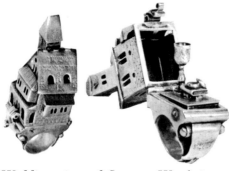

Wedding ring of Samson Wertheimer, Eisenstadt, Austria, 1690, closed and open. Inscribed are the names of the owner and Rabbi Meir ben Isaac, who performed the ceremony.

MORDECAI MEISELS THE SHTADLAN

Mordecai Meisels (1528-1601) was a wealthy financier who used his influence with the Hapsburg rulers to protect the Jews of Prague. With his own money, he built a beautiful synagogue, the Jewish Town Hall with the dual Roman and Hebrew clock, a public bath-house, and a shelter for the poor and needy. His financial ability brought him to the attention of the emperor who depended upon him for advice on financial matters. For many years, he served the emperor honestly and faithfully. Three years before his death, he received a guarantee from the emperor that his estate would pass on to his heirs. But when Meisels died in 1601, the emperor simply confiscated all his wealth. The following excerpt describes the emperor's confiscation of Meisel's estate.

From Prague, the 5th Day of April, 1601.
A short time ago there died here the Jew Meisels. He died during the night between the 13th and 14th of March. Notwithstanding that he had left his imperial Majesty 10,000 florins, and much cash also to the hospital for poor Christians and Jews, his imperial Majesty on the following Saturday, viz., the Sabbath of the Jews, ordered Herr von Sternberg, at that time president of the Bohemian Chamber, to enter the Jew's house forcibly and to seize everything there was. The widow of Meisels handed this over willingly, for she had already set aside and hidden the best part of the treasure. That which was taken away came to 45,000 florins in cash, besides all manner of other things, such as silver plate, promissory notes, jewels, clothes, and all kinds of coins. After this, however, the president, against whom the Jewess and the sons of the two brothers of Meisels had raised a strong protest to the privy councillors, was not satisfied with all this money and booty, and no doubt at the command of his Majesty, once more broke into the house at night. The son of one of the brothers was taken prisoner, secretly led away, and tortured in such guise that he confessed to the executioners, as a result of which 520,000 florins was handed to the Bohemian Chamber.

In those days Meisels was considered a millionaire.

30,000 Salzburg turnip ducats of 2 florins apiece make	......	60,000 florins
10,000 Styrian ducats of 2 florins apiece make	....	20,000 florins
60,000 silver thalers of 70 kreuzer apiece make	....	70,000 florins
Together with the above-mentioned	....	45,000 florins
Make altogether	....	516,250 florins

WHAT DO YOU THINK?

I. Was Meisels aware of the duplicity of the emperor whom he had faithfully served?
2. How did Meisels try to protect the finances of his suvivors?
3. What are promisory notes?
4. Do you think the emperor would try to collect on Meisels's promissory notes?
5. The Arabs, after the establishment of Israel, drove almost a million Jews out of their countries and confiscated their property. Have they repaid the Jews for their property and valuables?

The Jews of Turkey

Doña Gracia Mendes

In the 14th and 15th centuries, the Ottoman Turks conquered Anatolia, the Fertile Crescent, and many European lands, including Greece, Albania, Bulgaria, Romania, Bosnia, and Serbia. Their capture of Constantinople in 1453 ended the long history of the Byzantine Empire.

There had been Jews living in the Ottoman territories since ancient times. After the expulsions from Spain and Portugal, their numbers were greatly increased by exiles seeking a new home, and in the 16th century, a flourishing Jewish community developed in the Ottoman domain. The port of Salonica in northern Greece became a major center of Jewish life and commerce.

The Turkish sultans welcomed the Jewish merchants, bankers, and physicians from Spain, and put their talents to good use. Jews rose to high positions at the Ottoman court, serving as ambassadors and advisors.

Solomon Ashkenazi / 1520–1600

It was as if the golden age of Spanish rule had returned once more in the lands of the East. Jewish diplomats were sent from Constantinople to the courts of Europe. Solomon Ashkenazi, a learned Jewish physician, became Turkey's ambassador to Venice, where he negotiated a peace treaty in 1571. Later, he offered Turkey's help to Venice in case of war with Spain.

When the Jews of Venice were threatened with expulsion, Ashkenazi pressured the Venetian government to revoke the order. Thanks to his efforts, the Jewish community was saved.

The Mendes Family

Gracia Mendes (1510–1569) was a Portuguese Marrano who sought refuge in Italy. The beautiful widow of a wealthy and famous banker, she had taken over her husband's business after his death.

A Jewish merchant in Turkey.

When she left Portugal, she was accompanied by her daughter Reyna and her nephew and business advisor, Joseph Nasi.

They settled in the great port of Antwerp in Belgium, which was then under Spanish rule. But when they were denounced to the Inquisition as heretics, Gracia Mendes and her family fled from Antwerp and found refuge in Venice.

There again, Gracia Mendes was denounced as a heretic who had abandoned the Catholic Church. She was imprisoned and all her wealth was confiscated. Many of her debtors cancelled their obligations, including the king of France, who owed the Mendes family great sums of money, but declared he would not pay his debt.

A Jewish wedding in Turkey

Joseph Nasi / 1520–1579

Joseph Nasi was determined to rescue his aunt and his cousin. He went to Constantinople and enlisted the help of Sultan Suleiman I. The sultan, impressed by Joseph Nasi's ability and connections, sent a letter to Venice demanding the release of Gracia Mendes.

Thanks to the sultan's intervention, Gracia Mendes was released from prison and her confiscated property was returned. She went from Venice to Ferrara, where she openly rejoined the Jewish community. When her confiscated property was returned, she proved to be a generous and compassionate woman, giving much of her time and fortune to aid troubled Jews and Marranos who were returning to Judaism. From Ferrara, Gracia Mendes and her daughter journeyed to Turkey, where Joseph Nasi and Reyna were married.

Joseph in Palestine

Joseph Nasi became the sultan's financial advisor. The young man's intelligence, tactful counsel, and charming manner made him one of the most respected personalities at the sultan's court. Joseph's knowledge of languages and his connections in many lands

Suleiman the Magnificent receiving Christian vassals as his army besieges the Hungarian town of Szigetvar.

made him an ideal diplomat, so Joseph Nasi was appointed to represent Turkey in conferences with many foreign ambassadors.

After the death of Suleiman, Joseph served his son, Selim II. The new sultan heaped many honors upon Joseph. In addition to making him duke of Naxos, a beautiful island in the Aegean Sea, he granted him the ancient city of Tiberias, in Palestine, where once the rabbis of the Mishnah had taught. Joseph hoped that large numbers of Jews and Marranos would settle in Tiberias, where they would be free from fear and oppression, and could build a new life in the land of their ancestors.

Joseph Nasi's Vision

Joseph Nasi's vision had a practical side. In Tiberias he hoped to found a new industry that would bring profit to both the Jewish settlers and the Ottoman Empire–the manufacture of silk. He rebuilt the houses and streets of Tiberias, and planted mulberry trees for the silkworms to feed upon. However, his plans were not realized. Only a few Jews were able to reach the Holy Land, for a war had broken out between Venice and Turkey and ships could not sail the Mediterranean safely. Yet, Joseph Nasi was not discouraged. At a time when few wealthy men put the ideals of charity into action, he continued to devote much of his wealth and energy to the service of his suffering brethren.

View of Istanbul, 17th cent.

JOSEPH NASI

Joseph Nasi was a friend of Sultan Selim II of the Ottoman Empire, who rewarded him and made him duke of Naxos. The sultan gave him a grant of the city of Tiberias in Palestine. Joseph endeavored to make the city self-supporting through the production of silk. The following is a selection from the book Vale of Tears *by Joseph ha-Kohen (1486-1518).*

Don Joseph Nasi came to Ferrara with those who had escaped from the iron furnace, Portugal. He lived there and then went on to Turkey, where he found favor in the eyes of Sultan Suleiman. The sultan gave him the ruins of Tiberias and seven of the villages about it, appointing him prince and chief over them at that time. Don Joseph sent Rabbi Joseph ben Ardut, his agent, there to rebuild the walls of the city.

Ardut went and found favor also in the eyes of the Prince Selim. The sultan sent eight of his own household with him, together with an order, written and sealed with the royal signet, recommending him to the pashas of Damascus and Safed, as follows: "Do everything that this man requires of you." Hence an order was issued by authority of the sultan, as follows: "All builders and laborers in those villages must report for the rebuilding of Tiberias. He who does not appear will be punished."

But the Arabs were envious of them and a certain old noble arose and cried out to the inhabitants of that region: "Don't allow them to rebuild this city, for there will be trouble later. I have indeed found written in a very old book that when the city, whose name is Tiberias, is rebuilt, our religion will be destroyed, and we shall be the sufferers." They heeded him and refused to go on with the building of the walls, with the result that the work on the walls of Tiberias ceased.

Joseph ben Ardut, being very grieved, went to the pasha of Damascus and complained before him: "I regret, my lord, but the inhabitants of the villages absolutely refuse to obey the command of the Sultan." The pasha hastened to send men there who seized two of the leaders and executed them in order that those left might see and be afraid. Again they started to dig in order to rebuild the walls of the city. The circumference of the city of Tiberias, which they rebuilt, was 500 cubits, and the work was finished in the month of Kislev, in the year 5325. And Don Joseph rejoiced very much and gave thanks to God. At his command they planted very many mulberry trees there to feed silk worms. He also ordered wool to be brought from Spain to manufacture garments just like the clothes they made in Venice, for the man Don Joseph was very great, and his fame spread throughout the land.

WHAT DO YOU THINK?

l. Was Tiberias a built-up city?

2. Why was it necessary to build walls around Tiberias?

3. Why did the pasha give Rabbi Ardut his signet ring?

4. The Arab notables incited the inhabitants to sabotage the rebuilding by the Jews because they were destroying their religion. What modern-day event reminds you of the same claim?

5. Maimonides in his Ladder of Tzedakah says that the greatest mitzvah is to help someone earn a living. How did Joseph Nasi perform this mitzvah?

Pioneers and Mystics

Magic formula from *Sefer Raziel*. This kabbalistic book was printed in Amsterdam in 1701.

Lag Ba-Omer is celebrated on the 33rd day of the counting of the Omer. It is a time for singing, dancing, bonfires, picnics, hiking, and playing with bows and arrows.

On Lag Ba-Omer Jews remember the heroes who fought the Romans, especially Simeon bar Yohai. He and his son studied Torah in a cave high on Mount Meron. Students carried bows and pretended to be hunting so the Romans would not arrest them. For 13 years, Rabbi Simeon bar Yohai was hidden in his cave. This brave rabbi died on Lag Ba-Omer.

Today, in Israel, many Jews travel to Meron on foot and by car to visit his grave.

Immigrants to Palestine

Throughout the centuries a trickle of Jewish settlers made their way to Palestine from Germany, France, Italy, and Turkey. In the aftermath of the expulsion from Spain, new immigration came to the ancient communities of Galilee in northern Palestine. A few of the Spanish refugees established themselves in Tiberias. Others went to Jerusalem, but it was in the town of Safed, in the mountains of Galilee, that the most renowned new community was founded.

Safed: City of the Kabbalah

Most important among the books that the kabbalists studied was the Zohar. To the kabbalists of Safed, Simeon bar Yohai, the tanna to whom the book was attributed, was a beloved figure. On Lag Ba-Omer, said to be the day of Simeon's death, the Jews of Safed made a pilgrimage to his grave in Meron to honor his memory with prayer, song, and dance. This practice is still followed in modern Israel.

On the Sabbath, they would dress in special garments and joyously celebrate the day of rest. The famous hymn Lekha Dodi, "Come, My Beloved," which is still chanted in the synagogue on Friday nights, was composed by Solomon Alkabetz (1505–1584), one of the great kabbalist teachers of Safed.

Moses de Leon / 1250–1305

The body of mystical lore that comprises the Kabbalah developed over centuries. In the 13th century, all these teachings were compiled in a book called the Zohar by Moses de Leon of Castile, Spain. According to Moses de Leon, the Zohar dated back to the 2nd century C.E. and had been written by Simeon bar Yohai. He claimed to have found it in the cave in which Simeon bar Yohai and his son Eliezer had hidden for 13 years during the Hadrianic persecution.

The Sefirot

The kabbalists maintained that every aspect of the Torah, even including the shapes of the letters and unusual spellings, has a secret meaning that can be uncovered through study. The hidden meanings in the Torah are set forth in the Zohar, written in Aramaic and organized as a commentary on the Torah. The Zohar retells biblical stories and events, such as the creation of the world, the divine chariot of Ezekiel, the various names of God, and the powers of angels, explaining them in a mystical way.

Individual Responsibility

The Zohar also teaches that every act of every human being on earth has an effect on the world above. When we perform good deeds, we crown the day with goodness and it becomes our protection in the world-to-come. But if we sin, it has a negative effect on the day and will destroy us in the world-to-come. Thus, good and bad deeds can build or destroy the balance of the earth. Some of the symbols developed by the mystics have been utilized in the prayer-book. The blowing of the shofar is introduced with a kabbalistic prayer. The prayer before reading the Torah, the Berikh Shemei, is from the Zohar.

Rabbi Isaac Luria

The greatest teacher of Kabbalah in Safed was Rabbi Isaac Luria (1534-1572). Born in Jerusalem, he lost his father when he was a child, but was brought to Cairo, where he was educated under the care of his uncle.

When Rabbi Isaac Luria came to Safed, he found many devoted, enthusiastic students there devoting themselves to the joys of mystical speculation, prayer, and the time of eternal peace.

Rabbi Luria's personality and unique approach to kabbalistc study won him the affection and loyalty of Safed's mystical community. After he died at the early age of 38, they preserved his teachings and transmitted them to later generations.

Luria's disciples referred to him as the Ari, an acronym for Adoneinu Rabbi Yitzhak ("Our Master

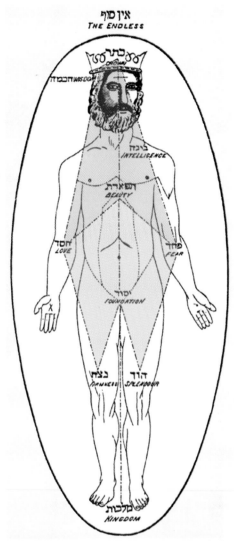

According to the Kabbalah, each of the sefirot of the Tree of Life corresponds to a part of the human body. These power centers are energy spheres which control the physical, mental, and psychological functions of the human being. When they are operating properly, they provide the individual with special abilities of perception and creativity.

THE TEN SEFIROT

Binah	=Understanding,
Hokmah	=Wisdom,
Hesed	=Mercy,
Hod	=Splendor,
Gevurah	=Strength,
Keter	=Crown
Malkut	=Kingdom,
Netzah	=Might,
Tifarah	=Beauty,
Yesod	=Foundation.

Hebrew emblem of the Italian printer Abraham Usque.

Title page of Don Isaac Abravanel's commentary to the Later Prophets.

Title page of the Shulchan Arukh. It lists 20 different commentators. Included is the commentary by Moses Isserles.

Rabbi Isaac"). Ari is the Hebrew word meaning "lion," and the disciples of Rabbi Isaac considered him to be mighty as a lion in mystical knowledge.

Two Approaches to Judaism

Many talmudic scholars at first regarded the kabbalists as dangerous. The kabbalist life-style, they said, differed from the life of the scholars. As time went on, the conflict between these two approaches to Judaism diminished and Kabbalah became widely accepted. But in Safed, in the days of Rabbi Isaac Luria, they existed peacefully side-by-side.

Rabbi Joseph Caro

Safed was also the home of Rabbi Joseph Caro (1488–1575). Born in Spain just a few years before the expulsion, Rabbi Joseph wandered through many lands before finding peace in Safed. After settling in Safed, he undertook a gigantic task: the compilation of an encyclopedic code of talmudic law that would be easier for Jews everywhere to use and follow than earlier legal codes and the original books of the Talmud.

A Handy Reference Book

Caro based his explication of Jewish law on the *Turim*, a code composed by Rabbi Jacob ben Asher (1270–1340) in Spain. He brought the *Turim* up to date by adding rabbinic decisions made in the two centuries since Jacob ben Asher and including Sephardic legal decisions and customs as currently enforced. For 30 years, Joseph Caro worked on his commentary on the *Turim*. He then prepared a shorter, well-defined version in which he discussed every phase of Jewish life and all its rituals. Joseph Caro's code is called the *Shulchan Aruch* ("Prepared Table"). It proved a handy reference work for those seeking guidance on Jewish practice and custom. In spite of initial opposition among Ashkenazic rabbis, it won full recognition after the glosses of Rabbi Moses Isserles (1530–1572) were added to it.

The *Shulchan Aruch* was used by Jews in many lands. It was especially helpful in small communities where there was no scholar to turn to for guidance.

THE SHULCHAN ARUCH

When rabbis are questioned about Jewish law, they usually consult the Shulchan Aruch. To this day, some seminaries, before they ordain rabbis, question them on their knowledge of the rulings in the Shulchan Aruch.

THE FIFTH COMMANDMENT: HONOR THY FATHER AND MOTHER, THAT THY DAYS MAY BE LONG UPON THE LAND WHICH THE LORD THY GOD GIVETH THEE [EX. 20]. YOU SHALL FEAR FOR YOUR MOTHER AND FATHER [LEV. 19].

1. What is fear? It is forbidden to stand or to sit in the seat which belongs to the father at the time when he has a meeting with his members or at the time when he is at prayer in the synagogue or when he is sitting in his home, and one shall not contradict or second his words and shall not call one's parents by their first names either if they are alive or dead but only "My dear Father or Mother."

4. What is honor? To honor is to give the parents drink, food, clothes to cover them and assist them in going and coming, wait on them, and do it all cheerfully and happily and gladly. If these things are done for the parents with a sour face, then the children are subject to receive great punishment.

7. The above rules apply only when the children have enough support for the day. If, however, they have not enough support for the day, they are not bound to give their time for the service for the parents.

8. If the children are all rich, the expenses of treating the parents must be borne by each of them according to the amount of their wealth. If some of them are rich and some poor, the expenses of the treatment of the parents must be borne by the ones that are rich, but the personal services must be shared by all the children.

22. It is the duty of the parents not to trouble their children too much, to pardon them if they neglect to honor them, and not cause them to sin.

23. If a father smite his grown son about 22 years of age, the father can be excommunicated by the court because he violates the law not to place a stumbling-block in front of a blind man.

24. It is the duty of a man to honor the wife of his father even though she is not his mother; to honor the husband of his mother even though he is not his father.

26. A man is bound to honor his father-in-law or mother-in-law.

28. If a student wishes to go to another place to study because of better opportunity and his father forbids him on account of the dangers in the city, the son need not obey the father.

29. If the parents are against their child's marriage to a certain party, the right is with the child, provided the marriage is not against religion.

WHAT DO YOU THINK?

I. Why was it necessary to compose a simple book of laws like the Shulchan Aruch?
2. On what book was the Shulchan Aruch based?
3. Why were the Ashkenazi Jews opposed to the Shulchan Aruch?
4. What is the Fifth Commandment?
5. Name several ways of honoring parents.
6. Do you know of anyone who does not honor their parents. What don't they do?
7. How can you honor your parents after their death?
8. According to the Shulchan Aruch, do children also have rights?
9. The Shulchan Aruch was written more than 400 years ago. Do you think the rules still apply today? What is your opinion of paragraph number 29?
10. How can a child honor his or her parents?
11. Should a child also have the same attitude toward his or her grandparents?

False Messiahs

The term *meshiach*, meaning "anointed one," was first applied to high officials and kings who were anointed with oil. In Jewish literature it is the Prophet Elijah who will announce the coming of the Messiah and then anoint him with sacred oil. During the Passover seder and the Birkat Hamazon (Grace after Meal) we pray for the coming of the Messiah to bring peace and harmony to the world. Rabbis say that the Messiah will be a descendant of King David. Why David? This is explained by the charismatic personality of the king who captured Jerusalem, enlarged the national boundaries, and authored the Psalms.

Bar Kochba

Belief in the Messiah received a boost during the first century, when Rome ruled Judea. Rabbi Akiva electrified the Judeans when he presented Bar Kochba as the anointed one, the Messiah, who would free the Judeans from the suffocating embrace of the Romans. Bar Kochba's rebellion failed and thousands of Jews died or were sold as slaves.

Because of this disaster the rabbis disapproved of mystical speculation about the coming of the Messiah. Calculations regarding the time of his appearance were disproved because they led to false hopes, disappointments, and disasters. Misfortunes always plagued the Jews in the wake of false Messiahs when from time to time they made their appearance.

David Reubeni /1490-1537

One day in the year 1524, a strange, dark man rode into the city of Rome on a white Arabian steed. Jews and Christians alike ran after him as he went to the palace of the pope for an audience. This man, who called himself David Reubeni, claimed to be the son of the king of the ancient Israelite tribe, of the tribe of Reuben, deep in the lands of Arabia.

Reubeni proposed a alliance to Pope Clement VII. If the pope would equip a Christian army to liberate

The false Messiah David Reubeni presented this letter to Pope Clement VII: "I am David, the son of King Solomon (may the memory of the righteous be blessed), and my brother is King Joseph, who is older than I, and who sits on the throne of his kingdom in the wilderness of Habor and rules over thirty myriads of the tribe of Gad and of the tribe of Reuben and of the half-tribe of Manasseh. I have journeyed from before the king, my brother and his counselors, the seventy elders. They charged me to go first to Rome to the presence of the pope, may his glory be exalted."

Jerusalem and place him in command, Reubeni would muster the fighting men of the tribe of Reuben to join forces with it. Together they would free the Holy Land from the Ottoman yoke.

Times were difficult for the Catholic Church. The Reformation was taking hold in many lands and curbing the power of Rome. A new crusade that would take the Holy Land from the Turks seemed a worthwhile project. The pope arranged for Reubeni to visit the king of Portugal, who was expected to aid in this ambitious plan. In Portugal Reubeni was received with honor and the king gave consideration to his plan.

Solomon Molcho /1501/1532

Diego Pires, a prominent young Marrano, was deeply moved by Reubeni. Openly returning to Judaism, Diego left Portugal and went to Palestine to study the Kabbalah, changing his name to Solomon Molcho. In time he became convinced that he was meant to be a messenger of God on earth, sent to proclaim the coming of the Messiah. Solomon Molcho traveled to many lands, and finally appeared in Rome.

By this time, Charles V of Spain had decided that both men represented a danger since they were inciting both Christians and Jews to rebellion. Molcho was imprisoned by the Inquisition and put to death. Reubeni likely died as a prisoner of the Inquisition.

Shabbatai Zevi

As the 17th century progressed, messianic fervor spread among Jews. Among those affected by the messianic yearning was Shabbatai Zevi, the son of refugees who had settled in the Turkish town of Smyrna (Izmir) after the expulsion from Spain. As a boy he studied the Kabbalah and became deeply involved in unraveling its intricate mysteries.

Shabbatai the Messiah: 1626-1676

In 1648, the year which was supposed to bring the Messiah, 22-year-old Shabbatai stood up in the synagogue of Smyrna and pronounced the Ineffable Name of God, something only permitted to the High Priest on the Day of Atonement.

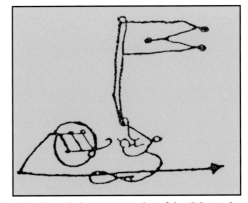

David Molcho was another false Messiah, who excited the imagination of Jews everywhere. This is his signature on his victory pennant.

Shabbatai Zevi

Nathan of Gaza, a kabbalist and disciple of Shabbatai Zevi.

The messianic fervor convinced some Jews to sell their belongings and leave for Jerusalem where the Mesiah was to apear. This picture shows the Jews of Vienna on their way to Israel.

Title page of a Shabbatean prayerbook called *Tikkun*, printed in Amsterdam in 1666. It contains readings for each day and night of the year.

By this revolutionary act Shabbatai clearly declared himself to be the Messiah.

Shabbatai Zevi returned to Smyrna where his followers took over the community. He then went to Istanbul supposedly take over the throne. Shabbatai the was forced to leave Smyrna so he went to Israel to study and become more involved in messianic thoughts. In 1665 he sought advise from Nathan of Gaza who proclaimed Shabbatai as the messiah.

Even rabbis and scholars came under the spell of Shabbatai Zevi. New prayerbooks with prayers for Shabbatai as Messiah were printed in Amsterdam. Many Jews settled their affairs and prepared to leave for Palestine on Shabbatai's command.

Shabbatai and the Sultan

In 1666 the Ottoman sultan, concerned about the unrest spreading through his empire, gave Shabbatai a choice between death and conversion to Islam. To everyone's amazement the would-be Messiah, accepted conversion and became a Muslim! Jewish communities everywhere were dumbfounded. Many found it impossible to believe that Shabbatai Zevi had really been nothing but an impostor.

Jacob Frank

There were still some extremists, however, who clung to the Messianic hopes. They gathered around a leader who proclaimed that he was possessed by the spirit of the dead Shabbatai. In Polish Ukraine, One of these groups was led by Jacob Frank (1726-1791) who, a hundred years after the appearance of Shabbatai Zevi declared himself to be the latter's successor. A council of rabbis excommunicated this extreme group and declared that only masters of talmudic wisdom or mature students over the age of might engage in the study of the Zohar.

Frank and hundreds of followers were baptized as Catholics in Poland, in 1759.

A 15th century German painting illustrates the Messanic hope of the coming of the Messiah to Jerusalem

David Reubeni claimed to be an ambassador of his brother Joseph who was king of a group of Jewish tribes living in a faraway land. Reubeni claimed that he was sent by Joseph to obtain arms so as to recapture Jerusalem from the Turks.
The following shortened account comes from the book Vale of Tears which Joseph Ha-Kohen completed in 1575.

In those days there appeared at the court of the king of Portugal a Jew, David by name, from a distant land, J. And David said to him: "I am a Hebrew and I fear the Lord God of the heavens. My brother, the king of the Jews, has sent me here to you for help. Help us that we may go to fight Suleiman the Turk, so that we may take the Holy Land out of his power."

The king answered "Let thy coming be in peace. Now go and I will send you to the archbishop and I will do whatever he says." So David left him and spent a short time in Lisbon. The Marranos believed his words, saying: "He is our redeemer, for the Lord has sent him," and many gathered about him and they honored him.

David came also to Bologna, Ferrara, and Mantua and declared that with the consent of the Christian kings he was going to take all the Jews in those cities with him back to his homeland.

A shoot came forth from Portugal-Solomon Molcho was his name-of the stock of the Jews who had been scattered there since the days of the forced conversions. He was at that time a very young man, one of the secretaries of the king. When Solomon saw this man David, God touched his heart; he returned to the God of our fathers, and he circumcised himself. In those days Solomon knew nothing of the Holy Writings; but after he was circumcised, God gave wisdom to him, and almost immediately he became wiser than all other men. He went to Turkey. Then he returned to Rome, where he spoke with Clement, the pope, who showed him favor in spite of the wishes of the theologians of the church.

And it came to pass after this that Solomon undertook to speak to Emperor Charles V, on religious matters.

The emperor would not listen to him, and even issued an order to put him and his friend Prince David and his men into prison. They remained there for a few days until the emperor returned to Italy. Then he brought them back, shackled on wagons, to Mantua where they were put in jail. The emperor then spoke with his advisers, and when they found Solomon guilty and deserving death, the emperor commanded: "Take him out and let him be burnt."

WHAT DO YOU THINK?

1. *Why were people ready to accept an individual who claimed to be a Messiah?.*
2. *How did Shabbatai Zevi draw attention to his presence.*
3. *How did people prepare for the coming of the Messiah?*
4. *Did any individual or group of people oppose Shabbatai Zevi?*
5. *Why did the Turks imprison Shabbati?*
6. *How did Shabbati followers interpret his removal to a better prison?*
7. *What choice did the sultan offer Shabbatai?*
8. *What effect did Shabbati's conversion have on some Jews?*
9. *How did Shabbatai ingratiate himself into the good graces of the Turks?*

The Marranos

Rabbi Jacob Sasportas (1610–1698). In 1681, he was appointed Chacham in Amsterdam. He was a bitter opponent of Shabbatai Zevi.

Engraving by Adolf van der Laan (ca. 1710) showing the Portuguese synagogue on the left and the two Ashkenazic synagogues on the right in Amsterdam.

The Netherlands

In the 15th and early 16th centuries, the Netherlands were under the dominion of Spain. The Protestant Dutch hated the Catholic Spaniards and their ways. Charles V, who ruled both Spain and the Holy Roman Empire, was determined to suppress any stirrings of revolt; he wanted his far-flung domains united in loyalty to church and crown, and therefore sought to crush Protestantism wherever he encountered it.

But Spanish rule could not maintain its grip on the freedom-loving Dutch. The people of the Netherlands fought Spain bitterly, and in 1581, declared their independence.

Meanwhile, Protestant England, also wary of Spain, was on the way to becoming a nation of seafarers, merchants, and colonists. Spain set out to conquer England, but in 1588, under Queen Elizabeth I, the English navy defeated and destroyed the Spanish Armada.

Marranos in Holland

After the Netherlands won their independence, large numbers of Marranos from Portugal and Spain fled to Amsterdam and Antwerp, where they reverted to their ancestral religion. The local Christians treated them with friendliness and tolerance, and before long, major Sephardic communities had developed in the great trading cities of Holland and Belgium.

The Dutch Jerusalem

Throughout this era, the city of Amsterdam was often called the Dutch Jerusalem, a name coined in 1596, when a group of Portuguese Marranos there returned to Judaism in a solemn public ceremony. From that time on, Amsterdam was one of the great centers of European Jewry. Jewish communities also grew up in the other cities of the Netherlands. Many Portuguese and Spanish Marranos became successful and respected traders in their new homeland and contributed to the growing power of the Netherlands.

Jews in Germany

The Portuguese Marranos who settled in Amsterdam had trade connections with Jewish merchants in the German city of Hamburg. At first, the Marranos in Hamburg were simply known as Portuguese, but after a time, they openly professed their Judaism. Since they had become very useful to the merchant city, they were permitted to remain, although they had to accept the restrictions imposed on all Jews in Germany. Under the influence of the Portuguese immigrants, Hamburg became a center of active Jewish life.

Jews in the Dutch Colonies

Holland eventually gained a foothold in the New World, both in the West Indies and in Brazil, which was a Portuguese possession until the Dutch conquered it in 1631. There were many Marranos in Brazil, especially in the city of Recife. Under Dutch rule, they openly returned to the Jewish

Resolution of the Amsterdam Portuguese Jewish community granting pioneer Isaac da Costa a Sefer Torah for Curaçao in the West Indies, 1659. The Jews of Holland helped the new overseas communities in many ways.

Minute book, written in Portuguese, of the Spanish and Portuguese Jewish congregation in Amsterdam, 1656.

Portrait of Rabbi Manasseh Ben Israel, painted by Rembrandt.

Letter from the Jews of London to Oliver Cromwell, dated March 24, 1655, pleading that "we may with security meet privately in our houses for our devotions."

A painting of a Dutch Jewish merchant dressed in high fashion, 1681.

Portrait of Oliver Cromwell.

faith, dedicating a synagogue where they proudly worshipped in the Sephardic tradition and brought a rabbi from Amsterdam to serve their community.

When Portugal began the reconquest of Brazil, the Jewish settlers fought side by side with their Dutch neighbors and many of them died in battle.

Rabbi Manasseh Ben Israel / 1604–1657

One of the most important rabbis in the Dutch Jerusalem was Manasseh Ben Israel. The son of Spanish Jews, he was steeped in Jewish learning. Many Christians in those days wanted to study the Bible in its original language rather than in translation, and they often turned to Manasseh Ben Israel for guidance.

Manasseh Ben Israel was a student of the Kabbalah. Like many Jews of his day, he believed that the coming of the Messiah was near. A keen observer of political developments, he noted the great changes that had taken place in England since its break with Catholicism. In 1649, Oliver Cromwell and the Protestant Puritans had come into power and deposed the king. Many of England's political leaders looked to the Bible for inspiration. They seriously studied the workings of the Sanhedrin for guidance in conducting their own Parliament.

Manasseh Meets Cromwell

No Jews had lived openly or legally in England since the expulsion in 1290, but Manasseh Ben Israel felt the time for change was nigh. In 1655, after a difficult journey, he arrived in London and met with Cromwell. England's Protestant ruler was inclined to grant the rabbi's request, but many of his political associates were not so favorably disposed. As a result, the rabbi's plea was rejected. Still, his journey had not been wholly in vain. The following year, a group of Marranos who were already living secretly in England returned to the religion of their ancestors and were granted the right to worship as they pleased. Eventually they were joined by other Jews, and Jewish communities arose again all over England.

THE NETHERLANDS

After the Expulsion from Spain, the Marranos used Holland as a way station, on the road to freedom. From Spain they moved to Holland and from there, they would go to Italy or Turkey. About 1600, the Dutch allowed the Jews to establish a synagogue and acquire a cemetery. Soon, Amsterdam had a large Jewish community with rabbis, schools, and community officials. The following is a brief survey of the curriculum of a Jewish school in Amsterdam in 1680. This excerpt is from the book Sifte Yeshenim *by Shabbatai Bass, Amsterdam.*

Some time ago I came here to the holy congregation of Amsterdam and I visited the schools of the Sephardim a number of times. There I saw "giants in scholarship tender children as small as grasshoppers," "kids who have become he-goats." In my eyes they were like prodigies because of their unusual familiarity with the entire Bible and with the science of grammar.

There is a teacher in every room and there are pupils by the hundreds. In the first class the younger children study until they are able to read the prayerbook; then they are promoted to the second class. There they study the Pentateuch with the melody of the cantillation marks until they are well versed in the Five Books of Moses down to the last verse.

Then they enter the third class, where they study the Pentateuch until they can translate it fluently into their mother tongue, Spanish.

Then they go on to the fourth class, where they study the Prophets and the Hagiographa in order, with the melody of the cantillation marks.

Then they go on to the fifth class, where the lads are trained to study the mishnaic law by themselves until they acquire understanding and intelligence and reach the category of *bachur.* In that class they speak in no other tongue but Hebrew except to explain the law in Spanish.

They then move on to the sixth class, to the talmudic college, to the academy of the rabbi and chief judge—may his Rock and Redeemer guard him. There they sit in class and every day study one law thoroughly with Rashi and Tosafot. They also discuss the matter by further consulting the legal comments of Maimonides, the *Tur*, the *Bet Yosef*, and the other authorities on law.

During hours when the lads are at home, every householder has a tutor who teaches his child to write the vernacular and Hebrew and who reviews the class work with him at the house.

The above-mentioned rabbis and teachers are chosen and appointed by the community and paid out of the treasury of the Holy Brotherhood which is known as the Talmud Torah Association. This "Study of the Torah" Association was established in 1616.

WHAT DO YOU THINK?

1. *Why did the Christians in Holland readily welcome the Jewish Marranos?*
2. *How did the Marranos in Holland try to ensure that their children would follow the Jewish religion?*
3. *What do you think of the school curriculum?*
4. *Who paid for the upkeep of the school?*
5. *Why were there no girls in the schools?*
6. *How did the Talmud Torah Association show its appreciation to the teachers?*
7. *Why did the school not allow books to be taken out of the building?*
8. *Does your Hebrew school library allow you to take books home?*
9. *What has changed between the year 1620 and the year 2004?*

In Eastern Europe

The Old-New Synagogue (Altneuschul) in Prague, built in the late 13th or early 14th century, in the heart of the Jewish quarter. Brick gables were added in the 15th century.

A painting by the artist Arthur Szyk shows King Boleslaw issuing the Statute of Kalisz. In 1264, the king issued the Statute of Kalisz as a charter of Jewish rights to attract Jews to build up the towns of Poland that had been ruined by the Mongol armies in the 1240s.

Early Russian Beginnings

According to some traditions, the first Jews to settle in areas that later became part of the Russian Empire arrived there after the destruction of the Temple in 586 B.C.E. They were brought to these regions when Nebuchadnezzar of Babylon deported large numbers of Jews to territories in Armenia, the Caucasus region, and along the shores of the Black Sea.

A sprinkling of Jewish settlers settled in Eastern Europe in Roman times, when Jewish traders traveled along the great rivers and brought their wares to many distant lands. Others moved into Russia from Persia and Arabia. Around 800 C.E., some the Khazars, a Turkic people who lived beyond the Black Sea, converted to Judaism. It is possible that only the royal family and some of the nobility converted. They continued to practice the Jewish religion until the mid-10th century, when the Russians overran their kingdom.

Beginnings of Polish Jewry

Most of the Jews of Eastern Europe, however, came from Germany. Toward the end of the Middle Ages, they began wandering eastward to Poland, which, at that time, included Ukraine and Lithuania, in order to escape persecution in the cities and towns of Germany. The Polish kings eagerly welcomed them, for there were many merchants and artisans among the Jewish migrants, and Poland badly needed their commercial and technical expertise.

The populace of Poland at the time consisted of two classes—nobles who owned the land and peasants who worked it; there was virtually no middle class. The kings of Poland hoped that the newcomers would build cities and bring commerce and industry to their realm. To encourage the Jewish immigrants, they made them directly subordinate to the crown rather than to the nobles in the regions where they settled. This gave the Jewish settlers a special legal status that protected them from many manifestations of anti-Semitism and enabled them to live under their own laws.

Drawn by the opportunities Poland offered, ever greater numbers of Jews moved eastward. As cities grew, Jewish communities sprang up. In time, large and prospering Jewish communities flourished in Warsaw, Vilna, Lublin, Posen (Poznan), and Cracow, as well as many smaller towns.

Polish coins with Hebrew inscriptions.

King Casimir the Great

The charter granted to the first Jewish settlers was renewed by King Casimir the Great, who reigned from 1333 to 1370. Casimir was renowned for building many new cities, and was often referred to as king of the serfs and the Jews, for he was a very tolerant ruler who was genuinely concerned about the welfare of the serfs and his Jewish subjects.

A Russian cavalryman.

A model of a Polish synagogue built about 1600.

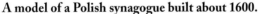

Stately house of Simcha Menahem, Jewish physician to King John III Sobieski of Poland.

With the arrival of so many skilled immigrants, Poland experienced an era of rapid progress and development. Many non-Jews joined the movement eastward, and, unfortunately, they brought to their new homes not only their skills, but also their traditional prejudices. They were eager to restrict their Jewish neighbors, whom they regarded as rivals, just as they had done in Germany, and often found allies in the church. But Poland's kings defended the Jews, and for some 300 years, Polish Jewry enjoyed an era of peace and freedom.

The Jews as Assets

The Jews proved to be an asset to Poland. They set up a banking system and minted Poland's first money. Some of these early coins bear the names of the Polish kings of the time printed in Hebrew letters.

Many Jews in Poland were employed as managers of estates, tax collectors, and financial advisors to the nobility, and the nobles valued their services. Jews were also active in the export of grain, salt, timber, and other natural resources, and imported goods needed from abroad. In addition, they owned and operated many of the country's inns, taverns, and stores, were active in transporting merchandise from place to place, and played a major role in many of the skilled crafts so essential to a pre-industrial economy.

Replica of an interior section of the Great Synagogue that was built in Vilna in 1572. This reproduction is in the Diaspora Museum in Tel Aviv.

THE STATUTE OF KALISZ

In the year l264, Boleslaw the Pious issued the Statute of Kalisz for governing the Polish Jews, many of whom had sought a haven in Poland after fleeing for their lives from the crusaders and other terrors against them in Western and Central Europe. In this celebrated charter, the only one of its kind in the history of Christendom, the king made plain his resolve to give the same protection to Jews as to Christians, and to guarantee to them full freedom of worship. Moreover, he forbade Christians, on pain of severe punishment, to desecrate, injure, or wreck the Jews' synagogues, religious schools, or cemeteries.

The following are sections from the Statute of Kalisz.

First of all we affirm that the testimony of a Christian alone may not be admitted in any matter which concerns the money or property of a Jew. . . In every such instance there must be testimony from both a Christian and a Jew.

Similarly if a Christian brings a complaint charging that he gave a Jew security and the Jew denies the charge and the Christian does not accept the statement of the Jew. . . let the Jew take an oath on an article equal in value to the alleged security and he will be exempt. . .

Likewise, if a Jew should charge without producing witnesses to that effect, that he lent a certain sum to a Christian, and the Christian denies the claim, the Christian may take an oath and exempt himself.

In the case of strife or quarrel between one Jew and another, no matter what the cause, the local magistrate may not bring judgment. Only we, our palatine or his court may sit in judgment in such an instance. In capital cases only the royal court may sit in judgment.

If a Christian injures a Jew in any which way, the accused shall pay a fine to the royal treasury or to our palatine . . .

If the Jew is carrying any goods or materials, he is obliged to pay duty at each customs station. The duty he is to pay shall be the same as that paid by other citizens of the city in which the Jew is resident at the time.

If the Jews should transport, as is their custom, one of their dead from one city to another, or from one district to another . . . we decree that our customs collectors take nothing from them.

If anyone should intentionally throw stones at a synagogue, it is our desire that he pay our palatine two stone-weight of pepper.

If a Jew should do injury to another Jew, he may not refuse to pay the fine to his judge.

If a Jew be murdered in secret, in such a manner as there are no witnesses to the deed and there is no way of knowing the murderer; and if after an investigation the Jews begin to suspect someone, we shall provide the Jews with a prosecutor against the suspect.

WHAT DO YOU THINK?

1. *Why did King Boleslaw invite the Jews to Poland?*
2. *What incentives did the king offer the Jews?*
3. *What did the king expect the Jews to do for his country?*
4. *How did the king protect the Jews from the local rulers?*
5. *With what specific injustices did the royal charter deal?*
6. *How did the Jews help build up the Polish economy?*
7. *In what fields of economic activity were the Jews involved?*
8. *How did the non-Jews benefit from Poland's renewed development?*
9. *What was the atttitude of the non-Jewish merchants toward the Jews?*
10. *During the 20th century millions of Jews lived in Poland.*
    How many Jews now live in Poland? Why are there so few Jews left?
11. *What was the attitude of the Poles toward the Jews during the Holocaust?*

The Jews of Poland

The Jewish community enjoyed a self-sufficient economy and had its own merchants, farmers, and tradesmen. These paintings by Arthur Szyk picture a Jewish blacksmith and baker at work.

Meeting place of the Council of the Four Lands, Lublin, 16th and 17th centuries.

The Kahal

The Jews of Poland constituted a separate social class. They were neither nobles nor peasants, nor city-dwelling burghers like the Christian merchants and artisans. In recognition of their status, King Sigismund Augustus issued a charter in 1551 that guaranteed the Jews of Poland the right to govern themselves.

The Jews of the four provinces ruled by the Polish kings—Greater Poland, Little Poland, Volhynia, and Lemberg—were organized into self-governing communities headed by a Kahal (assembly) known as the Va'ad Arba Aratzot (Council of the Four Lands), whose members were the elected representatives of Poland's many Jewish communities.

The Council of Four Lands

Whereas the Jews of ancient Babylonia had been ruled by an individual, the exilarch, Polish Jewry was ruled by an elected council. The Va'ad Arba Aratzot met twice yearly at Lublin and Jaroslaw, negotiated with the king's representatives, and collected the taxes levied on the country's Jews. It enforced the law in the Jewish communities and was in charge of Jewish courts, schools, trade guilds, and communal charities. When necessary, it appointed a spokesman or advocate (shtadlan) to represent it in dealings with Christian officials.

Although the Jews of Poland were only allowed to live in certain areas, they managed to build up an independent communal life. They had their own bankers and merchants, farmers and laborers, and their own craft guilds of butchers, bakers, and printers.

The Yiddish Language

The Jews of Poland evolved a language of their own. In medieval Germany their ancestors had spoken German with a significant admixture of Hebrew. The migrants from Germany who settled in Poland continued speaking this language in their new homeland. Over time, Polish words and expressions were added.

The language that evolved from these developments is known as Yiddish.

The Yiddish language, written in Hebrew letters but ultimately derived from medieval German, soon came to be the main form of intercommunication among the Jews of Eastern Europe. By 1700, Yiddish was playing an important role in religious, intellectual, literary, and personal correspondence.

Jewish Education

The Jewish communities of Eastern Europe organized their own school systems. Boys from 4 to 13 years of age attended the *cheder* (elementary school). The better students went on to a yeshiva for advanced studies.

Russian Unrest

The 17th century was a time of unrest all over Europe. The peasants of Ukraine hated their Polish overlords. They were members of the Orthodox Church, whereas the Poles were Roman Catholics. The unfortunate Jews were caught in the middle, especially because most of the contact the peasants had with their Polish masters was through Jewish tax-collectors and estate managers. Thus, the Jew was identified with the hated landlord. When the Ukrainians revolted, they launched their first attacks against the Jews.

The Cossacks Spread Destruction

The Ukrainian uprising was spearheaded by fierce peasant-soldiers known as Cossacks. Their commander, Bogdan Chmielnicki, led his troops against the hated Polish landlords and the Jews of Ukraine and Poland. Many thousands of Jews were killed within a few months. Even in the few instances when Poles and Jews united in defense of their towns, it was to no avail, for the Cossacks swept through the land like a hurricane, spreading death and destruction. In the town of Nemirov, on June 10, 1648, the Cossacks, after a Polish betrayal of the Jews, massacred more than 6,000 Jewish men, women, and children. Similar scenes occurred in many other towns.

The Jews in this Polish synagogue are wearing fur hats called *streimels* that were worn on holidays and special occasions. This rabbi and his disciples are praying in front of a desk called a *shtender*. The texts are located in shelves above them. The Yiddish word for "standing" is *shtayt*, hence the Yiddish word *shtender*.

The Cossack leader Bogdan Chmielnicki killed thousands of Ukrainian Jews in the revolt he led in 1648.

A street in Lublin, a major economic center for the Jews of Poland from the 16th century. Lublin also became a center for the study of Torah, and was nicknamed the Jerusalem of Poland.

Catherine the Great was the daughter of a minor German ruler. In 1745, she married the Russian Tsar Peter III and soon after his mysterious death, in 1761, made herself the ruler of the greatest state in Europe. Domestically, she ruled with an iron hand and militarily, advanced Russian power. She acquired Lithuania and Ukraine from the Polish kingdom, and the Black Sea territories from the Ottoman Empire. Envious statesmen saw Catherine's success as the work of the Devil.

Expulsion from the Ukraine

The king of Poland, in order to make peace with Chmielnicki, named him prince of Ukraine. As a condition of this deal, Chmielnicki stipulated that the Jews were to be expelled from Ukraine. But peace did not come to the torn country even then.

By the time the Cossacks and the Poles signed a peace treaty in 1654, 700 Jewish communities had been destroyed and more than 100,000 Jews killed. The Council of the Four Lands had disintegrated. The surviving Jews were left impoverished and scattered.

To make things worse, the Orthodox Church increased its hostility toward the Jews. Blood-libel accusations by the church began to spread in which the Jews were accused of using the blood of Christian children in making matzot for Passover. Anti-Jewish riots terrorized the Jews in eastern Poland.

The last half of the 18th century was another stormy era both for Poland and for its Jews. Three times the land was invaded and partitioned by its more powerful neighbors. By 1796, nothing remained and Poland lost its independence altogether. The Jews of Poland now became subjects of either Russia, Prussia, or Austria. To further compound their difficulties, even before the partitions, Poland's last king, Stanislaw II Poniatowski, had abolished their two institutions of self-government, the Council of the Four Lands and the Council of Lithuania.

Catherine the Great

The ruler of Russia at this time was Catherine the Great whose subjects lived under extremely primitive conditions. Russia had a wealthy nobility and a merchant class composed of immigrants from Germany. The rest of the people were mostly serfs. The partitions of Poland brought Catherine the lion's share of Polish Jewry. In order to prevent this mass of Jews from expanding into other parts of the Russian Empire, she and her successors restricted their right of residence to the areas taken from Poland in which they were already living, a zone called the Pale of Settlement.

SIGISMUND II AUGUSTUS
Permission to Establish a Yeshiva in Lublin, Poland (August 23, 1567)

This document was signed into law to build a yeshiva but also encouraged Jewish scholars in the realm to choose the head of the new school. Students could attend tuition-free and the king exempted the yeshiva from all taxes.

As a result of the efforts of our advisors and in keeping with the request of the Jews of Lublin, we do hereby grant permission to erect a yeshiva . . . and a synagogue by its side . . . and to outfit the said yeshiva with all that is required to advance learning. The administration of the yeshiva is to be vested in a person who will be accorded authority and influence by the teachers and who will be capable of maintaining order and discipline among the students. All the learned men and rabbis of Lublin shall come together and from among their number choose one to serve as the head of the yeshiva. Let their choice be of a man who will magnify the Torah and bring it glory! To him shall be granted the right of supervision over teachers and students alike. We hereby grant him the honorary title of Rosh Yeshiva and assert that he shall not be subject to the authority of the present rabbi of Lublin nor to that of those who hold that position in the future. Not only that, we do here affirm that the Rosh Yeshiva shall be the superior of all the rabbis and learned men of the city.

And inasmuch as instruction in the said yeshiva is to be given without charge and at no cost to the student, we declare the Rosh Yeshiva to be exempt from all taxes and duties due our treasury and the treasury of the state.

WHAT DO YOU THINK

1. *What was the Kahal? What areas of Poland did the Kahal represent?*
2. *What were the responsibilities of the Kahal?*
3. *How did the Jews take advantage of the charter to build a Jewish community?*
4. *Do Jews in America need a special charter to build a Jewish community?*
5. *What guarantees the Jews the right to organize local communities?*
6. *What type of clearances did your synagogue need to establish a Jewish school?*
7. *Are Jewish communitues in America given special political status?*
8. *Are Jews in America a separate political class?*
9. *What motivated the king to issue such an unusal order?*
10. *Why did the king permit the Jews to erect a synagogue and a yeshiva?*
11. *Was it a good idea for King Sigismund to create a self-governing Jewish community?*

Tzadikim and Mitnagdim

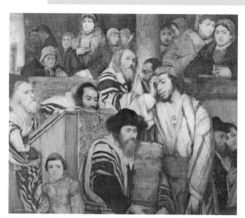

Day of Atonement in a shtetl synagogue. Oil painting by Maurycy Gottlieb, 1878.

The Vilna Gaon

Hasidic scholar wearing a *streimel*. A streimel is a fox fur hat worn by some Hasidic sects on holidays and special ocasions

Life in the Pale

The Pale of Settlement, the area the Russian government allowed Jews to live in, included eastern Poland, Ukraine, and Lithuania. In addition to its Jewish residents, it had a much larger population of Christians, many of whom were quite hostile to the Jews.

It was here, in the little towns and villages of the Pale, that most of Europe's Jews were to live for the next 200 years. Many harsh restrictions were placed upon them: they had to pay high taxes and could not move or travel without permission; they did not attend Russian schools and were barred from many other public institutions. Nonetheless, Jewish life in the Pale was active and full and the Jewish population increased. While all but a few of the Russian nobles were illiterate, even the humblest Jewish family sent its sons to the cheder to learn to read and write and engage in studying the Torah.

Jewish Life in Poland

After the Chmielnicki revolt, the Cossack wars, and the general disillusion that set in after the exposure of Shabbatai Zevi and his false messianic claims, Jewish life in Poland went into a decline. The institutions of self-government were abolished. Many thriving communities disappeared; others were reduced in size.

Despite these serious problems, and the accompanying demoralization, this period was to produce two great religious leaders, each quite different from the other and each concerned with a different way of life. One was Israel ben Eliezer, known as the Baal Shem Tov; the other was Elijah ben Solomon, the Gaon of Vilna.

Israel ben Eliezer

Israel ben Eliezer was born in a small town in Ukraine about 1698. When still a small child, he lost both his parents and was cared for by the community.

After graduating from the cheder, he worked at menial jobs while studying intensely. He became the assistant to his teacher. Israel liked children, and they, in turn, loved to listen to his stories. Israel was a bright young man with a charismatic manner and mystical disposition. He was also known as a healer and wonder-worker. Israel married a young woman called Anna, and they were given a house in Medzibozh by the community, along with a small stipend.

The Worship of the Heart

All around him, Israel could behold the beauty God had created. The humble lime digger was convinced that the holiness, or *Shekhinah*, of God dwelt within every living thing. All human beings, he believed, had the ability to see and experience the Shekhinah within and around themselves. Everyone, he asserted, could reach spiritual heights by prayer and communing with God. The "worship of the heart" through joy and ecstasy, he taught, is of greater importance than dry, routine, ritual observance. Israel infused religious zest and vigor into the hearts of the physically downtrodden and spiritually impoverished masses.

Israel learned to make healing salves and ointments from plants and herbs, for he wanted to help the sick and the suffering. He also kept an inn which his wife managed while he devoted himself to teaching and healing. Faithful students flocked to him.

Israel's Teachings

Israel ben Eliezer's teachings appealed not only to students but also, in the next generation, to the humble classes of the Jewish community.

His followers told stories about the wondrous deeds he performed, and before long, the kindly Israel ben Eliezer was known as the Baal Shem Tov, the Master of the Good (Holy) Name, for it was said that he could heal people by writing amulets for them to wear. He is also known as the Besht, an acronym made up of the first letters of Baal Shem Tov.

Hasid and his wife in holiday dress.

The synagogue of the Baal Shem Tov.

The Baal Shem Tov, the Master of the Holy Name.

Hasid with wife and daughter.

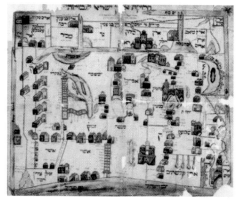

A map of the Land of Israel divided into tribal areas. The drawing is attributed to the Gaon of Vilna.

A painting showing two students discussing a controversial point in the Talmud.

The Hasidim

The followers of the Baal Shem Tov, who called themselves Hasidim ("pious ones"), would dance with joy in their synagogues when they welcomed the Sabbath. The leaders of the Hasidim in the generations after the Baal Shem Tov were known as Tzaddikim ("righteous ones"), and their disciples followed them with great fervor. As time passed, some of the Tzaddikim became men of great power and influence.

Elijah ben Solomon

The rabbis who fought against Hasidism were called Mitnagdim ("opponents"). Their leader was the Vilna Gaon—Elijah ben Solomon (1720–1797), the greatest among the many scholars of Vilna, a city known as the Jerusalem of Lithuania because of its great schools. Elijah never accepted an official position as rabbi. He spent many hours in his quiet study at scholarly work,

Like the great scholars of earlier days, the Vilna Gaon studied mathematics and astronomy in addition to the works of Jewish mysticism. Some of his disciples encouraged the study of the sciences as essential for a proper understanding of Torah.

Conflict Between Hasidim and Mitnagdim

In the days of the Vilna Gaon, the conflict between Hasidim and Mitnagdim became very bitter. The Tzaddikim had become very powerful, for their followers had come to regard them as intermediaries between the ordinary Hasid and God. The Mitnagdim, on the other hand, maintained that all human beings were personally responsible to God and therefore no intermediary was needed.

The Vilna Gaon took up the fight against Hasidism, going so far as to excommunicate its leaders and forbidding his followers to intermarry with its adherents. In time, the two ways of Judaism made peace with each other. Hasidim and Mitnagdim persisted in their different ways, as they do to the present time, but each group came to respect the other.

HASIDIM AND MITNAGDIM

This comparison is from the book **Aliyot Eliyahu**, *published in the city of Vilna in 1875.*

The Baal Shem Tov

The sect sprang up in Klezibiz in Podolia and its founder was a fanatical rabbi who exploited the superstitious peasants who are always in search of miracles. He succeeded in becoming known as a prophet and boasted that it was within his power to cure any illness by means of the Kabbalah. The simple people streamed to his house to find remedies for their health. . . But they found only deception. Despite this the number of his disciples has grown...

During the decade between 1750 and 1760 a certain rabbi called Israel achieved great prominence in the city of Medzibozh, which is in Ukraine. He was an ambitious man but because he was not learned in the Talmud and other matters, he had no hope of influencing others through his spiritual qualities. And so he chose another way: He began to "exorcise spirits," and it is from this that his name "Baal Shem" is derived. . .

The cloud of "secret knowledge" in which he enveloped himself and the attraction which this "hidden wisdom" holds for human beings drew more than 20,000 souls, whom he calls Hasidim, to Israel Baal Shem in a short period of less than ten years.

The Gaon of Vilna

He who was to surpass the most learned men of his time was born on Tuesday, the first day of Passover 1720, From the very day of his birth it was clear that he was to be a source of joy for generations to come. He was instructed by a teacher only until the age of six. By the time he was nine years old he was already steeped in Bible, Mishnah, and Gemara. He was well versed in arithmetic, algebra, and geometry, and after that he learned the theory of music, for he believed that without it one could not understand the poems of the Levites or the cantillation of the Torah. In medicine he had a knowledge of surgery as well as of drugs and their effects. From the day of his thirteenth birthday he let nothing distract him from study. He never slept more than a half hour and then he would rise like a lion, wash his hands, and begin to study in a loud voice. Later he would sleep for another half an hour and that is how he slept—for three hours during the night and one hour during the day.

While still young he took upon himself a vow of exile. He wandered from place to place for several years in holiness and purity. Great things were said of him in every place through which he passed. His keen intelligence and devotion to the service of the Lord permitted him to withstand all manner of trial and freed him of care and worry. He was thus able to serve God with joy and with fullness of his heart all the days of his life.

WHAT DO YOU THINK?

1. Where was the book **Aliyot Eliyahu** *published?*
2. What does this tell you about the author?
3. What was the name of the Gaon of Vilna?
4. Whom did the author favor?
5. Why does the author favor the Gaon of Vilna?
6. How did the Baal Shem Tov influence his followers?
7. Have you ever come across or read about a person who claimed hidden wisdom and secret knowledge?
8. What were the differences between the Hasidim and the Mitnagdim?
9. If you had a choice, which group would you join? Why?

Spinoza and Luzzatto

Spinoza's house in The Hague. The plaque records that he lived there from 1671 to 1677.

Baruch Spinoza (1632–1677) was a Jewish philosopher. In 1656, he was excommunicated for his shocking ideas.

Baruch Spinoza / 1632–1677

Among the Jewish merchants and craftsmen in Amsterdam there were many brilliant and unusual people. Some were learned in the Talmud; others were immersed in the study of the Kabbalah. One of them was Baruch (Benedict) Spinoza (1632–1677). The son of refugees from Spain, Spinoza had studied the Torah and the Talmud like all the other Jewish boys of his day. He had also studied not only the great philosophers of Judaism, but also the secular works of the philosophers of ancient Greece and Rome. Spinoza was a brilliant young man, and his teachers, the rabbis of Amsterdam, hoped he would become their brightest disciple and successor.

But Spinoza gradually isolated himself from Jewish life. He did not follow all the laws of the *Shulchan Aruch,* and some of his ideas seemed shocking and sacrilegious. Spinoza wrote brilliant philosophical works in which he stated that God was present in all things and that humans could serve Him by being just and righteous to one another.

Spinoza also rejected the divine origin of the Torah, and that was considered shocking by the Jewish community of the 17th century. Spinoza's ideas seemed to threaten Jewish unity and survival, for fear of what Christians might say about his idea of challenging the Bible. Therefore he had to be rejected.

Spinoza Is Excommunicated

In 1656, the rabbis of Amsterdam excommunicated Spinoza, and as a result, he was regarded as an outsider by the official Jewish community. Spinoza earned his living by making lenses for spectacles. He liked this work, and after his excommunication, he took his tools and moved to the little village of Rijnsberg on the outskirts of Amsterdam. Here he lived quietly, devoted to his studies and writings. Many of the great scholars of the time came to visit the hum-

He died at the age of 45, a lonely man. In later years Spinoza came to be universally recognized as one of the greatest philosophic minds.

Moses Hayim Luzzatto / 1707–1747

Another unusual personality who caused a stir in the Jewish community of Amsterdam, some years later, was the poet and mystic Moses Hayim Luzzatto (1707–1747). Like Spinoza, he too earned his livelihood as a lens grinder. Born in the Italian city of Padua, Luzzatto made a name for himself by the age of 20 with a book of poetry patterned on the biblical psalms. Inspired by the spirit of the Renaissance, he wrote plays on biblical themes that had a lasting influence on the development of modern Hebrew literature. As he grew older, Luzzatto turned more and more to Kabbalah and the Zohar.

The Kabbalah Forbidden

In Luzzatto's time, the rabbis of Italy forbade young Jewish scholars to study the Kabbalah, because they felt that only mature men would be able to do so without falling victim to confusion and doubt. The rabbis strongly disapproved of Luzzatto's interest in mysticism. They were shocked when the poet ignored their warnings and wrote a book which he entitled *The Second Zohar*. As a result, Luzzatto was compelled to leave Italy in 1733. He went to Amsterdam to begin a new life, grinding lenses for a living, but here, too, he was not able to write works on Kabbalah.

Luzzatto in Israel

As Luzzatto grew older, he began to see the Holy Land as his salvation, as the place where he could pursue his kabbalistic studies and write in peace. He and his family managed to translate their yearning into reality and, after an arduous journey, settled in Tiberias. Unfortunately, soon after their arrival, the entire family was wiped out by an epidemic of plague that ravaged the country.

Besides his psalms, poems, and plays, Luzzatto also wrote a book on Jewish ethics called *The Way of the Righteous Mesillat Yesharim*. This much-studied book has become a classic and has been translated into several languages.

Title page of the English edition of *Mesillat Yesharim.*

The front page of the first issue of the *Jewish Daily Forward*, Wednesday, September 8, 1897. At that time, the price of a newspaper was one cent.

First Stirrings of Democracy

During the 18th century, more tolerant ideas first advanced in the Renaissance took on new life. Europe was slowly outgrowing the idea of absolute monarchy in which a king ruled supreme and an aristocracy had the right to subject the rest of the people. Universities began to rise in the cities of Europe, attended by the sons of nobles and wealthy burghers. Writers and poets put forth new and stimulating ideas.

The Reformation had stimulated widespread interest in the Bible, and many Christians had become aware that the Hebrew Scriptures were part of their religious heritage. Despite this, the Jews, whose ancestors had given the Bible to the world, were among the most despised people in Europe.

The Court Jews

Frequently, a court Jew would speak to the prince on behalf of his community. Sometimes, Jewish merchants who had helped free city in time of war would be invited to settle there with their families and friends. In this way, some Jewish communities increased in size. But there also were small communities surrounded by the high walls of the ghetto from which a Jew could go forth only when he had to do business.

The Yiddish Language

Developments outside the ghetto were foreign to the Jews of the 17th and 18th centuries, except insofar as they affected their lives directly in the form of persecution or war. So isolated was the life of the Jews in Germany that their spoken language was not the German of everyone else but Judeo-German, medieval German closely interwoven with Hebrew words, the same dialect that in Eastern Europe had evolved into Yiddish.

BARUCH SPINOZA

Spinoza was schooled in Talmud and Kabbalah. He pursued a broad line of inquiry, which included physics, mathematics, philosophy, political science, and theology. Spinoza was concerned with the relationship of spirit to matter, mind to body, and of God to creation. He preached that all beliefs must be directed to a supreme being whom all must obey and worship by practicing justice and charity. In 1656, he was formally excommunicated by the Sephardic community in Amsterdam. Spinoza opposed religous authority, pointed out contradictions in the biblical text, and argued that nothing was supernatural. One of his arguments was that the government must ensure free thought. The following is an excerpt from one of his books.

. . the ultimate aim of government is not to rule, or restrain, by fear, nor to exact obedience, but contrariwise to free every man from fear, that he may live in all possible security; in other words, to strengthen his natural right to exist and work without injury to himself or others.

No, the object of government is not to change men from rational beings into beasts or puppets, but to enable them to develop their minds and bodies in security, and to employ their reason unshackled; neither showing hatred, anger, or deceit, nor watched with the eyes of jealousy and injustice. In fact the true aim of government is liberty.

Now we have seen that in forming a state the power of making laws must either be vested in the body of the citizens, or in a portion of them, or in one man, for, although men's free judgments are very diverse, each one thinking that he alone knows everything, and although complete unanimity of feeling and speech is out of the question, it is impossible to preserve peace unless individuals abdicate their right of acting entirely on their own judgment. Therefore, the individual justly cedes the right of free action, though not of free reason and judgment; no one can act against the authorities without danger to the state, though his feeling and judgment may be at variance therewith; he may even speak against them, provided that he does so from rational conviction, not from fraud, anger, or hatred, and provided that he does not attempt to introduce any change on his private authority.

WHAT DO YOU THINK

1. *According to Spinoza, the individual cedes the right of free action but not of free reason. What is the difference between free action and free reason?*
2. *What can an individual do if his free reason is at odds with free action?*
3. *How do people give up the right to differ with the government?*
4. *Can a democracy exist if individual cedes the right to free action?*
5. *Does free action mean permission to physically destroy property so as to attain the goals of free reason?*
6. *What do you think about groups that revolt against democratic governments to achieve their goals?*
7. *What if the goals of free reason goals are contrary to what is desired by a democratically elected majority?*
8. *Why did the community excommunicate Spinoza? Was the fear justified?*

New Horizons

The old synagogue in Berlin.

Moses Mendelssohn

Moses Mendelssohn playing chess.

Moses Mendelssohn / 1729–1786

Moses Mendelssohn was a small man who spoke with a slight stammer, but he had a dynamic spirit and a brilliant mind. The son of a Torah scribe, Mendelssohn was born in the German town of Dessau and studied with a rabbi there. When he was a boy of 14, his beloved teacher moved to Berlin. The boy followed him, and on paying the tax required of Jews, he succeeded in gaining admission to the city.

Mendelssohn Finds a New World

Mendelssohn found a new world in Berlin. Even though most of the city's Jews lived much as their brethren did in other German communities, there were quite a few enterprising Jewish merchants and financiers in Berlin who enjoyed special privileges and were in contact with the world outside the ghetto. Young Mendelssohn continued his Jewish studies with his mentor, but broadened his education by taking up a variety of other subjects as well.

Mendelssohn secured employment as tutor to the children of a wealthy silk manufacturer. In his spare time, he began to write on philosophy and current issues, expounding his ideas in a pure, flowing German. Moses Mendelssohn was the first German Jew of his day whose writings and intellectual interests transcended the ghetto walls. Berlin's intellectual and cultural elite became very much interested in this unusual man.

The First German Torah Translation

Facility in German, Mendelssohn felt, was essential. Few German Jews knew the language well, and virtually none could read it. To provide them with a learning resource, Mendelssohn translated the Five Books of Moses into German. He had it printed in Hebrew characters, however, so that Jews could read it even if they did not know the German alphabet. The translation appeared with a Hebrew commentary prepared by Mendelssohn in collaboration with a biblical scholar.

The new translation was published with the permission of the rabbis of Germany, and at first, it was widely accepted. Since most Jews already knew and had read the Bible in Hebrew, the translation satisfied an important need. It became a learning tool for everyone who wanted to learn German; copies found their way even to the Yiddish-speaking villages of far-off Russia where isolated students sought to master German as the first step on the road to enlightened self-improvement.

Before long, however, the rabbis decided that Mendelssohn's German Bible and modern commentary were dangerous innovations; the old, traditional way of teaching was safer and more desirable. This did not deter those who were eager to learn German from continuing to rely on Mendelssohn's Bible.

Wilhelm von Dohm and the Edict of Tolerance

No explicit laws to better the lot of the Jews were passed in the German states during Mendelssohn's lifetime. But the new ideas had paved a path for new hopes and attitudes.

Among Mendelssohn's many Christian friends who were favorably disposed toward the new concepts of liberty and tolerance was Christian Wilhelm von Dohm, a Prussian lawyer. When the Jews of Alsace asked Mendelssohn to write a petition requesting the authorities to remove some of the heavy restrictions placed upon them, it was to Dohm that Mendelssohn turned, asking him to draft the text of the memorandum. Dohm not only complied with his friend's request, but also wrote a plea for freedom and equality for all the Jews of Western Europe.

Dohm's plea helped influence Joseph II, the emperor of Austria, to proclaim the famous Edict of Tolerance (1782). While this law did not lift all restrictions from the Jews of Austria, it eased their burden considerably and opened doors hitherto closed to them. They no longer had to pay special poll taxes and wear the yellow badge; they were allowed to

Title page of the Book of Psalms, translated into German by Moses Mendelssohn.

Edict of Frederick the Great with regard to the conversion of Jews.

Medal commemorating Joseph II's Edict of Tolerance, Vienna, 1782.

HEBREW LITERATURE

Among the great exponents of Russian Haskalah were the following Hebrew authors whose works have left an indelible mark in the annals of modern Hebrew literature and culture: Abraham Mapu (1808–1867), pioneer Hebrew novelist famed for *Ahavath Zion*, a biblical romance written in superb biblical Hebrew style; Judah Leib Gordon (1830–1892), greatest of 19th-century Hebrew poets, who fought valiantly against some harsh survivals of manners and customs, while remaining loyal to Jewish tradition as a whole; Yitzhak Ber Levinsohn (1799–1860), erudite author of works demonstrating the complete harmony of Torah and the scientific spirit.

YIDDISH LITERATURE

Many authors wrote in Yiddish, the everyday language of the Jewish people of Russia and Poland. One of the best-loved Yiddish writers was Sholem Yaakov Abramovich (1836–1917), or Mendele Mokher Sefarim, "Mendele the Bookseller," as he was known. He started his career as a Hebrew author, and in fact, he is also considered one of the founders of modern Hebrew prose. It was, however, as a Yiddish writer that he gained special fame. He painted a vivid picture of life in the towns of the Pale, and his books were read with great enthusiasm. The writings of Mendele and others of his day revealed Yiddish for the first time as an expressive language, capable of reflecting the thought and character of the Jews of Eastern Europe. Among the other great luminaries of Yiddish literature were Sholem Aleichem and Isaac Leibusch Peretz.

The play *Fiddler on the Roof* was taken from a story by Sholem Aleichem

engage in trade and manufacturing and to become apprenticed to Christian master craftsmen. However, when Joseph died in 1790, most of the restrictions were revived.

The Maskilim

Mendelssohn was not a voice crying in the wilderness. His call to the Jews to participate in West European culture while remaining loyal to the Jewish religion awakened a group of active diciples of enlightenment (Maskilim). They published a Hebrew magazine to bring literary culture to the Jews. In 1778, while Mendelssohn was still alive, the Jewish Free School of Berlin was established, and here secular subjects were taught as well as the German language.

Haskalah

As early as the days of Tsar Nicholas I (1825-1855) the new ideas that had risen in the West managed to find their way into the Pale of Settlement, and some Jews of Russia became interested in learning about the world around them. Jewish schools founded with government support began to teach history, Russian, and the new sciences in addition to religious subjects. Instruction was given also in the Hebrew language and Hebrew grammar. Although the Jewish masses stood by their rabbis and opposed these schools. The Haskalah made rapid progress. In the western part of Europe, "enlightenment" tempted many Jews away from their, heritage but not so in the East. There the Haskalah, as enlightenment was called in Hebrew, took the direction not of assimiliation, but of a more intense cultivation of the Hebrew language and modern Hebrew literature along with knowledge of the Western world. Thus began the rebirth of Hebrew as a living language. Hebrew and Yiddish writers applied their talents to immortalize the folkways and customs of the Jews of the Pale, their ideals and their daily lives. In their works, both prose and poetry, they described the negative as well as the positive aspects of life in the traditional Jewish community.

The philosophy of the Enlightenment found a happy match in the person and principles of Joseph II (1742–1790), the emperor of Austria. While still young, he was deeply moved by the suffering of the peasants in the provinces of his realm and upon his succession to the throne, he initiated reforms which were intended to create a measure of social equality and security for the disadvantaged, poor.

The Edict of Tolerance, which he issued in 1782, marked a radical departure from the previous practice of the House of Hapsburg toward the Jews.

We, Joseph the Second, King in Germany, Hungary, and Bohemia, make known: The laws and the so-called Jewish Regulations pertaining to the Jewish nation prevailing in Our hereditary countries in general and particularly in Vienna and Lower Austria are not always compatible with these Our most gracious intentions. We hereby will amend them. As it is Our goal to make the Jewish nation useful and serviceable to the State, through better education and enlightenment of its youth by directing them to the sciences, the arts and the crafts, We hereby grant and order:

8. Graciously, that the tolerated Jews may send their children in such places where they have no German schools of their own, to the Christian primary and secondary schools so that they have at least the opportunity to learn reading, writing and counting.

10. We hereby most graciously permit them from now to learn all kinds of trades here as well as elsewhere from Christian masters.

11. We hereby further grant to the Jewish nation the license to carry on all kinds of trade, to be carried on by them freely. Painting, sculpture and the exercise of other liberal arts are equally permitted to them as they are to Christians.

16. In order to facilitate the tolerated Jews in their trades also with regard to the question of servants, it shall be permitted to them from now on to employ as many Jewish as well as Christian servants as their business requires.

18. By this present decree We hereby permit the existing restrictions with regard to definite Jewish houses to lapse and allow tolerated Jews to lease at their choice their own residences in the city as well as in the suburbs.

19. We hereby completely abolish the head-toll hitherto levied on foreign Jews and permit them to enter Our residence from time to time in order to carry on their business...

23. Besides, We hereby completely remove the double court and chancellery fees hitherto in force only for Jews.

25. Since by these favors We almost place the Jewish nation on an equal level with adherents of other religious associations, in respect to trade and domestic facilities.

Vienna, the second day of January, 1782.
Jewish Emanencipation:
A Selection of Documents *by R. Mahler*

1. *What was a tolerated Jew?*

2. *How did the edict help Jews make a living?*

3. *How did the Austrian courts discriminate against the Jews?*

4. *Could Jews, before the edict, send their children to German schools?*

5. *Emancipation and Enlightenment gave the Jews new opportunities, but they also threatened the Jewish way of life. Do you agree or disagree?*

6. *Can you acquire a Jewish education without studying Hebrew?*

7. *What were the beneficial results of the Haskalah? Were there any bad results?*

8. *What ideas of the Maskilim do most Jews accept today?*

The Jews of Germany

The synagogue of Regensburg appears on a 16th-century copper engraving by the artist Albrecht Altdorfer.

Printed handkerchief showing an open-air service on the Day of Atonement, 1870, outside Metz.

Reform Judaism

Those calling for radical changes in Judaism founded the Reform movement. They felt that if Judaism was to have a meaningful function in the modern world, it was necessary to eliminate old ceremonies and ideas, which seemed antiquated or inappropriate or which reflected the sensibility of the narrow life of the medieval ghetto.

One of the leaders of this new movement, headed by Rabbi Abraham Geiger (1810–1874), proposed a different form of service. They introduced sermons and prayers in German, the everyday language of the people, and shortened Hebrew prayers that seemed too long. References to the return to Zion and the coming of the Messiah were omitted. Believing that a "reformed" Judaism would adjust Jewish life to the demands of the times, they set aside the authority of the Talmud and the *Shulchan Arukh*. The Reform movement took root in some of the larger German cities, and the first Reform temple was dedicated in Hamburg.

Orthodoxy

Many Jews steadfastly resisted the changes proposed by the reformers, maintaining that any break in the chain of tradition would endanger the very foundations of Judaism. Their approach is now known as Orthodox Judaism. The most influential early opponent of reform was Rabbi Moses Schreiber (1763–1839), who was born in Germany and later became known as the Chatam Sofer, after the title of one of his many works. From his position as rabbi in Pressburg, Hungary, he rallied traditionalist-minded Jews against any changes in the synagogue service. Orthodoxy, which held the loyalty of most German Jews, had a number of brilliant spokesmen. In the next generation, the most prominent among them was Rabbi

Samson Raphael Hirsch (1808–1888). Hirsch was convinced that Jews could be good citizens, steeped in the culture and learning of their country, and still remain loyal to the laws that had come down through the ages in the Bible and Talmud.

The Nineteen Letters

In 1836, Rabbi Hirsch wrote the *Nineteen Letters of Ben Uziel*. The book was an intellectual presentation of Orthodox Judaism in which he defended all of its institutions and ordinances. It is written in the form of an exchange between two young men. Benjamin is the spokesman for the "perplexed" and Naphtali represents tradtional Judaism. Benjamin expresses the doubts of a young intellectual, while Naphtali, the representative of traditonal Judaism, formulates his answers in 19 letters.

Rabbi Zechariah Frankel

The Historical School

A third group took a midway position between Reform and Orthodoxy. Led by Zechariah Frankel (1801–1875), the president of the rabbinical seminary in Breslau (Wroclaw), this movement was known as the Historical School, and eventually became what is today called Conservative Judaism. It emphasized the importance of the historical continuity of the Jewish heritage. The adherents of the Historical School knew that change was inevitable and acknowledged that Judaism had undergone changes throughout its history, but they insisted that innovations had to be within the framework of Jewish tradition. Radical reform, they felt, was not in keeping with the evolving spirit of Judaism.

The "Science of Judaism"

A group of young German Jewish university graduates believed that the best way to ensure the survival of Judaism was to make its history and values better known. To this end, they began to apply the same analytical methods to the study of the Jewish heritage that were used in studying any other ancient culture.

A Jewish Wedding by Moritz Oppenheim, 1861. Painting of a German marriage ceremony, showing a tallit serving as a huppah canopy.

Leopold Zunz

Heinrich Graetz, professor and leading modern historian.

This group, headed by Leopold Zunz (1794–1886), called itself the Society for the Scientific Study of Jewish Culture; its approach is often referred to as the "Science of Judaism" *Wissenschaft des Judentums.*

Heinrich Graetz, Historian

Among the adherents of Zunz's school was Heinrich Graetz (1817–1891), a man of great talent and imagination. Graetz, a professor at the rabbinical seminary of Breslau, devoted 17 years of his life to the task of writing a well-documented history of the Jews. One of the first works of its kind, based on solid research and analysis of sources, it is still widely read to this day.

The Struggle for Democracy

As the first half of the 19th century drew to a close, Europe was shaken by uprisings and revolts. When the Revolution of 1848 in Germany was crushed, many of the disappointed freedom fighters left their homeland. Thousands of them crossed the Atlantic to settle in the United States.

The cause of civil liberties in Germany was greatly advanced by the unification in 1871 of all the German lands and provinces into one nation, under the leadership of Prussia. All Germans were recognized as free citizens with equal rights and liberties, including the freedom to worship as they chose. At last, the Jews of Germany were free.

LEOPOLD ZUNZ

Leopold Zunz (1794–1886) was one of the founders of the "Science of Judaism" movement. Zunz believed that acquainting the Christian world and its leaders with the true nature of Judaism could lessen the curse of anti-Semitism. His books were known for their objective and detailed research. Leopold Zunz, besides his Jewish studies, took an active role in the political events in Germany.

It is high time that the Jews of Europe, particularly those of Germany, be granted rights and liberties–not some paltry, humiliating privileges, but complete and uplifting civil rights. The neglect of Jewish scholarship goes hand in hand with civil discrimination against the Jews. Through a higher intellectual level and a more thorough knowledge of their own affairs, the Jews could have achieved a greater degree of recognition and thus more justice. Furthermore, much bad legislation, many a prejudice against Jewish antiquity, much condemnation of new endeavors are a direct consequence of the state of neglect in which Jewish literature and Jewish scholarship have been for about seventy years, particularly in Germany. And even though writings about the Talmud and against the Jews mushroomed overnight and several dozen Solons offered themselves to us as reformers, there was no book of any consequence which statesmen could have consulted, no professor lectured about Judaism and Jewish literature, no German learned society offered prizes in this field, no philanthropist went traveling for this purpose… Religion and scholarship, civil liberty, and intellectual progress require schools. Seminaries and synagogues must enlist the efforts of capable community leaders, competent teachers, well-trained rabbis. If emancipation and scholarship are not to be mere words, not some tawdry bit of fancy goods for sale, but the fountainhead of morality which we have found again after a long period of wandering in the wilderness, then they must establish institutions, high-ranking educational institutions, religious instruction for everyone, dignified religious services, suitable sermons. Such institutions are indispensable for the needs of the congregational totality of the Jews: but to establish them we need religious zeal and scholarly activity, enthusiastic participation in the entire project, benevolent recognition from the outside.

WHAT DO YOU THINK?

1. *What does Zunz mean when he says that the lack of Jewish scholarship goes hand in hand with discrimination against the Jews?*
2. *How has the modern Jewish community taken Zunz's criticism and rectified the situation?*
3. *Can you name some Jewish institutions that endeavored to acquaint the Christian and secular world with the history and customs of the Jews?*
4. *If you were in a position of authority, how would you acquaint the outside world with your religion?*
5. *Zunz preached that Judaism needs schools, seminaries, community leaders, trained teachers, and well-trained rabbis. How are Jewish institutions following Zunz's advice? Name some institutions and tell how they function.*

The Jews of France

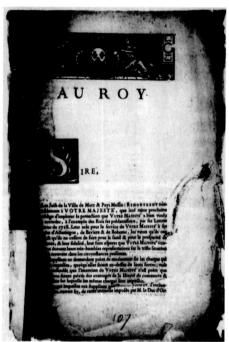

First page of a petition by Metz Jews to Louis XV in 1745, requesting permission to engage freely in commerce and industry.

Napoleonic decree ordering the Jews of France to adopt family names and first names, July 20, 1808.

Jews first made their appearance in France sometime in the 4th century. Although in the rest of Europe their presence was restricted, in France, the Jews were active as merchants and as doctors.

In 1096, members of the First Crusade attacked and killed Jews, and local bishops and rulers were powerless to protect them.

The 11th and 12th centuries are called the Golden Age of France. Scholars such as Rashi, Rabbenu Gershom, and the tosafists established schools and produced a treasure house of important literature. Unfortunately, anti-Semitism in the form of forced conversions, blood-libels, and accusations of well-poisoning plagued the Jewish communities and often led to murder, expulsion, and book-burnings.

In 1306, King Philip IV banished more than 100,000 Jews and seized their business assets and properties. Ten years later, they were readmitted and once again active Jewish communities sprang to life in many French cities. However, in 1394, Charles VI once again expelled the Jews, and for 200 years they were almost non-existent in France.

Following the expulsion from Spain in 1492, Marranos began to arrive and because of their skills and business connections were welcomed with open arms. In 1648, the Chmielnicki massacres in Ukraine sent a wave of Jews into Alsace–Lorraine. By 1800, there were about 40,000 Jews living there, and by decree they were freely allowed to practice their Judaism.

The French Revolution / 1789

For a hundred years, France had set the trends in Europe. In Germany, Poland, and Austria, and even in Russia, French was the language of the nobility, the educated, and the wealthy. French ideas and styles were adopted and imitated.

On July 14, 1789, the people of Paris stormed the

Bastille, a fortress in which many of those who had been unable to pay the high taxes were imprisoned. This was the start of the French Revolution, an upheaval in which the people came to power.

In 1789, the year the Revolution began, the French National Assembly proclaimed the Declaration of the Rights of Man. This document, which is similar to the American Declaration of Independence, declared that all human beings are born free and entitled to equal rights.

In 1790, the primarily Sephardic Jews of Bordeaux were granted equality. A decree passed in 1791 gave all French Jews the rights and privileges of full citizenship. But then the new French republic became involved in war.

A short time later, the French armies themselves became armies of conquest. They were led by a young general named Napoleon Bonaparte.

Napoleon Bonaparte

The Reign of Napoleon

Napoleon was a brilliant strategist. A highly ambitious man, he had dreams of great conquest. He hoped to carry the ideals and the new freedom of the young republic of France to every country in Europe.

Wherever his conquering armies took over, serfs and Jews were freed. The ghetto walls of Germany, Austria, and Italy fell. Many Europeans regarded Napoleon as a great liberator. The liberation of the Roman ghetto and the removal of the yellow badge were a way of demonstrating to the Vatican his power over the church.

His ambition was to be the undisputed ruler of the French state, the crowned conqueror of Europe. In 1804, he became emperor of France.

Napoleon Convenes a Sanhedrin

Eager to gain the loyalty of the Jews and also to exercise a measure of control over them, Napoleon convened an assembly patterned on the ancient Sanhedrin. All together, 71 representatives, 46 rabbis and 25 laymen, were chosen to settle legal and religious questions and to demonstrate loyalty to Napoleon's France.

In 1806, Napoleon convened an assembly of Jewish notables and announced that Jews were now officially citizens of the French nation. The emperor is shown raising the Jewish woman while the rabbis kneel at his feet.

The Declaration of the Rights of Man, 1789.

Napoleon became the ruler of France after the turmoil of the French Revolution. During his regime, France conquered much of Europe. In 1821, he died in exile on the tiny island of St. Helena.

The Sanhedrin was soon dissolved, but it served to emphasize some of the fundamentals of Judaism to the non-Jewish world.

Reaction

Eventually the allied countries of Europe defeated Napoleon. With Napoleon defeated and banished, the Jews lost many of the freedoms he had granted them. In some parts of Germany and Austria, they had to return to the ghettos, and the peasants were forced to revert to serfdom.

Having had a taste of freedom, the Jews found it difficult to readjust to the old restrictions. Some German and Austrian Jews had attended universities and embarked upon brilliant careers; they were now respected bankers and merchants, or high-ranking government officials. Some of them, concluding that there were many advantages to be gained from converting to Christianity, underwent baptism in order to be able to keep their positions.

Changes Within

Most of the Jews of Germany and Austria continued to follow the ways of their ancestors. But, like everyone in the 19th century, they, too, had to adjust to the radical changes that were occurring in their time.

Patriotism and nationalism reached new heights. The Jews were proud of their newly won rights of citizenship in the countries in which they lived. And this brought them face to face with a new problem: how to remain faithful to the traditions of Judaism and still be loyal, active citizens of the countries that had accorded them freedom and equality.

Impelled by a desire to eliminate the differences between themselves and those in whose midst they lived, many Jews were anxious to change Judaism itself.

NAPOLEON AND THE JEWS

The slogan of the French Revolution (1789) emphasized Liberty, Equality, and Fraternity for all society. These ideals brought the Jewish question into the forefront. In 1806, Napoleon convened a Sanhedrin to answer 12 questions. The Sanhedrin was organized according to tradition with 71 members, a majority of whom were rabbis. Napoleon asked the Jewish representatives to answer 12 questions. The Sanhedrin cooperated with Napoleon and answered all of his questions. However, the rabbis refused to officiate at mixed marriages. The Jews had little choice but to answer yes to the questions asked by Napoleon. All they were prepared to grant was a declaration that intermarriage, if legalized by the civil authorities, would be respected by the Jewish community.

QUESTIONS

1. Is it lawful for Jews to have more than one wife?

2. Is divorce allowed by the Jewish religion?

5. What conduct does Jewish law prescribe toward Frenchmen not of the Jewish religion?

6. Do the Jews born in France, and treated by the law as French citizens, acknowledge France as their country? Are they bound to defend it?

10. Are there professions from which the Jews are excluded by their law?

ANSWERS

1. In conformity with the Decree of Rabbenu Gershom, polygamy is forbidden to the Israelites.

2. Divorce by the Jewish law is valid only after previous decision of the civil authorities.

5. Every Israelite is religiously bound to consider his non-Jewish fellow citizens as brothers, and to aid, and protect them.

6. The Israelite is required to consider the land of his birth or adoption as his fatherland, and shall love and defend it when called upon.

10. Israelites can engage in agriculture, manual labor, and the arts,

WHAT DO YOU THINK?

1. *Why did Napoleon go out of his way to try to assimilate the Jews? Jews were a tiny part of the population. What difference did it make to him?*
2. *How did Napoleon try to test the resolve of the Jewish representatives?*
3. *How did the representatives finesse Napoleon's trick?*
4. *Napoleon submitted 12 questions and the representatives were to answer yes or no. How did the questions reflect the prejudices against the Jews?*
5. *Are some of these predjudices used today by the anti-Semites? Name two.*
6. *Why did the Jews refuse to allow rabbis to officiate at mixed marriages?*
7. *What is a Sanhedrin?*
8. *Anti-Semites usually ask American Jews: What would be your attitude as an American Jew if called upon to fight against Israel? Would your loyalty be to Israel or America?*
9. *Suppose you were a scientist at a supersecret American installation and you were approached to spy for Israel. What would you do?*

The Jews Resettle in England

New Synagogue, Great Helen Street, London, 1860. It is Sukkot. The man on the left is carrying the Torah. The person next to him is holding a lulav and etrog. On each side of the sanctuary is a prayer for the Royal Family, in English and Hebrew.

Coat of arms adopted by the Rothschild family in 1817.

England became a major world power. This land of seafarers and merchants attracted many Jewish immigrants ever since the days when Rabbi Manasseh Ben Israel first came from Holland to plead for the readmission of Jews.

The first Jews to settle in England in the 17th century were Marranos. They were followed by Sephardic Jews from Italy and Ashkenazim from Germany and Poland. By the 19th century, a sizable Jewish community existed in England.

The Rothschilds

Among the leading members of Britain's Jewish community was Nathan Mayer Rothschild (1776–1836). His father, Mayer Amschel Rothschild (1743–1812), had built up a major banking business in the German city of Frankfurt. The oldest of Nathan's five brothers remained in Frankfurt to run the bank there, while the other three established branches in Paris, Vienna, and Naples. Nathan Rothschild settled in London, where he became a major figure on the stock exchange and acted as a financial agent for the British government during the Napoleonic Wars.

Moses Montefiore

Another prominent British Jew serving in the war against Napoleon was Nathan Mayer Rothschild's brother-in-law, Moses Montefiore (1784–1885), whose family had come to England from Italy. After his discharge from the British army, Montefiore returned to his business.

Champions of Civil Liberties

Rothschild and Montefiore were both ardent champions of freedom. When England decided to abolish slavery, they assisted the government with a large loan to make the enforcement of the new law possible.

At that time, Jews in England still could not receive academic degrees and were barred from most public offices because, with the exception of the post of sheriff of London, they entailed an oath requiring an affirmation of the "true faith of a Christian."

Neither Montefiore nor Rothschild and the other Jewish leaders were satisfied with these conditions. They fought for the elimination of the oath and for the right of Jews to hold public office.

The First Jew Enters Parliament

The son of Nathan Rothschild, Baron Lionel de Rothschild (1808–1879), was elected to Parliament four times in ten years, but resigned each time because the required oath of office was Christian in form. In 1858, the rules were finally changed so that Rothschild could take an oath on a Hebrew Bible on the faith of a Jew. He was the first Jewish member of Britain's House of Commons. Eventually a special oath was devised so that Jews could be sworn in to all public offices and hold professional positions.

Benjamin Disraeli (1804–1881) was a symbol of the new position of the Jew in England. Although he had been baptized a Christian at an early age, he was proud to be descended from Spanish Jews who had fled from Spain in 1492. A brilliant statesman and trusted advisor to Queen Victoria, Disraeli also wrote novels and political essays.

Moses Montefiore

In 1838, Moses Montefiore was knighted by Queen Victoria, becoming the first Jew to attain this honor. Although active in public affairs, Sir Moses devoted much of his time and effort to the Board of Deputies of British Jews.

The Damascus Libel

In 1840, Sir Moses Montefiore learned that the Jews of Damascus in Syria had been falsely accused of murdering a monk. Jews there were being arrested and tortured, and Jewish children had been imprisoned to compel their parents to confess to a crime they had not committed. The British government sent Montefiore

Mayer Amschel Rothschild.

The Rothschild Family at Prayer, **by Moritz Daniel Oppenheim.**

Windmill in Yemin Moshe, a community in Israel named after Moses Montefiore. Much new building has taken place since the time of this photograph, but the windmill is still there.

to Egypt to press for the release of the prisoners and for an official acknowledgment of their innocence.

The incident in Damascus aroused indignation all over the world, and protest demonstrations took place in many countries, including the United States. In the end, the Egyptian government bowed to public pressure. The prisoners were released and their innocence was publicly proclaimed.

Sir Moses and the Tsar

While restrictions were being lifted throughout the rest of Europe, the situation of Russian Jewry was deteriorating. The Jews were still forced to live in the Pale of Settlement and were subjected to humiliating restraints. Now the tsar wanted them to abandon their customary occupations and relocate to the provinces of Astrakhan and the Caucasus region as farmers.

Moses Montefiore hoped to prevent this cruel decree from being put into effect. In 1846, he and his wife made the long journey to Russia, bearing with them a letter of introduction from Queen Victoria. They made another visit in 1872. Each time they were received courteously at the imperial court. The tsar permitted the Jews to remain in the Pale of Settlement, but nothing was done to ease their hardships.

Sir Moses and Palestine

Sir Moses dreamed of the return of the Jews to the Land of Israel. He visited Palestine six times, and each time brought assistance and support. To attract settlers, he planted vineyards and olive groves, and opened an experimental agricultural school. On the outskirts of the Old City of Jerusalem, Montefiore built a group of homes that became the nucleus of what is now called the New City.

Sir Moses Montefiore lived to the prodigious age of 101. His 100th birthday, in 1884, was marked by elaborate celebrations and parades, for his name had come to be known far and wide as a symbol of charity, progress, and love of liberty.

British philanthropist Sir Moses Montefiore. He encouraged many of the early Jewish settlements in Palestine.

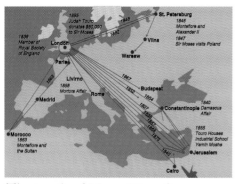

The travels of Moses Montefiore to protect the rights of the Jews. Note the seven trips to the Holy Land.

THE JEWISH RELIEF ACT

Obstacles in the way of Jewish communal and financial activity had long been removed. However, Jews still had not achieved political equality. Jews who were elected to Parliament refused to take the oath which stated "upon the true faith of a Christian." Lionel Rothschild and David Salomons were elected several times, but were prevented from taking their seats in the House of Commons because of the oath. Finally, in 1858, the Jewish Relief Act was passed and Lionel Rothschild was sworn in as a member of the House of Commons. He was sworn in with a Hebrew Bible. The following section is from the Jewish Relief Act. Note the specific language.

The Houses of Parliament
The Jewish Relief Act (July 23, 1858)
Be it enacted by the Queen's Most Excellent Majesty, by and with the Advice and Consent of the Lords Spiritual and Temporal, and Commons, in this present Parliament assembled, and by the Authority of the same, as follows:

1. Where it shall appear to either House of Parliament that a Person professing the Jewish Religion, otherwise entitled to sit and vote in such House, is prevented from so sitting and voting by his conscientious objection to take the Oath which by an Act passed or is to be passed in the present Session of Parliament has been or may be substituted for the Oaths of Allegiance, Supremacy, and Abjuration in the Form therein required, such House if it think fit, may resolve that thenceforth any Person professing the Jewish Religion, in taking said oath to entitle him to sit and vote as aforesaid, may omit the words "and I make this Declaration upon the true Faith of a Christian," and so long as such Resolution shall continue in force the said Oath, when taken and subscribed by any Person professing the Jewish religion of the Oath so modified shall, so far as respects the Title to sit and vote in such House, have the same Force and Effect as the taking and subscribing by other Persons of the said Oath in the Form required by the said Act.

2. In all other Cases, except for sitting in Parliament as aforesaid, or in qualifying to exercise the Right of Presentation to any Ecclesiastical Benefice in Scotland, whenever any of Her Majesty's Subjects professing the Jewish Religion shall be required to take the said Oath, the words "and I make this Declaration upon the true Faith of a Christian" shall be ornitted.

WHAT DO YOU THINK?

1. *Why were Jews barred from most public offices?*
2. *Why did Baron Lionel de Rothschild refuse to serve in Parliament?*
3. *Who was the first Jewish member of the House of Commons?*
4. *What phrase were Jews permitted to omit when taking the oath of office?*
5. *Are American elected officials sworn in on a Bible?*
6. *On what kind of Bible are Christian officials sworn in?*
7. *On what kind of Bible are Jewish officials sworn in?*

Looking for a Refuge

Isaac Aboab, the first rabbi in the Western Hemisphere. In 1642, he was called to the Dutch Jewish community of Recife, but he returned to Amsterdam when the Portuguese conquered the colony and brought in the Inquisition.

The expulsion from Spain in 1492 began a long period of wandering for many thousands of Jews.

Those exiles who went to Portugal found themselves betrayed by King Manuel. Thousands were forced to convert to Christianity.

Marranos who were able to leave Portugal often sought refuge in free countries like Holland. Throughout the 16th and 17th centuries, small numbers of devoted secret Jews made their way to Brazil, the West Indies, Mexico, and other New World colonies.

The Colony of Recife

When the Dutch conquered the Portuguese colony of Recife in Brazil in 1630, the Marranos living there fully resumed the faith of their ancestors and openly, began to teach their children Torah.

To serve as their religious leader and teacher, they invited Rabbi Isaac Aboab da Fonseca (1605–1693). Born to Marrano parents in Portugal, Aboab had escaped with his family to Holland and there had studied for the rabbinate. In 1642, he came to Recife from Amsterdam, becoming the first rabbi in the Western Hemisphere.

The freedom of the new Jewish community did not last long. In 1654, the Portuguese reconquered Recife and reintroduced the Inquisition. The Jews, who now were considered heretics, or traitors to the Christian faith, were forced once more to flee for their lives. Isaac Aboab and a few others returned to Amsterdam. Some of the refugees went to the Dutch Caribbean colonies of Surinam and Curaçao.

First Jews in North America

Twenty-three of the exiles from Recife sailed first to the West Indies, and then, in a vessel named the *Saint Charles,* up the North American coast to the Dutch colony of New Amsterdam. Robbed on the way

Artist's impression of Recife in the 1600s, showing the wall of the settlement and the church.

by pirates, the penniless group arrived in September of 1654 at the port that was later to be named New York.

Peter Stuyvesant

Peter Stuyvesant, the governor appointed by the Dutch West India Company, let the new arrivals know that they were not welcome. He "required them in a friendly way to depart," but allowed them to remain temporarily while he awaited instructions from Amsterdam. After some months, a letter arrived stating that because the Jews of Recife had fought for Holland, and because the Dutch West India Company had many Jewish shareholders, the newcomers were to be permitted to remain, "provided the poor among them shall not become a burden to the company or to the community, but be supported by their own nation."

Burgher Rights

These instructions did not find favor in the eyes of Stuyvesant and his council. Although the company had specified that the Jews were to be treated like everyone else, he denied them the right to stand guard with the colony's other residents, and instead required that they pay a special tax. This policy was abandoned when two Jewish colonists, Jacob Barsimson and Asser Levy, took legal action. Three years after they first landed, the Jews of New Amsterdam were granted citizenship. This did not mean that they enjoyed every civil right. They were not permitted to build a synagogue, being required to "exercise in all quietness their religion within their houses."

Through their outspoken demands for justice and freedom, and their faithfulness to Jewish tradition, this small group of Jews proved themselves worthy ancestors of the American Jewish community.

This chart for counting the Omer between Passover and Shavuot was used in the synagogue.

The Chatham Square Cemetery in New York City is one of the oldest Jewish cemeteries in the United States. It was founded in 1656.

The Mill Street Synagogue of the Shearith Israel Congregation of New York, erected in 1730.

Exterior of the Touro Synagogue. It was design by the architect Peter Harrison and was completed in 1763.

Interior of the beautiful Newport synagogue, first permanent synagogue in the New World. Named Yeshuat Israel, the congregation and its building were supported for many years by Judah Touro.

Asser Levy

In 1657, Asser Levy became the first Jew in New Amsterdam, and therefore in North America, to enjoy the full rights of citizenship. He became the colony's first Jewish landowner when he purchased a plot of land on William Street which is now in the heart of the Wall Street financial district. He was also accorded the privilege of becoming one of the colony's six licensed butchers.

The First Synagogue

In 1664, the British captured New Amsterdam and renamed it New York. Now Asser Levy expanded his business enterprises. In addition he bought a house on Mill Street to be used as a synagogue. Congregation Shearith Israel ("Remnant of Israel"), which had been meeting in private homes, now had its first official building.

Jews in the Colonies

The earliest Jewish settlers in North America were Sephardim, or, as they designated themselves, "of the Portuguese nation." The first synagogue in North America, Shearith Israel in New York, still follows the Spanish and Portuguese minhag, the Sephardic order of prayer.

During the 18th century, small numbers of Jews came to America from Europe, making their homes in Philadelphia, Charleston, Savannah, and other cities along the eastern seaboard.

Rhode Island, the colony founded by Roger Williams as an outpost of religious freedom, was a favorite destination. Among the prominent Jewish residents of Newport, its most important city, was Aaron Lopez (1731–1782), son of an old Marrano family in Lisbon, who became a wealthy merchant-shipper in the New World. The Newport Synagogue building, one of the earliest to be erected in America, is now a national shrine. It is often called the Touro synagogue in honor of Isaac Touro, its first spiritual leader.

PETER STUYVESANT AND JEWS

In 1620, a war broke out between Spain and Holland, and the Dutch took over the Portuguese colony of Recife, on the Brazilian coast. The Marranos in Recife immediately threw off their masks and openly returned to Judaism. Unfortunately, in 1654, Portugal reconquered Recife, and the Jews fearing the return of the Inquisition, scattered. Some returned to Holland, and returned to Catholicism, and some fled to other Dutch colonies in the Carribbean. Twenty-three Jewish refuges sailed to the Dutch colony of New Amsterdam in North America. On the way, they were robbed by pirates and arrived penniless to New Amsterdam. Peter Stuyvesant let the Jewish refugees know that they were unwelcome guests. This is his letter to the directors of the West Indian Company.

The Jews who have arrived would nearly all like to remain here, but learning that they with their customary usury and decitful trading with the Christians were very repugnant to the inferior magistrates, as also to the people having the most affection for you; the deaconry which takes care of the poor: also fearing that owing to their present indigence due to the fact that they had been captured and robbed by pirates they might become a charge in the coming winter, we have, for the benefit of this weak and newly developing place and the land in general, deemed it useful to require them in a friendly way to depart; praying also most seriously in this connection, for ourselves as also for the general community of your worships, that the deceitful race—such hateful enemies and blasphemers of the name of Christ—be not allowed further to infect and trouble this new colony, to the detraction of your worships and the dissatisfaction of your worships most affectionate subjects.

WHAT DO YOU THINK?

1. *Why didn't Stuyvesant want the Jews to settle in New Amsterdam?*

2. *How did Stuyvesant describe the Jewish refugees?*

3. *Did the directors of the West India Company accede to Stuyvesant's request?*

4. *What restrictions did the directors place on the newcomers?*

5. *What is a "burgher"?*

6. *Why was it important for the Jews to have a burgher certificate?*

7. *Did the Jews in Holland have burgher rights?*

The Revolutionary War

Aaron Lopez, distinguished citizen of Newport, Rhode Island. He came from a Marrano family in Portugal in 1752.

When the 13 American colonies revolted against England, many volunteers came from across the ocean to join the fight for freedom. Among them were Lafayette from France, Pulaski and Kosciusko from Poland, and Baron von Steuben and Baron Johann de Kalb from Germany. The latter, who died in action, commanded a unit of 400 men, so many of whom were Jews that it was sometimes called the Jewish regiment.

Most Canadian colonists remained loyal to England, but a few of them sympathized with the American rebels. David Salisbury Franks (1743–1793), a resident of Montreal, was arrested for making a slighting remark about a statue of King George. After he was released, he left Canada and joined the American army.

Haym Salomon

Service beyond the call of duty was rendered by Haym Salomon (1740–1785), a Jewish broker who came to New York from Poland in 1772. Imprisoned for supporting the revolutionary cause, he managed to escape to Philadelphia. There he worked with Robert Morris, superintendent of finance, extending loans and arranging credit to pay for the costs of the war. Though in America only a few years, he was an ardent patriot, never hesitating to risk his own funds to bring about victory for the cause of right.

There were about 3,000 Jews in the British colonies at the time of the American Revolution. Many of them fought for the patriotic cause. Francis Salvador (1747–1776), a Jewish planter born in England, was chosen a member of the provincial congress in South Carolina in 1774. Two years later, he gave his life in one of the Revolution's first battles.

Among the many other Jewish soldiers was Benjamin Nones (1757–1826), who came from France in order to participate in the battle for freedom and human rights, which he felt the Revolution represented.

Chicago's memorial to Haym Salomon, seen standing to the right of George Washington while Robert Morris stands on his left, both supporting him in his fight for freedom.

He rose to the rank of major, and afterwards served the new country as a legislator.

Gershom Mendes Seixas

Supporters of the American cause were in danger of imprisonment when the British army occupied New York and Newport. Gershom Mendes Seixas (1745–1816), minister of Shearith Israel, was so outspoken a patriot that he had to flee the city when the British troops landed. Taking the Torah scrolls with him, he reestablished the congregation in Stratford, Connecticut, and then set up a new one, Mikveh Israel, in Philadelphia. In New York after the war, he was honored as a leading religious figure, took part in George Washington's presidential inauguration, and served as a trustee of Columbia College.

Isaac Touro, accompanied by many members of his congregation, fled from Newport when the British occupied it. Aaron Lopez, rather than collaborate with the British, left his wealth and holdings and settled in a small town in Massachusetts until the patriot forces were victorious.

Words of George Washington

When the new nation came into being, and George Washington became its first President, the Jews of Newport were one of the many groups to send a message of good wishes. They expressed their appreciation for "a Government which to bigotry gives no sanction, to persecution no assistance," and their thanks to God for "all the blessings of civil and religious liberty."

In answer, President Washington stated, "The citizens of the United States of America have a right to applaud themselves for having given to mankind examples of an enlarged and liberal policy. All possess alike liberty of conscience and immunities of citizenship." He continued with a clear statement of the position of the new nation on human liberty:

"It is now no more that toleration is spoken of, as if

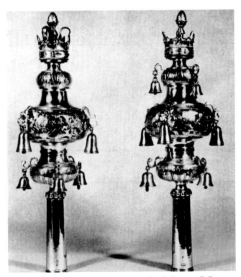

The talented silversmith Myer Myers (1723-1795) made synagogue ornaments as well as items for the general trade. These silver Torah rimmonim were specially made by Myer Myers for Congregation Mikveh Israel in Philadelphia.

Tombstone of Private Moses Judah, a soldier in the Revolutionary War. He served in the Pennsylvania Militia.

This painting by Ferris shows the forging of the Liberty Bell. It was cast by the Whitechapel Bell Foundry in England and cost £100. The inscription on the bell is from Leviticus, the third book of the Bible. It reads "Proclaim liberty throughout the land to all the inhabitants thereof". The Liberty Bell is now in Philadelphia.

Reverend Gershom Mendez Seixas (1745–1816) of Congregation Shearith Israel, a portrait copied by J. F. Brown from a miniature made in his lifetime. This picture hangs at Columbia University of which Seixas was a trustee 1787 to 1815.

it was by the indulgence of one class of people, that another enjoyed the exercise of their inherent natural rights. For happily the Government of the United States, which gives to bigotry no sanction, to persecution no assistance, requires only that they who live under its protection should demean themselves as good Citizens, in giving it on all occasions their effectual support."

Freedom of Religion

The United States was the first country in the world to guarantee full freedom of religion. The First Amendment to the Constitution begins: "Congress shall make no law respecting the establishment of religion, or prohibiting the free exercise thereof." Although some states still had laws restricting the right of holding office to those of recognized Christian faith, all of these were soon challenged and revoked. Jews were able to take their place as active citizens of the new democracy.

THE LETTER FROM THE HEBREW CONGREGATION IN NEWPORT TO GEORGE WASHINGTON

The following letter was addressed by the Hebrew Congregation of Newport, Rhode Island, to George Washington on the occasion of his visit to the city in 1790. It reflects the concern of the Jews for safeguarding the freedom for which they had found in America and which they did not enjoy abroad.

Sir: Permit the Children of the Stock of Abraham to approach you with the most cordial affection and esteem for your person and merits—and to join with our fellow-citizens in welcoming you to New Port.

With pleasure we reflect on those days—those days of difficulty and danger, when the God of Israel, who delivered David from the Peril of the sword—shielded your head in the day of battle—and we rejoice to think that the same Spirit, who rested in the bosom of the greatly beloved Daniel, enabling him to preside over the Provinces of the Babylonish Empire, rests, and ever will rest upon you, enabling you to discharge the arduous duties of Chief Magistrate in these States.

Deprived as we have hitherto been of the invaluable rights of free citizens, we now, (with a deep sense of gratitude to the Almighty Disposer of all events) behold a Government erected by the Majesty of the People, which to bigotry gives no sanction, to persecution no assistance—but generously affording to all liberty of conscience, and immunities of citizenship—deeming everyone, of whatever nation, tongue, or language, equal parts of the great governmental machine.

For all the blessings of civil and religious liberty which we enjoy under an equal and benign administration we desire to send up our thanks to the Ancient of Days, the great Preserver of Men—beseeching him that the Angel who conducted our forefathers through the wilderness into the promised land, may graciously conduct you through all the dangers and difficulties of this mortal life—and when like Joshua full of days and full of honor, you are gathered to your Fathers, may you be admitted into the heavenly Paradise to partake of the water of life and the tree of immortality.

Done and signed by order of the Hebrew Congregation in New Port, Rhode Island, August 17, 1790.

WHAT DO YOU THINK?

1. *Why did the Jews send George Washington a letter? What was their concern?*
2. *The contents of the letter had many biblical references. What do these references tell us about the Jews and the Christians? What did they value?*
3. *What does the phrase "to bigotry give no sanction" mean?*
4. *To what event does the letter compare the victory of the colonists against the British?*

Men and Women of Prominence

Judah Touro, philanthropist of New Orleans, in his old age.

The Touro Infirmary, endowed by Judah Touro in New Orleans. He gave continuously for health services during his life as well as for religious, cultural, and patriotic causes, and help to the poor.

Mordecai Manuel Noah (1785–1851), writer, politician, and well-known public figure.

Judah Touro

One of the many civic-minded Jews was the wealthy New Orleans merchant Judah Touro (1775–1854), who willed his entire fortune to synagogues, schools, hospitals, and orphan homes in 18 cities. A patriotic soldier who was seriously wounded in the battle of New Orleans during the War of 1812, Touro gave the largest contribution, $10,000, for the building of the Bunker Hill Monument. A large portion of his estate went to build homes for the poor in Jerusalem, under the direction of Sir Moses Montefiore.

Mordecai Manuel Noah

A quite different public figure was Mordecai Manuel Noah (1785–1851), well known as a politician, playwright, and newspaper editor. For a short time he was American consul at Tunis, there learning about the poverty and persecution suffered by the Jews of North Africa. Noah rallied support and proclaimed the establishment of Ararat, a settlement on Grand Island in New York's Niagara River, as a "city of refuge" for the oppressed Jews of the world. Until the ancient homeland in Palestine was restored, he declared, the United States, as the world's premier free nation, would be the proper host for the persecuted of Israel.

The Jewish Commodore

A top-ranking officer in the United States Navy, Uriah Philips Levy (1792–1862), showed courage both in his naval career and in his fight against discrimination and abuses in the service. He asked that these words be inscribed on his tombstone: "He was the father of the law for abolition of the barbarous practice of corporal punishment in the United States Navy."

The spirit of adventure and a sense of justice captivated Uriah Phillips Levy throughout his life. At the age of 10, he ran off and enlisted as a cabin boy on a sailing ship. By 20, he had become a master seaman and commanded a U.S. warship, the *George Washington*.

Adventure and Bravado

When the United States and Britain went to war in 1812, Levy was assigned to the warship *Argus*. It sank or captured more than 10 British cargo vessels. Levy was put in command of one of the captured ships and ordered to sail it to Philadelphia. Again, the spirit of adventure got the better of him. On the way, he attacked a heavily-armed British warship. His ship was sunk and Levy became a British prisoner.

After sitting out the rest of the war in an English prison, Levy was repatriated and commissioned a lieutenant in the U.S. Navy. During the course of his career he was court-martialed five times on various charges, but was always cleared.

Levy Challenges Naval Justice

Sailors on U.S. ships were regularly flogged and starved even for minor infractions. Levy refused to use corporal punishment on ships he commanded. He went on to persuade Congress that something had to be done to stop this sadistic practice. In 1850, thanks to Levy's heroic efforts, Congress abolished corporal punishment in the navy.

Many naval officers resented what Levy had done. In retaliation, they had him court-martialed on trumped-up charges. He was acquitted and returned to active duty with the rank of captain. Two years later, he was promoted to commodore.

Respect and Honor

Despite the insults and hardships, Uriah P. Levy loved America. A great admirer of Thomas Jefferson, he purchased his home at Monticello and restored it as a historical shrine. In 1943, the Navy honored his

Uriah Phillips Levy (1792–1862) Fighting sailor and admirer of Thomas Jefferson. He helped abolish corporal punishment in the U. S. Navy.

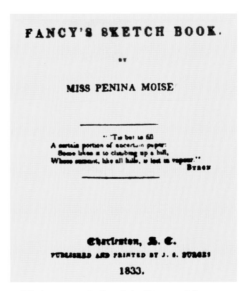

Title page of a book by Penina Moïse.

Portrait of Rebecca Gratz by Thomas Sully.

Jewish women in this country were active in the fields of education and good deeds. Lovely Rebecca Gratz (1781–1869), of a distinguished Philadelphia family, founded the first Jewish Sunday School in America, and worked for orphanages and other welfare institutions. It is thought that she was the inspiration for the virtuous heroine who bears her name in Sir Walter Scott's *Ivanhoe*.

Emma Lazarus (1849–1887), Jewish poet of New York, who was aroused by the plight of the Russian Jews to study her people's history and language and to write about their life and faith.

memory by naming a new destroyer the U.S.S. *Levy*. In 1959, the Jewish chapel at the naval base in Norfolk, Virginia, was named the Commodore Levy Chapel.

Penina Moïse

Penina Moïse (1797–1880), an educator and writer, supervised the Jewish Sunday School in Charleston, South Carolina, and composed poems and hymns throughout her life, even though she became blind in middle age. Penina Moïse was for many years the poet laureate of Charleston.

For many years she was the superintendent of the Sunday School of Congregation Beth Elohim in Charleston. Though she wrote poetry for newspapers and magazines, her favorite was writing hymns based on the psalms. Her long life was one of reading, writing, and teaching, activities which she continued, as much as possible, during her last 25 years, when she was blind and bedridden.

Emma Lazarus

The outstanding Jewish writer of this period was Emma Lazarus (1849–1887), whose early poetry on themes of nature and mythology won the praise of Ralph Waldo Emerson. The persecution of the Jews of Russia, and the steady stream of immigrants from Eastern Europe, made the young woman more aware of her people and faith. She studied Hebrew and Jewish history, gaining new pride and loyalty and a powerful theme for her later writings.

Songs of a Semite and *By the Waters of Babylon* are collections of poems by Lazarus expressing sympathy for her people's past and hope for the future. "Let but an Ezra rise anew," she wrote, "to lift the banner of the Jew!" Her best-known poem is "The New Colossus," inscribed on a plaque in the base of the Statue of Liberty in New York harbor.

MORDECAI M. NOAH

In 1825, Mordecai M. Noah announced a plan for the establishment of a Jewish settlement under the protection of the American Constitution. He picked the wooded Grand Island, close to the city of Buffalo, to be the center of a Jewish Republic. With several associates, some of whom were Christians, he named the colony Ararat, the mountain on which Noah landed after the flood. Noah announced his intentions in a proclamation to the Jews. He invited world Jewry to come to America and become citizens of Ararat.

On September 20, 1825, Noah dedicated Ararat's cornerstone.

The following selection is taken from Noah's proclamation to the Jews of the world.

I Mordecai Manuel Noah, citizen of the United States of America, announcing to Jews throughout the world, that an asylum is prepared and hereby offered to them, where they can enjoy that peace, comfort and happiness which have been denied them through the intolerance of former ages; an asylum in a free and powerful country, wealthy and with vast resources, the richness of its soil, of its climate; where industry is encouraged, education promoted, "a land of milk and honey," where Israel can repose in peace, under his "vine and fig tree," and where our people may so familiarize light of learning and civilization, as may glorify themselves. The desired spot in the State of New York, to which I hereby invite my people throughout the world, in common with those of every religious denomination, is called Grand Island, and on which I shall lay the foundation of a City of Refuge, to be called Ararat. Grand Island in the Niagara river is bounded by Ontario on the north, and Erie on the south, and within a few miles of each of these great commercial lakes. Deprived, as our people have been for centuries of a right in the soil, they will learn, with satisfaction, that here they can till the soil, reap the harvest, and raise the flocks which were unquestionably their own; and, in the full and unmolested enjoyment of their religious rights, with peace and plenty. In His name do I revive, renew and reestablish the government the The Jewish Nation, under the auspices and protection of the constitution and laws of the United States of America: confirming and perpetuating all our rights and privileges, our name, our rank, and our power among the nations of the earth, as they existed and were recognized under the government of the Judges. And I hereby enjoin it upon all our pious and venerable Rabbis, our Presidents and Elders of Synagogues, Chiefs of Colleges and brethren in authority throughout the world, to circulate and make known. my Proclamation, and give it full publicity, credence and effect.

WHAT DO YOU THINK?

1. *Why did Noah name his colony Ararat?*
2. *What motivated Noah to establish a Jewish Republic?*
3. *How would you describe "a land of milk and honey"?*
4. *Today, how would people react to Noah's proposal? Could he do this in the United States? Could he do this in any other country?*
5. *Is there still a need for a refuge for Jewish people? Why not?*
6. *Can Israel be a land of milk and honey? How can Israel make the dream of the prophets come true?*

Michael M. Allen, of Philadelphia, served as unofficial chaplain of Cameron's Dragoons, a Pennsylvania cavalry regiment. The regiment was commanded by Col. Max Friedman.

August Bondi (1833–1907), abolitionist. After leaving Austria following the Revolution of 1848, he, with Jacob Benjamin and Theodore Weiner, joined John Brown's anti-slavery army in Kansas.

The Union

The Civil War found most American Jews remaining loyal to the section of the country in which they lived. Jews were officers and fighting men on both sides.

In the years of controversy before the war, many Jews were active in the anti-slavery movement. Kansas Jews joined John Brown's army in the fight against slavery. Journalists like Moritz Pinner wrote articles in favor of abolition.

Moritz Pinner for the Union

Moritz edited the *Kansas Post*, a newspaper that tried to make Kansas a free state. This was a dangerous period, because a gang called "Border Ruffians," made up of people who wanted Kansas to be a slave state, attacked those who opposed slavery.

Pinner was a delegate to the Republican Convention in 1860 which nominated Abraham Lincoln for the presidency. He later refused a government post that would have taken him to Honduras; he wanted to stay and fight for the Union.

Rabbis for the Union

Rabbis Sabato Morais (1832–1897) of Philadelphia and David Einhorn (1809–1879) of Baltimore boldly preached against slavery despite strong opposition in their respective cities. The hostility against them was so intense that on one occasion, during the secession riots of 1861, Rabbi Einhorn had to flee Baltimore.

Soldiers for the Union

The surgeon general of the North was Jonathan Phineas Horowitz. The many Jewish officers in the Union army included several brigadier generals. One of them was Philip Joachimsen, who had helped to convict slave traders while serving as a U.S. attorney in New York.

Jewish Heroes

General Edward Solomon led an Illinois regiment in which there were over 100 Jews. After the war, he became governor of the Washington Territory. More than 6,000 Jewish soldiers served in the Union army, many of them in units that were predominantly Jewish. From Pennsylvania, came Cameron's Dragoons, commanded by Col. Max Friedman. Many Jewish soldiers died on the battlefield or in Confederate prison camps. Seven Congressional Medals of Honor were awarded to Jews in the Union army.

Order No. 11

General Ulysses S. Grant, in the second year of the war, took part in an action against Jews. He ordered all Jewish traders to leave the areas under his command along the Mississippi River:
"The Jews, as a class violating every regulation of trade established by the Treasury Department and also department orders, are hereby expelled from the department within twenty-four hours from the receipt of this order."

A leading Jewish citizen, Cesar Kaskel, went to Washington right away to protest to President Lincoln. The very next day, a message went out to General Grant revoking the order.

Abraham Linocoln's Relations With Jews

Lincoln acted quickly, but the hurt remained. It made it seem as if Jews were not to be trusted. Jews held many meetings of protest and articles were written for the papers to answer the false accusations. General Grant later made a public apology. This was not the only time that the Jews had to ask President Lincoln to step in. Early in the war, Congress had passed a law that would allow troops to have a chaplain. It said that each chaplain "must be a regular

Judah P. Benjamin (1811–1884), Confederate Secretary of War, and Secretary of State. After the war, he fled to England.

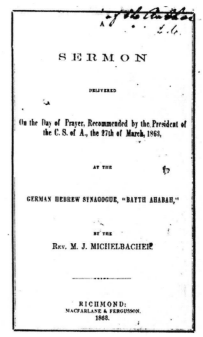

The President of the Confederate States of America, Jefferson Davis, on March 27, 1863, recommended a Day of Prayer. Rev. Michelbacher, of the German synagogue in Richmond, preached this sermon, to which he added a prayer for the Confederacy.

Captain Asher W. Garber.

Private Thomas Jefferson Goldman.

General Robert E. Lee's battle-tested Army of Northern Virginia included many Jewish soldiers. Captain Asher W. Garber was an officer in the Virginia Light Artillery and Private Thomas Jefferson Goldman served in the 44th Georgia Infantry.

List of Confederate Jewish soldiers buried by Rev. George Jacobs.

ordained minister of some Christian group."

Michael Allen, a Jew and chaplain of Cameron's Dragoons, had to resign. Arnold Fischel, of New York, went to Washington for the Jewish Board of Delegates to take the matter up with the government. Fischel appealed to both houses of Congress, saying that the law was not fair. It was against the Constitution, he reminded them, "to require a religious test as a qualification, for an officer under the United States." He was able to see Lincoln himself, who promised, "I shall try to have a new law broad enough to cover what is desired by you in behalf of the Israelites." The new law said that chaplains had to be ministers "of some religious denomination." This permitted rabbis to serve.

The Confederate Army

There were also thousands of Jewish soldiers on the Confederate side. The South's Secretary of War declared at one point that he could not give furloughs to Jewish soldiers for the High Holidays since there were at least 10,000 of them—more than could be spared from their posts.

The most important Jew serving the Confederacy was Judah Philip Benjamin of Louisiana (1811–1884). Elected to the U.S. Senate in 1852, Benjamin left Washington when Louisiana seceded from the Union. At various times, he served as the Confederacy's Attorney General, Secretary of War, and Secretary of State.

When the South began to lose the war, Benjamin's political enemies in the Confederacy placed the blame on his shoulders. After the war, he escaped to England and became an attorney.

FROM A RESOLUTION DURING THE CIVIL WAR

Like the rest of the country, the Jews, too, were divided in the conflict between the North and the South. The selection which follows is from a resolution of the Hebrew Congregation of Shreveport, Louisiana, in 1861. It reflects the conflict and indicates that there was no unanimous Jewish position on this question. The resolution was in response to an editorial in a magazine, the Jewish Messenger, *which appeared for support of the Union cause.*

Whereas, we received the "Jewish Messenger" on the 26th of April, a paper published in New York, in which an appeal has been made to all, whether native or foreign born, Christian or Israelite. An article headed "stand by the flag!" in which the editor makes an appeal to support the stars and stripes, and to rally as one man for the Union and the Constitution. Therefore be it

Resolved, That we, the Hebrew congregation of Shreveport, scorn and repel your advice, although we might be called Southern rebels; still, as law-abiding citizens, we solemnly pledge ourselves to stand by, protect, and honor the flag, with its stars and stripes, the Union and Constitution of the Southern Confederacy with our lives, liberty, and all that is dear to us.

Resolved, That we, the members of said congregation, bind ourselves to discontinue the subscription of the "Jewish Messenger," and all Northern papers opposed to our holy cause, and also to use all honorable means in having said paper banished from our beloved country.

Resolved, that while we mistook your paper for a religious one, which ought to be strictly neutral in politics, we shall from this hour treat it with scorn, as a black republican paper, and not worthy of Southern patronage; and that, according to our understanding, church and politics ought never to be mingled, as it has been the ruination of any country captivated by the enticing words of preachers.

Resolved, That we, the members of said congregation, have lost all confidence and regard to the Rev. S. M. Isaacs, Editor and Proprietor of the "Jewish Messenger," and see in him an enemy to our interest and welfare, and believe it to be more unjust for one who preaches the Word of God, and to advise us to act as traitors and renegades to our adopted country, and raise hatred and dissatisfaction in our midst, and assisting to start a bloody civil war amongst us....

Resolved, that papers friendly to the southern cause, are politely requested to publish the foregoing resolution.

WHAT DO YOU THINK?

1. *Why was there a divided Jewish opinion on the conflict between the North and the South?*
2. *What factors dictated the attitudes of the Jews in the North and South?*
3. *Where was the* Jewish Messenger *published?*
4. *Could a Northern newspaper support the Southern cause?*
5. *Do you think the* Jewish Messenger *should have remained neutral?*
6. *Do you think the Jewish newspapers or magazines should take political positions or stick to Jewish issues?*
7. *What was the argument of the Jews of Shreveport against the agenda of the* Jewish Messenger?
8. *Could there have been an alternative option available?*
9. *Suppose you lived in Shreveport during the Civil War, what would you, as a Jew have supported?*

Immigration and Westward Expansion

Julius Meyer (1851–1909) of Omaha. Nebraska, an Indian trader in the 1870s, with some of his Indian friends. Meyer spoke several Indian dialects.

The synagogue of Congregation Shearith Israel on Crosby Street, New York City. It was in use from 1834 to 1860, when it moved to a new and larger location.

A Jewish-owned firm on State Street, Salt Lake City, Utah, in the 1870s.

Encouraged by the promise of liberty and opportunity, great numbers of Europeans migrated to America during the 19th century. The Industrial Revolution was changing the way of life in the Old World, and many displaced workers and farmers sought new homes in the New World. The era of political reaction following the Napoleonic Wars and the failure of the revolutions of the 1840s in Central Europe led those who longed for freedom to turn their eyes across the Atlantic Ocean.

The Hand of Freedom

Millions of people in Europe saw the New World as the promised land of freedom. There had been revolutions in France and other countries, but the reactionary governments that gained power after Napoleon's defeat at Waterloo had no sympathy for the ideals of the French Revolution. They reinstated many of the old restrictive laws, and as a result, full equality and civil rights again became dreams.

As always, life was most difficult for Jews. Even in the 1820s and 1830s, but especially after the failed uprisings of 1848, Jews from Central Europe and the German states began flocking to America. At the time of the Revolution, there were about 3,000 Jews in the United States. By 1840, there were 40,000, the majority of them immigrants or the children of immigrants.

The newcomers became part of a growing country with open borders. When they arrived in America, they found well-established communities of fellow Jews in New York, Philadelphia, Baltimore, Richmond, Charleston, New Orleans, and many other cities. As early as the 1790s, adventurous Jews had traveled alone into the interior to set up trading posts or start new farms in such areas as Natchez, Mississippi, and Montgomery, Alabama. John Law, a Jew from Montreal, was trading with Indians at Green

Bay, Wisconsin, around the year 1800, and Samuel Solomon came to St. Louis in 1805.

The German Jews

Many of the new German immigrants, both Jewish and non-Jewish, settled in the Midwestern cities of Cleveland, Cincinnati, Milwaukee, and Detroit. All through the Midwest one could hear German spoken in the small Jewish communities. Synagogues were started in Cincinnati in 1824 and in Chicago in 1847.

Jewish immigrants worked at many different kinds of jobs. Their number included laborers, farmers, ranchers, watchmakers, tailors, doctors, lawyers, printers and editors, boatmen, and wagon drivers. A very substantial proportion were peddlers and storekeepers.

Jewish Peddlers

Many of the Jewish immigrants who came to these shores became peddlers. With settlements spreading far and wide across the country, there was a need for men to travel from place to place, bringing needed goods to people on farms and in villages too small to support a store. Some peddlers plied their routes through the countryside on foot, carrying their goods in backpacks; others drove small wagons. The wares they offered ranged from needles and pins, combs and mirrors, ribbons and cloth, to pots and pans, knives, and books. Depending on the circumstances and the area they worked in, some returned home every weekend, others only every few weeks or months.

Though they usually received a warm welcome from their customers, especially because they were important sources of news, the Jewish peddlers led a hard life. Travel was difficult and dangerous. They were lonely and homesick. They might go many weeks without meeting a fellow Jew or another person who could speak their native language.

A Jewish peddler exhibiting a variety of goods from his wagon.

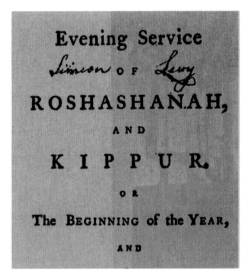

The first High Holiday prayerbook published in America.

Macy's, one of the world's largest department stores, was founded by Lazarus Straus in partnership with R. H. Macy. Straus moved to New York City from Atlanta because of the Civil War.

Levi Strauss

Levi Strauss (1829–1902) was a German-born immigrant who arrived in New York in 1848. Two years later, he caught the "gold fever" and sailed for San Francisco by way of Cape Horn, at the tip of South America. He arrived in California with a pack of needles, pins, string, sewing thread, and bolts of cloth. Strauss made all his canvas into pants. When these sold out, he ordered special denim cloth from France and dyed it blue. Levi Strauss's name appeared on a red tag on every pair of pants he manufactured, and before long a new term for those pants was added to the English language: Levi's. Today, the Levi Strauss Co. is a multinational enterprise with factories in many countries. Strauss's descendants are active in Jewish affairs and have contributed to the support of Jewish institutions all over the world.

Advertisement for denim work clothes produced by Levi Strauss & Co.

Workers in the Sutro tunnel.
Adolf Sutro (1830-1898), a German-born engineer, built the mine tunnel that carries his name in Nevada. He also served as mayor of San Francisco from 1895 to 1897.

A letter written by one peddler says that he was about to start the Sabbath on Friday afternoon, "unwashed, unshaven, in a gentile inn," far from home and friends.

The peddlers were ambitious and hardworking. Many of them went on to open stores in new settlements, especially places located near roads or river landings. They saved their money and, as soon as possible, sent for their wives, parents, and siblings in the old country.

Once a few Jewish families had settled in the same area, a Jewish community would come into existence. Almost always it began by purchasing a cemetery and holding weekly prayer services. Before long, a shochet would be hired to provide kosher meat, and a teacher engaged for the children. Larger groups would try to bring a rabbi or chazzan. With this done, the former peddlers came to feel at home in the new country.

Some Jewish storekeepers went on to become department store magnates. Among the many major stores founded or expanded by Jews were Filene's in Boston, Macy's in New York, Rich's in Atlanta, and Magnin's in San Francisco.

From Coast to Coast

From coast to coast, Jews did their share in the building of the towns and cities of America. They were only a tiny percentage of the country's population—by 1860, there were 200,000 Jews out of a population of 23 million. Nevertheless, it took their work as well as the work of other ethnic groups to make it the great country it is today.

As pioneers of the American frontier, Jews were indeed not very different from other people. They were part of a new land, learning its language, enjoying its rights and freedoms. Each group set up its own church, and the Jews set up their synagogues. All as they found their new homes and chose their own way of life helped settle the large stretches of land between the Atlantic and the Pacific Oceans.

CALIFORNIA

The earliest Jewish settlers traded with the Indians and participated in the western movement of the American frontier. With a pack on his back or with a wagon overflowing with general merchandise, the Jewish peddler followed the march of civilization. As the population increased, the peddlers opened general stores, which in a few cases became department stores. The gold rush stimulated the flow of Jewish immigration westward. Jewish entrepreneurs and immigrants helped to establish many of the towns in the god rush areas. In an article written in 1861, Henry J. Labatt, a lawyer who had migrated to San Francisco from New Orleans, describes the economic activity of the Jews in San Francisco.

On a first arrival in our city, it becomes a matter of astonishment to all who see the large number of mercantile houses conducted by Israelites, being much greater, in proportion to the commerce, than in any other city in America. Every line of business is engaged in by them, with credit to themselves and honor to the community.

Each mining town and city has a large representation, and everywhere you hear of their success and prosperity, which in turn they devote to the improvement of the place, by erecting substantial buildings and warehouses for the increase of their business, caused by industry, economy, and attention.

In all the great fires which have devastated the settlements of California, they have been great sufferers. Year after year, have they seen the hard earnings of their labor swept away by the ruthless conflagration, and yet with the indomitable energy of their race, have they toiled on to regain what they thus were deprived of by misfortune. Often, indeed, would they not lose what they had accumulated, but become reduced by being brought into debt by the destruction of their stock. Everywhere they seemed anxious to guard against this great affliction of our country and, by erecting substantial tenements, avoid another calamity.

In all commercial enterprises they keep pace with the marked improvements of the day, and, as merchants, are courted, admired—nay, even sometimes envied.

The almost universal success of the Jews, as merchants, in California, must be attributed to some peculiar reasons; for while many of all nations have succeeded in this State, yet, as a general thing, no class of people who began with so small a capital, have accumulated the same amount of fortune. Any close observer will find that their individual industry dispenses with the necessity for extra clerks, who, at the exorbitant rates necessary for their support, soon make sad inroads upon the monthly profit. They seldom pay unwarrantable rents, being willing to submit to many inconveniences rather than indulge in extravagance. Their method of conducting business is also worthy of consideration. They seem anxious to dispose of their stock in a short time, and at little profit, and you will generally find throughout the country, that their stores are known as the "cheap stores." This is a great secret of trade, and when once that reputation is acquired, the customer will seek that store.

WHAT DO YOU THINK?

1. *Why did the Jews who immigrated into the United States start as peddlers?*
2. *California was a land of opportunity. What opportunities were there for the Jews?*
3. *In what type of businesses were California Jews involved?*
4. *According to Labatt, were the Jews respected?*
5. *What type of catastrophes devastated the California settlements.*
6. *Were the Jews discouraged by the devastating fires?*
7. *According to Labatt, why did the Jewish mercantile houses succeed?*
8. *Does the method of doing business remind you of the type of stores that exist in your area?*
9. *What is a cheap store?*
10. *Is there a cheap store in your area?*
11. *Were the business practices of the California Jews respected?*

Rabbinical Leaders

Isaac Leeser (1806–1868), rabbi, teacher, translator, and organizer, did much to further Jewish education and raise the standard of Jewish communal life.

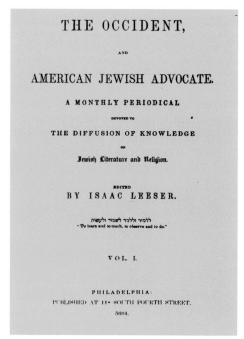

THE OCCIDENT,

AND

AMERICAN JEWISH ADVOCATE.

A MONTHLY PERIODICAL

DEVOTED TO

THE DIFFUSION OF KNOWLEDGE

ON

Jewish Literature and Religion.

EDITED

BY ISAAC LEESER.

"To learn and to teach, to observe and to do."

VOL. I.

PHILADELPHIA:
PUBLISHED AT 118 SOUTH FOURTH STREET.
5604.

For 25 years, Isaac Leeser edited and published the *Occident*, a leading Jewish periodical, which gave its readers essays, stories, poems, and news of Jewish communities all over the world.

Isaac Leeser (1806–1868), the most activist American rabbi of his day, set about almost single-handedly to try to remedy all the lacks in Jewish life and education. He published textbooks, and translations of the Bible and the prayerbook. In his Philadelphia congregation, Mikveh Israel, he delivered sermons in English, advocating education and Jewish unity. In 1867, with the help of Sabato Morais, he established Maimonides College, an institution for Jewish studies.

The *Occident*

Isaac Leeser made his greatest contribution as editor of the *Occident*, a magazine that appeared monthly from 1843 to 1869. Its pages tell of the interests and problems of American Jews in those years, including items ranging from the arrival of a new Hebrew teacher in New York to protests against the kidnapping of an Italian Jewish boy, Edgardo Mortara, by the Catholic Church in 1858. At times of crisis, magazines like the *Occident*, David Einhorn's *Sinai*, and Isaac Mayer Wise's *Israelite* served to inform and in some measure to unite the Jews of America.

The Reform Movement in the United States

The Reform movement in the United States became stronger in the 1840s with the arrival of large numbers of Jews from Germany, including several rabbis who agreed with the ideas expressed by Abraham Geiger. While upholding the ethics and moral law of Judaism, they wished to adapt to modern times by abolishing rituals and ideals that they felt no longer had meaning.

Rabbi David Einhorn (1809–1879) came to Baltimore, and Rabbi Samuel Hirsch (1815–1889) to Philadelphia, with radical ideas. They no longer considered Judaism's ritual laws to be binding. They felt that the age-old hopes for the coming of the Messiah and the return to Zion had no meaning for American Jews. They dropped many Hebrew prayers, substituting German readings and hymns.

The Conservative Movement

Sabato Morais (1823–1897) and a group of like-minded associates founded the Jewish Theological Seminary of America in 1886 in New York. They hoped that the rabbis ordained there, all of whom were to be English-speaking college graduates, would be able to keep Jewish youth loyal to their heritage. The movement that came into being with the founding of the Seminary is known as Conservative Judaism.

Alexander Kohut (1842–1894), Benjamin Szold (1829–1902), and Marcus Jastrow (1829–1903) were among the scholars who helped fashion this new religious denomination. From the start, the Conservatives differed with the Reform movement, upholding loyalty to Torah and Talmud, observance of the Sabbath, and dietary laws, Hebrew as the language of prayer, and the preservation of hopes for the return to Zion.

Solomon Schechter

From England's Cambridge University in 1902 came Dr. Solomon Schechter (1847–1915) to head the Seminary. Schechter was a dynamic teacher whose great learning combined East European devotion with modern scholarly discipline. He had become famous for his discovery of the Cairo Genizah, a storehouse of discarded ancient manuscripts that shed much light on Jewish history. Under Schechter's leadership, the Seminary became a first-rank scholarly institution. In the Conservative view, Judaism, like all other human institutions, has developed through the ages, not by sudden reforms but in response to the will and needs of its faithful adherents. The leading rabbis and congregations at the turn of the century, as well as the leading philanthropists, were mostly in the Reform wing of Judaism. Conservative and Orthodox rabbis and congregations were not as yet well-organized.

The Orthodox Movement

The great majority of Jewish immigrants from 1881 on were Orthodox in background. They attempted to set up the same type of communities as had

Rabbi David Einhorn (1809–1879), radical Reform leader and outspoken abolitionist, served pulpits in Philadelphia and New York after leaving Baltimore at the time of pro-slavery riots.

The Torah Ark of Congregation Beth Elohim, Charleston, South Carolina, is a replica of the one destroyed by fire in 1838. The original Ark was built in 1799.

Early photograph of the Jewish Theological Seminary of America in New York.

existed in their former homes. Each congregation, following Jewish tradition and the customs of its members, felt it could stand by itself without looking toward a central authority.

A group of Orthodox Jews in New York City made an attempt to attain unity under the leadership of Rabbi Jacob Joseph (1848–1902), whom they brought from Vilna in Lithuania to be the city's chief rabbi. He proved unable to bring order to New York's teeming Jewish community.

Umbrella organizations met with more success. In 1898, the Union of Orthodox Jewish Congregations was founded, thanks to the efforts of Rabbi H. Pereira Mendes (1852–1937) of the Shearith Israel Congregation in New York. A group of Orthodox rabbis joined together to form the Agudas Harabonim in 1902. One of their aims was to aid academies of learning, *yeshivot*, both in America and abroad.

Yeshiva University

The outstanding yeshiva in the New World was founded in 1896. Named for a great European scholar, Rabbi Isaac Elchanan, this New York institution began as a rabbinical seminary for students who had already steeped themselves in Jewish learning in European academies. Over the years, it expanded into a complete university. Under the presidency of Rabbi Bernard Dov Revel (1885–1940) and his successor, Dr. Samuel Belkin (1911–1976), it grew to include a high school, an undergraduate college, and a variety of graduate and professional schools, including the Albert Einstein Medical School, the Benjamin Cardozo Law School, Stern College for Women, and the Wurzweiler School of Social Work. Under Belkin's successor, Rabbi Norman Lamm (b. 1927), Yeshiva continued to grow. In the 1990s, it had 5,200 undergraduate and graduate students, and an additional 1,000 students at the affiliates. In 2003, Rabbi Norman Lamm retired and was succeeded by Richard M. Joel.

Solomon Schechter (1847–1915), scholar of Eastern Europe, Germany, and England, called from Cambridge University to head the Jewish Theological Seminary of America in 1902. He gathered the great faculty and library of the Seminary, and gave form to the Conservative movement.

THE DAMASCUS AFFAIR

In 1840, in the city of Damascus, in Syria, a Christian monk, Father Tomaso and his servant disappeared. Other monks directed suspicions to the Jews and accused them of murdering the Christians and using their blood to make matzot for Passover. Dozens of Jews, including children were arrested and tortured and several of them confessed. Jews all over the world were shocked. The French consul, and the authorities in Paris supported the ritual murder charge, hoping to strenghten their political influence among the Arabs. Meetings were held all over the world and governments sent protest messages to Mehemet Ali, Pasha of Egypt who controlled Syria at that time. Sir Moses Montifiore and Adolphe Cremieux fought to release the prisoners. In America, Rabbi Isaac Leeser the activist, organized protests against the charges. President Van Buren instructed the American consul, at Alexandria to use his influence on behalf of the prisoners. Finally Mehemet Ali freed the prisoners that were still alive and denounced the ritual murder charge. Now, in 1840, for the first time in American Jewish life, the Jews had organized themselves politically to help a Diaspora Jewry in distress. This endeavor strengthened the already effective national Jewish community. Their efforts were laudable since there were only 15,000 American Jews. Jews began to realize that in union there was strength.

Below is the consul's letter to the U.S. Secretary of State which indicates that he believed the charge against the Jews.

United States Consulate,
Beyrout 24th March 1840
On the 5th of February last the Revd Capouchin Thomas president of the Catholic Church of Damascus together with his Servant having, disappeared from that City H. E. Sherif pashaw Governor General of Syria and the French Consul of Damascus employed the pollice for making all strict inquiries after them, and some people having declared to have seen that priest and his servant enter on that evening in the Jews quarter, the suspitions of Government fall on the Jews, that they assassinated them. On that day Revd Thomas had put up against the wall of a Jew Barbers shop, an advertisement for some Articles to be sold by Auction, and was observed that the said advertisement had been removed from its place and put up again with different Wafers than these used by the priest. The Jew Barber was questioned and taken into prison, and after some torments on his person he confessed that the Revd Thomas had been beheaded in the house of David Atari a rich Jew, by Seven of his coreligioners of Damascus, and that, in order to take his Blood, it being ordered by their religion to make use of Christian Blood in their Unleavened Bread at Easter.

The Seven Jews thus accused, as well as all their high Priests; 64 Children, belonging to those families, and all their Butchers were immediately taken to prison, and after severe Tortures and threats several of them confessed also the fact of the murder, adding that they had since cut the body in small pieces and threw it in a Canal, after collecting all the Blood in a large Bottle for religious purposes.

The torments on the prisoners having continued, some of them confessed that the Servant also had been beheaded in the house of another jew, his Blood taken to the last drop, and his body cut in the same way like that of the Priest was thrown in another Canal. The Pashaw and the french Consul repared to the place and found that body also in pieces together with three sharp knives.

The french Consul is seizing all their religious Books with a hope of clearing that abominable secret. He found a Book printed in Latin, by "Lucio Ferrajo" in which the passages are found in the Talmoud, which I have the honor to accompany in french.

Several of the prisoners in prison have died of the torments, and others turned Turks and the rest in number Seventy two are sentenced to be hanged, but the french Consul has requested to postpone their death in hope of finding out through more torments the Bottle of Blood, which they pretend to have already distributed to their coreligioners in the different other City's.

In the place where the Servants remains were found a quantity of other human Bons of old date in small bits have been discovered, which proves that they were accustomed in that house to such like humane sacrifices. A Doctor bribed by the Jews declared the Servants Bons to be those of some Beast but the Pashaw having since called a Commission of several Doctors they pronounced them to be umane.

I have the Honor to be with great respect, Sir,
Your Most Obedient Humble Servant J. Chasseaud.

WHAT DO YOU THINK?

1. In1840, the French supported the murder charge to strenghten their influence among the Arabs. How are the French, in 2003, using their politics to gain influence among the Arabs

2.

Tsars Nicholas I and Alexander II

Sir Moses Montefiore speaking to Tsar Nicholas I in 1846 in St. Petersburg.

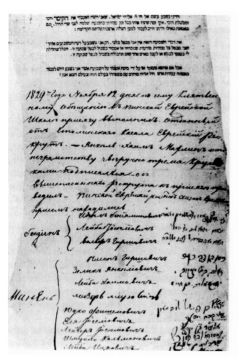

Oath of a Jewish recruit from Stolin, sworn in the synagogue of Pinsk, 1829. This Jewish youth, under the 1827 statute of Tsar Nicholas I, was forced to serve in the Russian army. The document is printed in Hebrew with handwritten additions in Russian.

Not even the intervention of so prominent a person as Sir Moses Montefiore could bring about an improvement in the situation of Russian Jewry. Tsar Nicholas I, who came to the throne of Russia in 1825, was bent on assimilating the diverse population of his empire into one vast Russian nation. During the reign of his brother, Alexander I (1777–1825), Napoleon's army had marched east, deep into the very heart of Russia. Russia had defended itself well and the French armies had retreated. But the new ideas of freedom and equality that had arisen in France had been carried by its soldiers into the lands of the tsar. Poland, which never had accepted Russia's rule gracefully, now chafed under its reins.

The Jew Laws

To gain greater control over the minorities in his realm, Nicholas I instituted a double administrative policy. On the one hand he lifted some of the restrictions that had been imposed upon them, but at the same time he sought to divest them of their identities as separate nationality groups. He dealt a severe blow to the Jews of the Pale of Settlement when he ordered the Kahal, the time-honored instrument of Jewish communal self-government, to disband.

The tsar wanted the Jews to give up their Yiddish language, their religion, and their traditions. He also wanted a large and powerful army, and to realize this aim in 1827 he instituted a draft of young men at the age of 18, for a term of 25 years. Jewish boys were conscripted as young as the age of 12, but were placed in military barracks or cantons until the age of 18, when they officialy began their 25 years of military service. Recruiters would come and take Jewish boys from their homes by force. Once they were in the army, they would be pressured to convert. Frequently they would be beaten and starved in an effort to persuade them to renounce their faith.

Crown Schools

As another means of hastening the disappearance of Russian Jewry as a distinct group, Tsar Nicholas I set up special schools in the Pale of Settlement. In these crown schools, as they were called, Jewish children were to learn Russian and be given an education that would wean them away from their traditional way of life and toward conversion to Christianity.

Despite the pressures brought upon them by the tsarist government, the Jews of Russia remained loyal to their heritage. The community was hard-pressed. Many were forced to leave the villages of the Pale and move to cities where they had no way to earn a living. When the tsar realized that his Jewish policy was not bringing about conversions, he invoked sterner restrictions.

Alexander II, a Liberal Ruler

Nicholas I died in 1855 and was succeeded by his son, Alexander II, a man of liberal leanings. In 1861, Alexander abolished serfdom, making it possible for peasants to buy land and establish farms. The Jews of the Pale of Settlement hoped that soon their lot, too, would be improved.

Their hopes were realized in great measure, for Alexander II abolished the draft of Jewish boys under the age of 18.

Alexander wanted to keep pace with developments in Western Europe by furthering the growth of Russia's factories and industrial centers. He permitted Jews to move from the Pale to the large cities and encouraged them to go into manufacturing, learn trades, become merchants, and take professional training at the universities.

Many educated Jews believed that a secular education was compatible with Jewish culture. Judah Leib Gordon (1831–1892), an important poet and journalist, coined the motto "Be a man outside, but a Jew in your own home."

No longer did all Jews have to live in the Pale of

Title page of *Tifilot Yisrael* the first prayer-book ever translated into Russian. The siddur was translated by Rabbi Joseph Hurwitz in 1869. It was published in Warsaw, the capital of the Polish provinces of the Russian Empire.

A cartoon showing Tsar Nicolas I extracting money from the Jews of Russia.

After the Pogrom by Maurice Minkowski (1881–1930). **The pogroms claimed thousands of Jewish victims.**

Settlement. Some became respected and successful merchants and manufacturers; others practiced law and medicine in the large cities. Still others became skilled workers in the new industrial centers.

Alexander II Assassinated

Russia was a hotbed of revolutionary movements. Despite the reforms, many Jewish youngsters joined the revolutionary parties. In 1881 Tsar Alexander II was assassinated. The assailant was caught and implicated his fellow plotters, one of whom was a Jewish girl named Gessia Helfman. Government officials used this incident to incite pogroms against the Jews. Over the next two years many Jews were murdered, and innumerable businesses and homes looted and destroyed. To make matters worse, the reforms instituted by Alexander were rescinded by his successor, and the government issued the May Laws, which restricted Jewish residence and professional rights.

The pogroms of 1881–82 in Russia and Ukraine were decisive in establishing Zionism as a major movement. The outbreak of violence on such a broad scale, and with government collusion, made many Jews feel that they could never lead a normal life in Russia. While some decided to emigrate to the United States, others concluded that the only viable solution was Eretz Yisrael, the Land of Israel.

Tsar Alexander II (1818–1881)

The anti-Semitic rioters have caught an unfortunate Jew and are in the process of murdering him. Note the police standing by and watching the rioters and doing nothing.

TSAR NICHOLAS I: JEW LAWS IN RUSSIA (1835)

Nicholas I was the tsar of Russia from 1825 to 1855. His reign was marked by oppression. In 1827, he introduced compulsory military service for Jews which was accompanied by the drafting of Jewish children at the age of 12 into the army. During his reign the area of the Pale of Settlement was reduced and the Kahal was disbanded. In 1835 Nicholas introduced the Jew Laws, which limited Jewish movement and commercial activities. The reign of Nicholas I is regarded as one of the darkest periods in the history of the Jews in tsarist Russia.

Jews in the Western districts may not settle in towns which are not at least 50 miles removed from the border.

Jews may not employ Christians as domestic servants.

Jews must use Russian or the language of their district in all official documents—under no circumstances may they use the Jewish language.

Jews engaged in legal commerce may not sell wine or other intoxicating beverages for credit on pain of cancellation of the debt.

Jewish merchants of the First Guild may leave the Pale of Settlement to attend fairs, but they may remain in the city only for the duration of the fair.

Jewish manufacturers who wish to ship products to the interior districts must affix their special sign on the goods.

Jewish craftsmen may register . . . in the places of their residence provided such a procedure is not contrary to the privileges granted the several cities.

Within the Pale of Settlement Jews may rent land . . . without thereby being classified as farmers . . .

The Jews are accounted members of the community of the city in which they live; in all affairs pertaining to them and for the distribution of taxes and other obligations which are theirs in particular let them appoint 3–5 representatives who shall constitute the Kahal.

The members of the Kahal shall be chosen only from among those Jews who can read and write Russian or the language used in that locality for official documents. The rnembers of the Kahal shall serve with the approval of the district officer for a period of three years.

It is forbidden to congregate in synagogues or houses of study for any purpose other than prayer or the practice of religious ceremonies.

Jewish children may be admitted to government schools in those places where their parents have the right of residence.

WHAT DO YOU THINK?

1. *Why were Jews not permitted to settle in towns less than 50 miles from the border? Was it an attempt to restrict Jewish merchants from importing cheaper merchandise from foreign sources?*
2. *What was the purpose of affixing a special sign to Jewish merchandise? Was it like the special clothing that Jews were forced to wear in medieval Europe? Was it like the yellow stars worn in Nazi Germany?*
3. *Was the government within its rights to expect Kahal representatives to read and write the language of the locality?*
4. *Why did the goverment specify that synagogues should only be used for religious purposes? What where they afraid of?*
5. *Why did the government insist upon the power to appoint Jewish teachers and civil servants?*
6. *The Jew Laws of Russia were a double–edged sword. Note that the law which grants a privilege also carries a restriction. List the privileges and restrictions?*
7. *Does the United States use such legislation to restrict its population?*

America Beckons

Polish Jews asking advice about emigrating to the United States at the information desk of the Hebrew Immigrant Aid Society in Warsaw.

The Statue of Liberty was a golden door and beacon of hope and freedom for all immigrants.

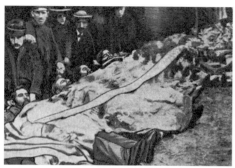

Jewish victims of the pogroms. Thousands of Jews were murdered in government-inspired bloodbaths.

Throughout its history, one country in particular opened its doors to the poor and wronged of all nations and creeds. Indeed, at the very gateway to this land stood a statue, the symbol of liberty, on which were engraved words written by Emma Lazarus (1849–1887), a compassionate and gifted Jewish poet.

Give me your tired, your poor,
Your huddled masses yearning to breathe free,
The wretched refuse of your teeming shore
Send these, the homeless, tempest-tost, to me.
I lift my lamp beside the golden door!

The May Laws

Jews suffered harsh oppression under the government of the tsars. The assassination in 1881 of Tsar Alexander II, who had attempted some reforms, brought on a rapid worsening of their condition. Government-inspired pogroms were followed by the May Laws of 1882, which expelled the Jews from many towns and many professions.

In 1905 a revolution took place in Russia. It was brutally crushed. As in 1881–82, there were bloody pogroms against the Jewish communities. Jews in Europe and America held out a helping hand to the refugees who poured out of Russia. Jews donated generous sums of money, and organizations were formed to aid the immigrants in establishing new homes in Western Europe or in South America, but most went to the United States.

About a quarter of a million Jews lived in America in the year 1880. In the next fifty years, two and a half million more came to these shores. This vast influx of immigrants came from Poland, Lithuania, and Ukraine, which were now under Russian rule.

The Great Exodus

Some Russians refugees went to France, Germany, and other West European countries. A small idealistic group went to Palestine, although they knew that Turkish oppression in an undeveloped land awaited them. The great majority of those fleeing the Old World wanted to go to the free country of America. After miserable voyages, these hopeful refugees arrived in the "Golden Land."

Helping Each Other

Poor as most of them were, the immigrant Jews never forgot their responsibility to one other. They set up free-loan societies, charities, and organizations for fellowship and mutual help. Many belonged to landsmanshaftn—societies made up of immigrants from the same European town.

Jews who were already established in the United States also helped the newcomers. Organizations like B'nai B'rith and the American Jewish Committee, supported largely by German Jews, fought anti-Semitism and protected the rights of new immigrants.

Poverty, crowded slum conditions, and unfamiliarity with the lifestyle of the New World were all handicaps for the immigrant. To make the younger people feel at home in America, educational and vocational courses and group social activities were sponsored by the Hebrew Immigrant Aid Society, the National Council of Jewish Women, the Educational Alliance in New York, and the YMHAs, and settlement houses.

The Love of Learning

The newcomers wished to live in cities, in communities where there were many fellow Jews, and where there would be synagogues and religious schools for their children. The Jews of Eastern Europe brought with them their love of learning. They wished in this new country to fashion the life of faith and piety they had known in Europe-even those who no longer strictly observed Jewish law and those who devoted them-

Jews who were established in America never forgot their responsibility and welcomed the newcomers.

Front page of the HIAS journal, the *Jewish Immigrant*. The lady is opening the gates of America to the wandering Jew.

A cartoon showing the relationship of the tsarist Russian government to the Jews.

The Educational Alliance in New York, 1895. Immigrants Jews in the New York area flocked to the Educational Alliance for its educational, social, and vocational activities

Jacob H. Schiff (1847–1920), outstanding Jewish philanthropist, gave support to universities, hospitals, and cultural activities both Jewish and general, helping religious institutions of all groups. His firm would not lend money to tsarist Russia because of its persecution of the Jews.

A 1915 Jews Relief Campaign poster

selves to secularist political movements had the Jewish love of learning. Jewish immigrants published and read more periodicals than any other immigrant group, before or since. They read Yiddish newspapers and Hebrew magazines, and flocked to the Yiddish theater and to public lectures and discussions.

The Jewish Tradition Weakens

The second generation, the children of the immigrants, were able to find better jobs and often to enter professions. In the free atmosphere of America, many of them left the old way of life. Many felt that the religion of their parents was not suited to modern America. World War I interrupted the flood of immigration which had increased the number of Jews in the United States to nearly 4 million. Immigrants who had entered the country during the past 33 years made up most of the Jewish population. They had learned how to live in the new land and had established themselves as citizens. Their children were growing up as Americans.

Following the war, when the flow of immigrants resumed, nationalist feelings in the United States were aroused, and resentment against foreigners grew. In 1924, Congress passed the Johnson Act, a restrictive immigration law that established a quota system favoring the Germanic countries and England, and severely limiting immigration from the countries of Southern and Eastern Europe. The Johnson Act reduced Jewish immigration to several thousand a year. After 1924, with the rate of immigration from Europe curtailed, the problem of preserving Jewish identity in America assumed new forms. The problem was not how to integrate the newcomers into America, but how to raise the native-born American Jewish citizen to a higher level of Jewish knowledge and awareness.

American Jewry had established its own institutions and was developing its own leaders and teachers, while the great Jewish communities of Europe faced a period of darkness and destruction.

THE KISHINEV POGROM

In April 1903, several days before Easter, rumors spread through the Kishinev area that the Jews had murdered a Christian boy to use his blood for making matzot. The local newspaper printed inflammatory articles accusing the Jews of the killing. For three days beginning on Easter Sunday, mobs attacked the Jews. Officials all over the world sent protests to Tsar Nicholas I, who denied that any massacre had occurred.

On May 2, the New York Times *printed an English translation of a Russian article describing the pogrom.*

The Central Commitee for the relief of the Kishineff sufferers said in a statement issued last night:

"The following from St. Petersburg Vuedemosti is an answer to the Russian official denial of the anti-Jewish riots in Kishineff, offering a remarkable picture of the outbreak. The Vuedemosti is subjected to strict censorship and therefore the account must be read in light of what the Goverment permitted to be published.

The account published on April 24 said:

"Since incendiary articles against the Jews were published in the Bessarabetz, Novoye and Swiet, rumors have been current that an ant-Jewish outbreak was imminent. The Moldavians are so peaceful that no credence was given these reports.

"In Kishineff all was quiet until Easter Sunday, when at noon [later reports proved that rioting actually began just after sunrise] the crowd on the Chuplinsky place, where amusement and other booths had been erected, became exited. Several Jews, who came to watch the Christians enjoying themselves, were attacked. They ran away. The cry 'Kill the Jews' was raised, and the mob, which swelled instantly, followed in hot pursuit, particulary through Alexandrowsky Street to the new bazaar, where a fearful riot took place.

"It is impossible to account the amount of goods destroyed in a few hours. The 'hurrahs' of the rioters and the pitiful cries of the victims filled the air. Wherever a Jew was met he was savagely beaten into insensibility. One Jew was dragged from a street car and beaten until the mob thought he was dead. The air was filled with feathers from torn bedding. About 3 o'clock in the afternoon the rioters were signaling and whistling in the principal streets. The miscreants began there by breaking windows.

At nightfall quiet was restored, at least in the centre of the city, and it was presumed that the disturbance was at an end. Police, troops, and mounted gendarmes patrolled the streets, but the real assault only began on Monday morning, when armed with axes and crowbars, the mob set upon its work of destruction, damaging the best houses and shops, clothing themselves in pillaged clothing and carrying away huge bundles of loot.

"The mob ignored the order of the patrols and the police to disperse, and continued to rob, destroy and kill. Every Jewish household was broken into and the unfortunate Jews in their terror endeavored to hide in cellars and under roofs. The mob entered the synagogues, desecrated the biggest house of worship, and defiled the scrolls of the law.

"The conduct of the intelligent Christians was disgraceful. They made no attempt to check the rioting. They simply walked around enjoying the frightful sport.

"On Tuesday, the third day, when it became known that the troops had received orders to shoot, the rioting ceased. The Jews then came out of their houses. The streets were piled up with the debris and they presented a horrible appearance. The big Jewish Hospital is filled with dead and wounded. Some bodies are mutilated beyond identification, From a distance there could be heard heart-rending groans and pitiable wailings of widows and orphans. The misery of the Jews is indescribable. There is an actual famine. The prices of all living commodities have gone up. Relief is being organized."

New York Times, **May 11, 1903**

WHAT DO YOU THINK?

1. *Why did the Russian officials deny the existence of the riots?*
2. *The Kishinev pogrom was fueled by the blood libel. Why are the Arabs using the same blood libel to inflame the Arab masses?*
3. *Why didn't the Russian police try to stop the riot?*
4. *Europe was a continent of terror for Jews throughout the generations. There were forced conversions, expulsions, blood libels, pogroms, and mass murders by the Nazis. What is it in the nature, education, or religion of the Europeans that promotes anti–Semitic violence?*

From Vision to Reality

The trial of Captain Dreyfus

Photograph of part of a letter Dreyfus sent to the Grand Rab-

Photograph of part of a letter Dreyfus sent to the chief rabbi of France from prison the day after he was found guilty.

French Jewry

The situation of French Jewry in the late 19th century resembled that of German Jewry. Although full civil rights had been extended to them by law, French Jews often found themselves face-to-face with prejudice when they sought to enter certain professions. The old picture of the Jew as a convenient scapegoat could not be wiped out by the enactment of liberal legislation. It was easier to pass laws proclaiming freedom and tolerance than to educate people to abide by their spirit.

Captain Alfred Dreyfus

In October 1894, Captain Alfred Dreyfus (1859–1935), a Jewish officer on the French general staff, was charged with espionage and arrested. Accused of giving military secrets to Germany, Dreyfus was tried, convicted of high treason, and imprisoned on Devil's Island. To the end, he insisted that he was innocent. When he was stripped of his military rank and honor, he cried, "Long live France! Long live the army!"

Emile Zola

Many people believed that Dreyfus was innocent—framed by anti-Jewish officers who had used forged documents to convict him. Among those who championed the captain's cause was Emile Zola, the great novelist, whose passionate crusade on behalf of Dreyfus was heralded in an essay entitled "J'Accuse," condemning the French government as unjust, intolerant, and corrupt.

Dreyfus Is Pardoned

In time it was found that the real culprit was one Major Ferdinand Esterhazy, who had sold information to the Germans. In 1899 Dreyfus was recalled from Devil's Island and granted a pardon.

Freedom-loving people in many lands had taken part in the fight to prove Dreyfus innocent. His fate had become a test case in a much larger struggle then taking place in Europe between those who clung to old prejudices and those who demanded civil rights and equality for all. In 1906, the French government finally admitted that Dreyfus was innocent of all charges and reinstated him in the army.

Caricature of the four army officers involved in the Dreyfus trial.

Theodor Herzl:
The Journalist at the Trial

Among the reporters at the Dreyfus trial in 1894 was Theodor Herzl (1860–1904), a young newspaperman from Vienna. The miscarriage of justice and the degrading treatment to which Dreyfus was subjected made a deep impression on Herzl. Up to that time he had led a fully assimilated life, but when he saw what harm anti-Semitic hatred could do even in a civilized country like France, he felt himself united in a bond of shared suffering with Dreyfus, the French Jew, and with all of his fellow Jews.

Influenced by the patriotic and nationalist ideas that were so strong in the 19th century, Theodor Herzl conceived a daring solution for the problems the Jews faced in their quest for equal rights. If they established a state of their own, he reasoned, they would once again be a nation like the other nations of the world. No one would be able to victimize or mistreat them. In 1896, Herzl explained his ideas in a book entitled *The Jewish State*.

The degradation of Captain Dreyfus

Herzl soon realized that there was only one possible site for the Jewish state he imagined: Palestine. In 1902, he set forth his vision of the return to Zion in a novel, *Altneuland* ("Old-New Land"). He and his associates, who called themselves Zionists, founded a periodical, *Die Welt* ("The World"), through which to publicize their program.

Theodor Herzl

The Zionist Movement

In 1897, Herzl convened the First Zionist

The land for the first settlements in Palestine was purchased by Keren Kayemet Le-Yisrael (Jewish National Fund), established in 1901 as the land-purchasing agency of the Zionist movement.

The Jewish National Fund depended on small sums of money collected from Jews throughout the world. The blue-and-white JNF box found a place in millions of Jewish homes.

Three Zionist leaders: Max Nordau, Theodor Herzl, and Max Mandelstamm. Farmer and the Western Wall are pictured on this 1906 wall decoration.

Congress in Basel, Switzerland, inviting Jewish representatives from all over the world who shared his vision. It was at this Congress that the Zionist movement was officially founded and its basic platform proclaimed—the establishment of a legally secure Jewish homeland in Palestine. Herzl became the first president of the World Zionist Organization.

Theodor Herzl dedicated his whole life and energy to the realization of this ideal. Since Palestine was then part of the Turkish Empire, he met with the sultan to obtain permission for Jews to resettle the Holy Land. When the sultan refused, Herzl despairingly approached officials in Egypt and England to see whether he could obtain some territory in East Africa as an alternative site for a Jewish homeland. This idea was soon dropped because of bitter opposition in Zionist circles.

Herzl inflamed the Jews of Europe with the Zionist idea and gave Zionism its basic organizational and political structure. His diplomatic efforts on its behalf won it international standing and recognition. Although he laid the essential groundwork, Theodor Herzl did not live to see even the beginnings of the realization of his plans. He died in 1904 at the age of 44, leaving his associates to continue the work he had begun.

The Gate of Hope

Herzl's most enthusiastic followers did not live in Austria, Germany, or France, but in Russia, where tsar and nobles ruled with a heavy hand, and Jews lived under very oppressive conditions. Herzl opened a gate of hope for many Russian Jewish young people, who looked to Palestine for a life of dignity and freedom.

THE DREYFUS CASE

The anti-Semitic press was used by the nobility to try to restore its social and political prestige. Army officers resented the control of the liberal French government. These two forces combined to show how corrupt the democratically elected Parliament was. They argued that the corrupt government was controlled by Jewish financiers, such as the Rothschilds. On October 15, 1890, Captain Dreyfus was arrested and accused of selling French military plans to the German government. The Dreyfus Affair split the country into two groups. A major turning point in the campaign for revision came on January 13, 1898 when the brilliant novelist Emile Zola challenged the French government and the army with his scandalous inditment, "J'accuse" blazed across the front pages of the newspaper La Aurore. *It brought Zola a conviction for slander, and riots against the Jews. However, in the end, it exonerated Dreyfus and he was reinstated in the army. The following is Zola's J'accuse."*

LETTER TO M. FELIX FAURE, PRESIDENT OF THE REPUBLIC

MONSIEUR LE PRESIDENT

I accuse Lieutenant-Colonel du Paty de Clam of having been the diabolical workman of judicial error.

I accuse General Mercier of having made himself an accomplice, at least through weakness of mind, in one of the greatest in iniquities of the century.

I accuse General Billot of having had in his hands certain proofs of the innocence of Dreyfus, and of having stifled them.

I accuse the war offices of having carried on in the press, particularly in *L'Eclair* and in *L'Echo* de Paris, an abominable campaign, to mislead opinion.

I accuse, finally, the first council of war of having violated the law by condemning an accused person on the strength of a secret document, in obedience to orders, in committing in its turn the judicial crime of knowingly acquitting a guilty man.

In preferring these charges, I am not unaware that I lay myself liable under Articles 30 and 31 of the press law of July 29, 1881, which punishes defamation. And it is willfully that I expose myself thereto.

As for the people whom I accuse, I have never seen them, I entertain against them no feeling of revenge or hatred. And the act that I perform here is nothing but a revolutionary measure to hasten the explosion of truth and justice.

I have but one passion, the passion for the light, in the name of humanity which has suffered so much. My fiery protest is simply the cry of my soul. Let them dare, then, to bring me into the Assize Court, and let the investigation take place in the open day.

I await it. Accept, Monsieur le President, the assurance of my profound respect.

EMILE ZOLA

WHAT DO YOU THINK?

1. Who was Dreyfus?
2. Why did the army officers pick on Dreyfus?
3. Why did Emile Zola involve himself in the Dreyfus Affair?
4. What influenced Theodor Herzl to became involved in Jewish affairs?

Zionism After Herzl

Hashomer, one of the first Jewish self-defense units in the Galilee (1904). Israel Shohat, its first commander, is in the center of the photo.

In 1909, Tel Aviv was nothing more than a series of sand dunes. This rare old photo shows the allocation of plots of land to the first residents of Tel Aviv.

Emblem of the 6th Zionist Congress, held in Basel in 1903.

Title page of the original statutes of the Bilu organization. The Hebrew motto means, "The little one shall become a thousand, and the small one a strong nation" (Isaiah 60:22).

Terrible pogroms were taking place in Russia, and thousands of Jews fled. Most of them made the long journey across the Atlantic and found new homes in the United States. Others went to the countries of Western Europe. Only a few were permitted to enter Palestine. Yet, Jewish immigration to the Holy Land continued and new settlements were founded.

The First Aliyah

The Hebrew word *aliyah* (lit. "going up") refers to the ascent of a person who is called upon to recite blessings during the reading of the Torah. The First Aliyah began in 1880 and continued until 1905. The first *olim* ("ascenders," a noun derived from *aliyah*) were the Bilu'im. Their numbers were reinforced by settlers stimulated by Herzl's writings and the establishment of the World Zionist Organization.

The Bilu Movement

After the pogroms of 1881–82, 17 young Russian Jewish students settled in Palestine. These young people, known as Bilu'im, were committed to the Zionist ideal. They labored long hours in the fields under the blazing sun in the new farm settlements.

The Bilu'im took their name from the initials of a four-word passage in the Bible, *Beit Yaakov lekhu venelkhah,* "House of Jacob, let us arise and go" (Isaiah (2:5.) They interpreted these words as encouragement to rise up from their diaspora homes and go to Israel to rebuild the Jewish homeland.

The Bilu Pioneers

They found a barren land, dry, rocky, and sandy, with many swampy areas. They saw that the desert would have to be irrigated before vegetables and trees could be planted. Most of the colonists were students and townspeople. What they lacked in knowledge of farming they made up in enthusiasm. The Jews of Europe followed the progress of the new settlements with keen interest. Wealthy men like Baron Edmond de Rothschild (1845–1934), the financier and philanthropist, generously contributed much-needed money to buy land and tools.

The settlers worked by day and stood guard at night with their guns, ready to defend themselves against Arab marauders. The men and women of the First Aliyah faced an enormous task. They literally had to make the desert bloom again. The settlers were called *chalutzim*, meaning "pioneers. They established settlements and created farmland from mosquito infested swamps .

Hovevei Zion

In 1881, Leon Pinsker, a physician, excited Russian Jewry with a pamphlet entitled *Auto-Emanicipation.* Pinsker maintained that no one could really emancipate the Jews except the Jews themselves. And the only way in which the Jews could secure their freedom and self-respect, he declared, was by returning to their ancient homeland. Pinsker's call gave rise to a society which took the name Hovevei Zion, "Lovers of Zion." The Hovevei Zion and the Bilu'im founded the first agricultural settlements in the Land of Israel, Rishon Le-Zion ("First in Zion") and Petach Tikvah ("Gate of Hope.") Nes Tziyonah, Zichron Yaakov, and several others soon followed.

The Revival of Hebrew

As settlers from many different places arrived in Palestine, the need for a common language became apparent. Hebrew was the obvious choice, for it had been the language of the Jewish homeland before the exile. The two most ardent champions of the Hebrew revival were Eliezer Ben-Yehudah (1858–1922) and Asher Ginzberg (1856–1927), who called himself Ahad Ha-Am ("One of the People").

Eliezer Ben-Yehudah

Eliezer Ben-Yehudah, considered the father of modern Hebrew, was a talented linguist and educator who foresaw the creative role that Hebrew could play in the

Eliezer Ben-Yehudah (1858-1922), the father of spoken Hebrew.

Hayim Nahman Bialik (1873–1934), the greatest Hebrew poet of modern times. Bialik's first poem was about his longing for Shivat Zion, the Return to Israel. Bialik supported himself as a businessman, teacher, and publisher.

In Israel today, Bialik is considered the national poet, just as Shakespeare is in English-speaking countries.

Poster promoting the study of Hebrew
The top two lines read: "One language, one people. For you and your children." The three bottom lines read: "Sign up today for evening lessons in Hebrew."

Mounted Shomrim on patrol

Members of the Second Aliyah opposed the practice of hiring Arab laborers to do their field work.

Women stood shoulder to shoulder with the men and shared the back-breaking work in the kibbutzim.

Alexander Zeid (1886–1938). He was a pioneer of the Second Aliyah and one of the founders of Hashomer. He was killed by Arabs while on guard duty in 1938. A statue of Zeid on horseback was erected in the settlement of Givat Zeid, named in his honor.

everyday life of the new Jewish homeland. Once he arrived in Palestine in 1881, Ben-Yehudah allowed only Hebrew to be spoken in his home, and his family and friends followed his example. He coined new words for tools and ideas that were unknown to ancient Hebrew. He embarked on the monumental task of compiling an dictionary of the Hebrew language which included many new expressions.

Ahad Ha-Am

Ahad Ha-Am was the leading essayist in modern Hebrew. He fashioned it into an instrument of articulate expression. He argued that the Land of Israel must be the spiritual and cultural center of the entire Jewish people. His writings inspired a generation of creative Hebrew writers, chief among whom was his close disciple, the poet of the Hebrew national renaissance, Hayim Nahman Bialik (1873–1934).

The Second Aliyah / 1905–1914

The Second Aliyah extended from 1905 until the outbreak of World War I in 1914. This wave of immigration marked the development of a new type of agricultural settlement in Palestine, the *kibbutz* or cooperative. The members of a kibbutz not only worked and lived together, but also owned everything jointly. The kibbutz supplied their food, clothing, and other necessities, paying for these goods with the proceeds from the sale of its agricultural products.

The Jewish National Fund

The land for the settlements was provided by the Keren Kayemet Le-Yisrael, or Jewish National Fund, which was established in 1907 as the land-purchasing agency of the Zionist movement. The JNF is still supported by contributions from Jews the world over.

The Histadrut

The pioneers in Palestine organized into a strong federation of labor unions known as the Histadrut Ha-Ovdim ("Federation of Workers"). Eventually the Histadrut evolved into a powerful organization which included all the Jewish working people in the country.

THE BILU MANIFESTO—1882

In the same year that saw the appearance of Pinsker's Auto–Emancipation, a group of Jewish university students in Russia banded together for the purposes of settling in Palestine and developing an agricultural colony there. Calling themselves "Bilu" (from the Hebrew initials of the verse in Isaiah 2:5: "House of Jacob, come, let us go") the young pioneers left for Palestine in 1882 and while in Constantinople issued the manifesto given here. The combination of zeal and Jewish nationalism which inspired the Bilu'im was not enough to overcome their ignorance of farming and the conditions then obtaining in Palestine. Instead of the cooperative colonies they planned, the Bilu'im were forced to work as hired labor in two recently established colonies. Despite the fact that the group soon disbanded, its example became a legend of Zionist history.

"If I help not myself, who will help me?"

Nearly two thousand years have elapsed since, in an evil hour, after a heroic struggle, the glory of our Temple vanished in fire. We lost our country where dwelt our beloved sires. Into the Exile we took with us, of all our glories, only a spark of the fire by which our Temple, the abode of our Great One, was engirdled, and this little spark kept us alive.

And this spark is again kindling and will shine for us, a true pillar of fire going before us on the road to Zion, while behind us is a pillar of cloud, the pillar of oppression threatening to destroy us. Sleepest thou, O our nation? What has thou been doing until 1882? The pogroms have awakened thee from thy charmed sleep. Thine eyes are open to recognize the cloudy delusive hopes. Canst thou listen silently to the taunts and mockeries of thine enemies?… Remember that thou wast a nation possessing a wise religion, a law, a constitution, a celestial Temple whose wall is still a silent witness to the glories of the past; that thy sons dwelt in palaces and towers, and thy cities flourished in the splendor of civilization, while these enemies of thine dwelt like beasts in the muddy marshes. Hopeless is your state in the West; the star of your future is gleaming in the East. Deeply conscious of all this, and inspired by the true teaching of our great master, Hillel, "If I help not myself, who will help me?" we propose to form the following society for national ends.

1. The Society will be named BILU according to the motto "House of Jacob, come, let us go."

2. The seat of the committee shall be Jerusalem.

3. WE WANT:

I. A home in our country. It was given us by the mercy of God; it is ours as registered in the archives of history.

2. To beg it of the sultan himself, and if it be impossible to obtain this, to beg that we may at least possess it as a state within a larger state; the internal administration to be ours, to have our civil and political rights, and to act with the Turkish Empire only in foreign affairs.

We hope that the interests of our glorious nation will arouse the national spirit and that everyone, rich or poor, will give his best labors to the holy cause.

GOD be with us! THE PIONEERS OF BILU.

WHAT DO YOU THINK?

1. What was the spark that kept Judaism alive?
2. What was the pillar of oppression that threatened to destroy the Jewish people?
3. Is that pillar of oppression still operating today?
4. Was Turkey interested in creating a Jewish homeland? Why not?
5. Turkey is a Muslim country. Has the attitude of the Muslims toward the Jewish state changed since 1882?

The Balfour Declaration

Chaim Weizmann

Weizmann seated next to Lord Balfour on a visit to Shefeyah, near Zikhron Ya'akov, in 1925. On their left stands Nahum Sokolow.

Chaim Weizmann

One of England's most brilliant chemists, Dr. Chaim Weizmann (1874–1952), was also a leader of the World Zionist Organization. Weizmann, who was born in Russia, settled in England in 1903, where he taught chemistry at the University of Manchester. During World War I, England had to cope with a serious shortage of acetone, a material required for the manufacture of explosives. Weizmann discovered a new formula for acetone, thus making an invaluable contribution to the Allied war effort.

When government officials asked Weizmann to name a price for his discovery, he refused to accept any payment, but asked that Britain allow unrestricted Jewish immigration into Palestine once the war was won. The British agreed, for they knew that the Jewish settlers, having no bonds with Turkey, could be relied upon to help England.

The Balfour Declaration

On November 2, 1917, Arthur James Balfour, the British Foreign Secretary, sent a letter to Lord Walter Rothschild asking him to inform the Zionist Organization of the British government's favorable attitude toward the proposed Jewish national home in Palestine. This letter, which is now known as the Balfour Declaration, brought rejoicing to Zionists the world over.

Shivat Tzion

The Balfour Declaration brought a sense of reality to the age-old dream of *Shivat Tzion* ("Return to Zion,") and *Kibbutz Galuyot* ("Ingathering of the Exiles").

All through the two thousand years of exile, the Jew never lost faith that someday they miraculously would return to Israel. Wherever they lived, they recited special daily Shivat Tzion prayers. They celebrated holidays according to the Israeli seasons and calendar. They prayed for rain at the right time and for a good and plentiful harvest.

For many painful years, the land of Israel was in the hands of conquerors. The Jews who lived there were not free. Yet, hope for freedom and independence never died. Now, the task of Shivat Tzion was on the horizon-now the age-old dream was coming true.

The Jewish Legion

In addition to the Jewish soldiers already serving in the British armed forces, all-Jewish fighting units were organized to fight under the blue-and-white Zionist flag. The first of these was the Zion Mule Corps, which served in the Gallipoli campaign in 1915. Its successor, the Jewish Legion, fought under General Edmund Allenby in the campaign to liberate Palestine from the Turks. One of the members of the Jewish Legion was a young immigrant from Russia, David Ben-Gurion, who later became the first Prime Minister of the State of Israel. Another was Vladimir Jabotinsky (1880–1940), the founder of Revisionist Zionism. It was largely thanks to his advocacy that the British agreed to form all-Jewish fighting units.

The Arabs

Many of Palestine's Arab inhabitants opposed the Balfour Declaration and Jewish immigration. Wealthy Arab landowners feared that Jews from Europe would bring in a standard of living much higher than that of the Arab peasants who tilled the soil of Palestine with the same primitive tools as their ancestors centuries earlier, causing them to become discontented with their lot. Arab marauders were incited to raid Jewish settlements in order to force the Jews to abandon them. But the Jews fought back. They worked their land by day and guarded it at night with their guns.

The Balfour Declaration

In 1917, the British Army under the command of General Allenby captured Beersheba from the Turks. This photograph shows the surrender of the city by the Turkish garrison to two British sergeants.

The Balfour Declartion was sent from Lord Balfour (1848–1930) to Lord Lionel Walter Rothschild, who played an important part in the discussions which led to the declaration. It recognized the right of the Jewish people to build a national home in Palestine. The declaration also supported the rights of non-Jewish citizens.

The Third Aliyah

The Third Aliyah (1919–1923) was spearheaded by young members of the Hechalutz movement in Russia and Poland who joined hands with the pioneers of the Second Aliyah.

Forty thousand more olim reached Israel in the years between 1919 and 1923. They believed in the same goals as the previous Zionist settlers: working and sharing, social justice, self-defense, and speaking Hebrew. The new wave of pioneers endured great hardships, but they persisted in the work of rebuilding Israel. Many new kibbutzim were established. Hebrew literature, journalism, and theater came into being.

The Haganah Is Established

The Haganah began in 1920 and was Israel's first military defense organization. Haganah members protected major cities in Israel as well as moshavim and kibbutzim. Despite the restrictions and the difficult living conditions, there were more than 80,000 Jews in the land.

The Balfour Declaration

Letter by Balfour to Lord Lionel Walter Rothschild.
Foreign Office November 2nd, 1917.

Dear Lord Rothschild,

I have much pleasure in conveying to you, on behalf of His Majesty's Government, the following declaration of sympathy with Jewish Zionist aspirations which has been submitted to, and approved by, the Cabinet.

"His Majesty's Government view with favour the establishment in Palestine of a national home for the Jewish people, and will use their best endeavours to facilitate the achievement of this object, it being clearly understood that nothing shall be done which may prejudice the civil and religious rights of existing non-Jewish communities in Palestine, or the rights and political status enjoyed by Jews in any other country."

I should be grateful if you would bring this declaration to the knowledge of the Zionist Federation.

Yours sincerely,
ARTHUR JAMES BALFOUR.

WEIZMANN AND BALFOUR

In 1903, the British government proposed to the Zionist Organization to establish a Jewish colony in British East Africa. The proposal was known as the Uganda Scheme. In the selection which follows, taken from his autobiography, Weizmann tells how he met Lord Balfour, the British statesman, for the first time and explained to him the meaning of Zionism and the reason for the rejection of a refuge in Africa.

I was brought in to Balfour in a room in the old-fashioned Queen's Hotel, on Piccadilly, which served as his headquarters.

I remember how Balfour sat in his usual pose, his legs stretched out in front of him, an imperturbable expression on his face.

The British Government was really anxious to do something to relieve the misery of the Jews; and the problem was a practical one, calling for a practical approach.

I dwelt on the spiritual side of Zionism, I pointed out that nothing but a deep religious conviction expressed in modern political terms could keep the movement alive, and that this conviction had to be based on Palestine alone....

I looked at my listener, and suddenly became afraid that this apparent interest and courtesy might be nothing more than a mask. I was ready to bow myself out of the room, but Balfour held me back, and put some questions to me regarding the growth of the movement.

Then suddenly I said: "Mr. Balfour, supposing I were to offer you Paris instead of London, would you take it?"

He sat up, looked at me, and answered: But, Dr. Weizmann, we have London.

"That is true," I said. "But we had Jerusalem when London was a marsh."

He leaned back, continued to stare at me, and said two things which I remember vividly. The first was: "Are there many Jews who think like you?"

I answered: "I believe I speak the mind of millions of Jews whom you will never see and who cannot speak for themselves, but with whom I could pave the streets of the country I come from."

To this he said: "If that is so, you will one day be a force."

Shortly before I withdrew, Balfour said: "It is curious. The Jews I meet are quite different."

I answered: "Mr. Balfour, you meet the wrong kind of Jews."

WHAT DO YOU THINK?

1. *Who was Lord Balfour?*
2. *Why were the British against the establishment of a home for the Jews? Was it political.? Was it anti–Semitic?*
3. *Could a Jewish homeland come into being without prejudicing the rights of a non-Jewish community?*
4. *Why did the Balfour Declaration specifically mention the Arabs?*
5. *Did the Balfour Declaration produce the present political problem between Jews and Arabs?*
6. *The Balfour Declaration mentioned the rights and political state of Jews in other countries. Could Jews be stripped of their rights because of the creation of a Jewish state?*
7. *Have the rights of Jews in Arab countries been compromised because of the State of Israel?*
8. *Have Arab Jews been compensated for their loss of properties, homes, and businesses?*

Heroes of Freedom

A Haganah member stands guard at a defense perimeter.

Joseph Trumpeldor was an officer in the Russian army. He lost an arm fighting in the Russo-Japanese War. In this photo, he is wearing his Russian uniform and the medals that he won for bravery in action.

During the First and Second Aliyot, there were many Arab attacks against Jewish settlements in Eretz Yisrael. Hundreds of Jews were murdered and much property was destroyed. In response, the Jews rose up and established Hashomer ("The Watchman"). This tiny defense force had only 100 members. But each of them was a deadly marksman, an expert horseman, and fluent in Arabic.

Joseph Trumpeldor

Joseph Trumpeldor (1880-1920) was an inspirational model for the Zionist pioneers. During his youth in Russia, Joseph Trumpeldor became a Zionist and dreamed of settling in Israel. He was drafted into the Russian army and lost an arm while fighting in the Russo-Japanese War.

Despite his handicap, Trumpeldor went to Eretz Yisrael, where he lived at Degania. He used his experience in the Russian army to organize defenses for the new Jewish settlements.

During World War I, he helped Vladimir Jabotinsky form the Zion Mule Corps, which fought with the British armed forces. He later became an officer in the Jewish Legion, the volunteer army which defended the settlements in Palestine.

The Jewish Legion was an army of volunteers from countries all over the world. Jewish Legion soldiers proudly wore the Magen David on their uniforms, spoke Hebrew, and saluted the Zionist flag as well as the British flag.

The Jewish Legion consisted of 2,700 volunteers from the United States, South Africa, Russia, Argentina, and Mexico. Among the recruits in the Jewish Legion was David Green, a young Jewish immigrant from Russia. As David Ben-Gurion, Green became the first Prime Minister of Israel.

After World War I, the Arabs began attacking the Jewish settlements in the Galilee. One-armed Joseph Trumpeldor led the defense of Kibbutz Tel Hai. Eight settlers, including Trumpeldor, were killed by Arab raiders. The dying words of this Jewish hero reveal his love of Israel: "It is good to die for our country."

A youth group was named in his honor: Betar, short for B'rith Trumpeldor, "The Covenant of Trumpeldor."

In Israel, the 11th day of the month of Adar is Tel Hai Day. Many Israelis make a pilgrimage to Tel Hai to honor the memory of Joseph Trumpeldor and the other heroes who died defending the homeland.

This photo was taken at Kibbutz Hanita in 1938. Left to right: Moshe Dayan, Yitzhak Sadeh, and Yigal Allon. Each of these young men became a high-ranking officer in the Haganah as well as an important political leader.

The Haganah Is Founded

In 1920, Hashomer was disbanded and a much larger defense force called Haganah ("The Defense") was established.

When Arab riots swept the country in 1929, Haganah volunteers saved the Jewish communities of Jerusalem, Tel Aviv, and Haifa from destruction. By 1939, the Haganah had 25,000 members armed with smuggled rifles, machine guns, and homemade grenades manufactured in secret factories.

After World War II, the British continued their pro-Arab policy of restricting Jewish immigration into Eretz Yisrael. The Haganah countered by destroying British radar stations, bridges, and other military establishments. Haganah's main activity during the period of 1945–1948 was the organization of illegal immigration into Palestine. Tens of thousands of so-called illegal immigrants were smuggled into the country. On May 31, 1948, the Haganah officially became Tzahal, the regular army of Israel.

Emblem of the Second Jewish Battalion, which fought in Italy in World War II

The Jewish Brigade

During World War II, the men and women of the Yishuv gave valiant aid to Britain in the fight against Nazi tyranny.

Six volunteers who were about to parachute into occupied Europe to help their fellow Jews. Most of them were captured and executed by the Nazis.

The Mufti and Hitler

The passport of Hannah Senesh

One of the Jewish heroes who operated in secret against the Nazis was Hannah Senesh (1921–1944). She had left her parents and a comfortable home in Budapest to live the life of a pioneer in Palestine. Hannah was parachuted into Yugoslavia, where she contacted the resistance and aided their underground operations. After this mission was accomplished, she made her way to Hungary to bring help to the Jews. There she was captured and put to death by the Nazis. Before Hannah Senesh died, she wrote a poem, "Blessed Is the Match," in which she compared herself to a fiery match, which kindles a flame and is itself consumed in performing this task.

Hannah Senesh wrote this short letter before she parachuted into Yugoslavia.

At the outset, David Ben-Gurion, the head of the Jewish Agency, spoke for all the Jews of Palestine: "We will fight the war as if there were no White Paper," he said, "and we will fight the White Paper as if there were no war."

The Mufti

Very few Palestinian Arabs fought in the war, but many Jewish settlers volunteered to serve in the British Army. The Nazis found many sympathizers among the extreme Arab nationalists who hated the British and opposed Jewish immigration to Palestine.

Eventually, the British permitted the Palestinian Jewish soldiers to organize their own Jewish Brigade and fight under their own blue-and-white flag, emblazoned with the Star of David.

Amin al-Husseini was a Palestinian leader who was active in the Arab nationalist movement. To appease the Arabs, Sir Herbert Samuel, the British high commissioner, appointed him Mufti (expert on Muslim law) of Jerusalem in 1921.

In 1940, Husseini moved to Iraq, where he took part in a pro-German rebellion. When the coup failed he escaped to Germany. Until the end of World War II, Husseini collaborated with the Nazis and recruited spies and saboteurs. After the defeat of Germany he escaped to Cairo, where he continued to direct the war against the Yishuv.

Behind Enemy Lines

Volunteers from the Haganah carried out dangerous assignments behind enemy lines. Several were dropped by parachute into Nazi-occupied territory to make contact with the local resistance movements.

The Jewish fighters from Palestine performed many missions for the Allies, as well as special missions for the Jewish people. Returning to their native lands using false names and false passports, they tried to organize ways to help Jews escape from the Nazi death camps. Many of them were captured and executed as spies.

THE YISHUV FIGHTS

The British were convinced that the 400,000 Jews in Palestine were a threat to the 1,000,000 Arabs. The Peel Report stated, "The Jewish National Home is already too large." In 1939, the British issued the White Paper and declared that the Jewish homeland was now completed and that during the next five years, only 75,000 Jews would be permitted to enter Palestine. It restricted Jewish immigration at a time when millions of Jews were facing destruction.

The British declared war on Jews entering Palestine outside the official quota. To enforce these policies, the British stationed troops that were desperately needed on the war fronts. The Germans, under the command of General Rommel, were threatening Egypt. If the Germans succeeded, the Allies would have lost the war in Africa. Yet they stubbornly kept some of their best troops in Palestine. On June 28, 1940, Winston Churchill wrote to Lord Lloyd, the Secretary of State for the Colonies.

The failure of the policy which you favour is proved by the very large numbers of sorely needed troops you have to keep in Palestine . . . the whole probably more than twenty thousand men. This is the price we have to pay for the anti-Jewish policy which has been persisted in for some years. Should the war go heavily into Egypt, all these troops will have to be withdrawn, and the position of the Jewish colonists will be one of the greatest danger. Indeed I am sure that we shall be told we cannot withdraw these troops, though they include some of our best, and are vitally needed elsewhere.

If the Jews were properly armed, our forces would become available, and there would be no danger of the Jews attacking the Arabs, because they are entirely dependent upon us and upon our command of the seas. I think it is little less than a scandal that at a time when we are fighting for our lives these very large forces should be immobilised in support of a policy which commends Itself only to a section of the Conservative Party.

WHAT DO YOU THINK?

1. Why didn't the British use all of their troops to fight Rommel?
2. What does this show about the British attitude toward the Jews?
3. Was their attitude anti-Semitic or stupid?
4. Why did the British refuse to arm the Jews? What were they afraid of?
5. Did Churchill agree with the anti-Jewish policy of the Conservative Party?
6. What was Ha-Shomer?
7. What was the Jewish Legion?
8. What were the primary activities of the Haganah?

The Palestine Mandate

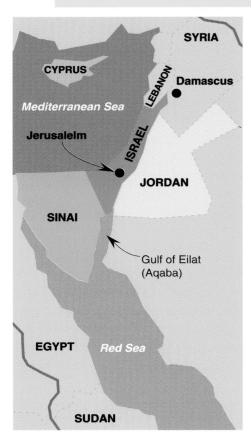

The British government in 1922 divided the promised Jewish homeland by cutting off three-quarters of the land area of Palestine. A new Arab state was created, called Transjordan. In 1946 Transjordan became independent. It is now called Jordan.

A 1930s Jewish National Fund poster in three languages: Yiddish, Hebrew, and Polish. It reads "Let us redeem the Jezreel Valley"

After the war, the League of Nations gave Germany's colonies and former Turkish territories in trusteeship to England and France to be guided and controlled until such time as they would be able to govern themselves. Palestine became a British mandate, and the Balfour Declaration was incorporated into the charter by which it was to be governed. This meant that the League endorsed the principle that Palestine was to become the Jewish homeland. Under the mandate, Hebrew became one of Palestine's three official languages (the other two were English and Arabic).

The Arab Situation

The progress the Jewish settlers were making was viewed with great anxiety by rich Arab landowners and many Muslim leaders. Arab propagandists stirred up hatred against the Jews, and anti-Jewish riots broke out repeatedly.

In 1936, the Grand Mufti of Jerusalem, religious head of Palestine's Muslim populace, helped to stir up a major Arab revolt. When the British tried to arrest him, he escaped to Lebanon and then to Germany. There he publicly endorsed Hitler's anti-Jewish program and spent the World War II years broadcasting Nazi propaganda to Muslims around the world.

As Jewish immigration increased, due to persecution in Europe, and Arab hostility intensified, the situation in Palestine became more and more difficult. In 1937, a British commission of inquiry proposed that the country should be divided into two parts, one Jewish, the other Arab. The Arabs rejected the proposed partition and stepped up their anti-Jewish activities. But the Yishuv kept right on growing.

New Immigrants

The population of the Yishuv was made up of Jews from many lands and many walks of life. It included

Jews from Iraq, Yemen, and North Africa who were very similar in culture to their Arab neighbors. There were many from Eastern Europe, and a few from the United States. In the 1930s, with Hitler in power, most of the new immigration was from Germany, Austria, and Czechoslovakia. As the Nazi terror spread, Jews came to Palestine from Poland, Romania, Bulgaria, and Yugoslavia. A few even managed to leave Russia, despite the danger of being arrested or killed by Communist border guards.

The people of the Yishuv learned to live together. To a great extent this was made possible by the fact that they had a common language-Hebrew. The language of the Bible had been transformed into a modern tongue. It was used by poets and writers, scientists, farmers and workers, cab drivers, and housewives doing their shopping. Newspapers were published in Hebrew, unions recruited members in Hebrew, and the Va'ad Leumi, the Yishuv's governing body, conducted its affairs in Hebrew.

In the land that had been the scene of biblical history, a new Jewish community was building a new life using the language of the Bible in everyday speech for the first time in 2,000 years.

A 1948 Histadrut poster issued after the War of Independence features the theme of physical labor and vigilance.

The Haganah

With the growth of the Yishuv, Arab resistance increased. The English, unwilling to antagonize the Arabs, could not deal with this friction between Arabs and Jews. The Jews secretly organized their own defense groups of men and women of the Yishuv, farmers and workers, city and country folk. These citizens trained to defend themselves against Arab terrorists who preyed upon settlements. This group of defenders took the name of Haganah ("defense").

Charles Orde Wingate

Charles Orde Wingate (1903-1944) was born in India to a family of Christian missionaries. He was a deeply religious man who always carried a Bible with

Lawrence of Arabia *(right)* arranged a meeting between Emir Feisal *(center)* and Chaim Weizmann *(left)*. Weizmann traveled by boat and camel to discuss the Palestinian situation with the emir. The two leaders developed a friendly respect for each other's views.

They issued a statement agreeing to the recognition of Zionist aims in Palestine if the Arabs were given independence in Syria and Iraq. The territories, which were then ruled by the French and the British, were not given independence and the Jewish-Arab alliance collapsed.

A stockade-and-tower settlement established during the 1930s. Despite British disapproval, the settlements were set up under cover of night. Walls provided protection against attacking Arabs.

The Haganah was trained by the British army officer Orde Wingate.

Wingate's job was to instruct the Haganah in night operations to protect the Iraq-Haifa oil pipeline, a favorite target of Arab bandits.

him so he could read it whenever he had a spare moment. Wingate became a British army officer and in 1936, was sent to Palestine to prevent Jewish immigration. After experiencing the agony of the Jewish immigrants, he became a strong Zionist and a supporter of the Jewish cause. In Palestine, he organized groups of Jewish volunteers known as Night Squads to detect and defeat Arab terrorist activities. The Jews called him Ha-Yedid, "the good friend."

However, some British officials disapproved of Wingate's activities and Zionist sympathies. They exiled him to the Far East, where in 1944, he was killed in Burma during World War II.

The Good Friend

Until his tragic death Wingate remained devoted to the Jewish people and to Israel. Israel has not forgotten, "the good friend." A forest, a college of physical education, and the children's village of Yemin Orde have been named after him.

During Israel's War of Independence, Wingate's widow arranged for his beloved Bible, together with supplies, to be dropped into the besieged village of Yemin Orde. In it she wrote a dedication to the defenders, "Orde Wingate is with you in spirit, though he cannot lead you in the flesh. I send you the Bible he carried on all his campaigns. May it be a covenant between you and him now and always."

DAVID BEN–GURION ON THE ARAB QUESTION: JANUARY 7, 1937
In the aftermath of the 1936 Arab riots, which began in Jaffa in April 1936, the Royal Commission, under the direction of Lord Peel, a former Secretary of State for India, examined the claims and grievances of both Arabs and Jews.

David Ben-Gurion, chairman of the Executive of the Jewish Agency, addressed the Royal Commission. Ben–Gurion was logical, positive, and sensitive to the historic importance of the moment. He was looking into future and saw a new nation, and a new time. He spoke steadily, making a case for independence.
This is a shortened version of Ben-Gurion's address.

A great deal was heard about the benefit which had accrued to this country from Jewish work, the improvement of agriculture in Palestine, better sanitary conditions, better education and so on. The benefit which is accruing to the country from our work is not the reason and the justification of our being here and of the Jewish National Home. We are here in our own right. Our right in Palestine is not derived from the Mandate and the Balfour Declaration. It is prior to that... the Bible is our Mandate, the Bible which was written by us, in our own language, in Hebrew, in this very country. That is our Mandate. Our right is as old as the Jewish people. It was only the recognition of this right which was expressed in the Balfour Declaration and the Mandate. It is stated in the Mandate that it recognizes the right of the Jewish people to reconstitute their National Home.

We are here to remove a historical grievance of the Jewish people against the whole Christian world. We do not intend to create in Palestine the same intolerable position for the Jews as in all other countries. Palestine is the only country in the world that the Jews, not as individuals, but as a nation and a race, can regard as their historic homeland.

The Palestinian Jews, however numerous they may be have no right to refuse to admit other Jews as long as there is a place in this country.

A National Home for the Jewish people is a much larger conception than a Jewish state. When the Balfour Declaration was made, there were 60,000 Jews here. It was not only the right of those 60,000. Now we are 400,000 and it is not only the right of these 400,000 and it is the only homeland of the Jewish people that we have rights in this country. We are returning to Palestine. Nothing shall be taken away from the inhabitants which they need for their well-being. We came to add, not to take away. If Palestine is our country, it is not to the exclusion of other inhabitants. We can come in without any limit except the limit not to displace the existing inhabitants. It means making the Jewish people masters of their own destiny as any other free independent people. It is our belief that a great Jewish community, a free Jewish nation, in Palestine, will be of great benefit to our Arab neighbors. We can benefit each other. We have never had a quarrel with the Arabs on our side, neither with the Arabs in Palestine, and no Arabs in other countries.

WHAT DO YOU THINK?

1. *Why do Jews have a historical right to live in Palestine?*
2. *Why is the Bible the Jewish Mandate?*
3. *Do the Jews intend to abrogate the rights of non–Jewish inhabitants?*
4. *Do Jews intend to limit the entrance of Jewish immigrants?*
5. *Do Jewish historical rights predate those of the Arabs?*
6. *Did the Arabs accept Ben–Gurion's assurances that their rights would be protected?*

Jews in Pre-Nazi Germany

Anti-Jewish poster issued by the Minister of Propaganda, Berlin, in 1940, with the slogan "Behind the enemy, the Jew" and in French, from 1942, with the slogan "And behind the Jew."

Members of the German general staff and Adolf Hitler.

The Weimar Republic

Germany's postwar government was known as the Weimar Republic. In the early 1920s, Jews became prominent in the arts, sciences, education, banking, and business. For a time it seemed as if the forces of progress would triumph. The Weimar Republic struggled valiantly to solve its problems but was hampered by nationalist military organizations. Their members, yearning for the "good old days," were unable to accept the fact that Germany had been defeated in the war.

Fascism in Italy

In Italy, too, many dreamed of a powerful military regime. In 1922, the Fascist Party, headed by Benito Mussolini, who called himself Il Duce ("The Leader"), seized power. The Fascists were extreme nationalists. Everyone who did not agree with them was conveniently silenced—by imprisonment; many opponents were tortured and put to death.

Hitler and *Mein Kampf*

The German general staff was not destroyed by the war. It just changed its name. In a short time, even though the postwar treaties forbade such weapons, German officers had made arrangements to manufacture tanks, aircraft, and even poison gas. By 1919, all of Europe was in a deep economic depression. Millions of unemployed Germans were looking for work. This was fertile ground for the evil genius of Adolf Hitler.

Hitler had been a corporal in World War I and won an Iron Cross for bravery After the war, he became the leader of a small political organization, the Nazi Party. In 1923, he attempted to overthrow the German government. Tried and convicted, Hitler spent nine months in jail, where he wrote the book *Mein Kampf* ("My Struggle").

No one should have been surprised by the political program Hitler adopted when he came to power, for it was detailed in *Mein Kampf*. But no one took him seriously, and few bothered to read his book.

Adolf Hitler and Nazism

A new kind of fascism now developed in Germany. In addition to the militarists, there were many other groups that disliked the Weimar government. Many were bitter about Germany's defeat in the war and its loss of territories and prestige. These groups, which fought the democratic builders of the new Germany, eventually found a leader in Adolf Hitler.

Adolf Hitler

Hitler promised the disappointed groups a different, powerful Germany—a Germany that would conquer the world and become an empire such as it had been under the Kaiser; indeed, he promised to make Germany even greater than it had been before.

The Nazis expounded the notion that the German people were a "master race," superior to all others. They and the other "Nordic" peoples, so the Nazis declared, were the master race of mankind which would lead and dominate the world and wipe out all inferior peoples. Hitler succeeded in winning more and more followers who were blindly devoted to their leader and his ideas.

The Nazi Rise to Power

Throughout the 1920s, the Nazis slowly gained in strength. But it was not until the late 1920s, which saw the combination of a decaying economic order and financial backing from some wealthy industrialists, that the party gained significant popular support. Hitler received funds from Fritz Thiessen of the German German steel trust, Emil Kidorf of the German coal industry, and other wealthy businessmen.

In the Reichstag elections of 1928, the Nazis won about 800,000 votes and 12 seats. By 1930, the Nazis had gained over 6 million votes and 107 seats. In 1932, the Nazis received almost 14 million votes, 120 seats, and became Germany's largest political party.

Racist attitudes in Germany developed from the idea that the Aryan-Nordic race was superior to all other races. To the Nazis, the Teuton stood for goodness, strength, courage, and beauty. Although the Aryan myth existed prior to the Nazis, they turned it into a reality which was readily applied to society.

Storm–Troopers

Nazi storm–troopers gathering Jewish books for destruction.

Following the example of Mussolini in Italy, the Nazi Party set up a quasi-military unit called the SA, or stormtroopers, to terrorize its opponents and disrupt their political activities. Dressed in military uniforms, trained like soldiers, the storm-troopers marched through the streets, shouting, singing, and breaking up orderly meetings of democratic groups. They started fights and made trouble. In addition to the SA, an elite group called the SS was organized to protect party leaders and maintain discipline among the members.

MY LIFE AS A GERMAN AND A JEW

Jacob Wasserman was a novelist who considered himself to be both a patriotic German and a good Jew, yet he felt that the Germans looked upon him as a foreigner. In 1921 he published a book entitled My Life As a German and a Jew *in which he discussed his feelings of hopelessness and despair as a non-German. The following excerpt sums up some of his sad conclusions.*

An aristocratic Dane once asked me: What is the reason for the German hatred of Jews? In my country the Jews are universally loved. They are known as the most reliable of patriots; they are known to lead honorable private lives: they are respected as a sort of nobility. **What do the Germans want?**

I should have answered: Hate. I should have answered: They want a scapegoat. Whenever they are badly off after every defeat, in every difficulty, in every trying situation they shift the responsibility for their distress upon the Jews. So it has been for centuries...

But what I did say was: A non-German cannot possibly imagine the heartbreaking position of the German Jew. German Jew—you must place full emphasis on both words. You must understand them as the final product of a lengthy evolutionary process. His twofold love and his struggle on two fronts drive him close to the brink of despair...

With the realization of the hopelessness of all efforts the bitterness in one's breast becomes a mortal agony....

Vain to adjure the nation of poets and thinkers in the name of poets and thinkers. Every prejudice one thinks disposed of breeds a thounsand others.

Vain to present the right cheek after the left has been struck. It does not move them to the slightest thoughtfulness: it neither touches nor disarms them. They strike the right cheek too.

Vain to interject words of reason into their crazy shrieking. they say: He dares to open his mouth. Gag him!

Vain to act in exemplary fashion. They say: We know nothing, we have seen nothing, we have heard nothing.

Vain to seek obscurity. They say: The coward! He is creeping into hiding, driven by his evil conscience.

Vain to go among them and offer them one's hand. They say, Why does he take such liberties, with his Jewish obtrusiveness. Vain to counteract the poison. They brew fresh venom.

Vain to live for them and die for them. They say: He is a Jew.

WHAT DO YOU THINK?

1. *Jacob Wasserman wrote his book in 1921. Since then, has there been any change in the attitude of the Germans toward the Jews?*
2. *What does the word "vain" mean?*
3. *In Wasserman's estimation, is it possible for the Jew to reason with the Germans and change their genetic hate at least into neutrality?*

Hitler Seizes Power

Walther Rathenau, German statesman.

Adolf Hitler

The Jews In Pre-Nazi Germany

Many Jews played a prominent and active role in the German republic which was created at a national assembly in the city of Weimar. Most prominent among the Jews in the German foreign service was Walter Rathenau (1867-1922), one of the great statesmen of his time. As Minister of Reconstruction, and later Minister of Foreign Affairs, Rathenau made every effort to improve relationships between Germany and France. He had a profound understanding of the political problems of Europe and hoped to help forge a thriving, peaceful new continent. But reactionary German forces disapproved of Rathenau and he was assassinated in 1922.

During the days of the Weimar Republic, German Jews became prominent also in the arts, sciences, education, banking, and business. It seemed to many that a new Golden Age of full emancipation had dawned.

Jewish scholars and philosophers made their contributions to Jewish learning. With the ideas of earlier Jewish scholars and philosophers and the wisdom of the modern world as a foundation, Jewish thinkers expounded new theories on the meaning of God and man.

For a time, it seemed as if the forces of progress in Western Europe would triumph. Yet, there were still many problems that needed solving. The Weimar Republic struggled valiantly to solve its problems, but it was hampered by old nationalistic military groups, disgruntled men, former army officers and impoverished aristocrats. These military groups, yearning for the old way of life they had known in the Germany of the Kaiser, were unable to accept the fact that Germany had lost its glorious empire and many of its territories. They sought to regain their own lost power in the government.

The Great Depression of the 1930s caused great suffering throughout the Western world. Many Germans were unemployed and desperate. During the years of the Depression, Hitler's following increased rapidly.

This beautiful Berlin synagogue was completely destroyed during Kristallnacht.

The Nazis in Power

In 1933, Adolf Hitler came into power, marking the end of the Weimar Republic. The Nazis took over the country. All democratic organizations were systematically dissolved. Germany was in the hands of uniformed men, the SA and the SS. The people were forced to spend their time in military parades and demonstrations to show their loyalty to Hitler—their Fuehrer, or "Leader."

The German people traditionally adored the tramp of massed men, the music of military bands, the waving of banners and the conquering songs of thousands. Hitler catered to this feeling, and in a short time, the Germans were ready for a war of conquest.

Behind this masquerade of zeal and devotion, the Nazis conducted a reign of terror. Aided by the police, Hitler's stormtroopers made thousands of arrests. No man or woman who had a different point of view or refused to support the new Nazi regime was safe.

Herschel Grynszpan

Germany: Land of Fear

Germany became a land of fear. People whispered stories of a new kind of prison—the concentration camp. In Hitler's first years of power, the Nazi concentration camps were filled mostly with political opponents. But from the very beginning, Hitler declared war on the Jews. He used them as a scapegoat, inciting latent anti-Semitic prejudices. Cruelties against Jews were encouraged, and one humiliating restriction after another was imposed upon them.

Hitler's main ambition was to forge a Germany that would follow him blindly into a great, victorious war. All obstacles hindering the unity and mindless obedience of such a Germany had to be removed. The German people became afraid to speak freely, even to

A vandalized Jewish department store in Berlin, Germany.

Kristallnacht was an anti-Jewish pogrom on November 9-10, 1938. Jewish property, businesses, and synagogues were attacked and burned by Nazi mobs.

Beginning in 1939, the passports of all Jews were marked with the letter "J". Also, the name Israel was added to the names of all Jewish males and Sarah to all Jewish females.

think. German history was shamelessly rewritten in accordance with the new Nazi viewpoint. Many respected educators and scientists were removed from their posts and replaced by loyal Nazis. The new replacements did as they were told, and helped fashion a Germany that would follow Hitler to war.

More and more Jews were subjected to restrictions. Jewish lawyers, physicians, teachers, scientists, journalists, and actors lost their jobs. Jewish places of business were boycotted by Hitler's party troops and stormed by angry mobs. Jews were insulted publicly and physically attacked. By 1939, Jews had been completely eliminated from the economic, cultural, and governmental life of Germany and Austria.

Kristallnacht / 1938

In 1935, the German Reichstag passed the Nuremberg Laws, which deprived Germany's Jews of citizenship and demoted them to an inferior status. During the next several years, Jewish businesses, homes, and property were expropriated.

On November 9, 1938, the Nazis staged a nationwide terror action that became known as Kristallnacht ("Crystal Night") because of the many broken windows. Synagogues in Germany and Austria were set afire, and about 10,000 Jewish businesses were destroyed and looted. Fifty Jews were murdered by organized mobs of bloodthirsty Nazis. Thousands of Jewish men were arrested and placed in concentration camps.

Herschel Grynszpan

The excuse for this outrage was the assassination of a German diplomat, Ernst vom Rath, by Herschel Grynszpan, son of Jewish refugees.

Grynszpan, in Paris, had received a letter from his sister in which she stated that the Grynszpan family, together with all Polish Jews living in Germany, had been arrested and deported. Seeking revenge for the suffering of his family, Grynszpan, who was 17 years old, bought a gun, went to the German embassy, and shot von Rath.

ANNE FRANK

Anne Frank was born in Germany in 1929 and emigrated with her family to Holland in 1933. During the Nazi occupation of Holland, the Frank family hid in an attic, and there Anne wrote her diary between 1942 and 1944. They were discovered by the German police in 1944 and taken away. Anne died in the Begen-Belsen concentration camp in March 1945. The following excerpt is taken from her diary, which was discovered in the attic after the war.

We have been pointedly remainded that we are in hiding, that we are Jews in chains, chained to one spot, without any rights, but with a thousand duties. We Jews mustn't show our feelings, must be brave and strong, must accept all incovenience and not grumble and we must do what is within our power and trust in God. Sometime this terrible war will be over. Surely, the time will come when we are people again, and not just Jews.

Who has inflicted this upon us? Who has made us Jews different from all other people? Who has allowed us to suffer so terribly up till now? It is God that has made us as we are, but it will be God, too, who will raise us up again. If we bear all this suffering and if there are still Jews left, when it is over, then Jews, instead of being doomed, will be held up as an example. Who knows, it might be even our religion from which the world and all peoples learn good, and for that reason only do we have to suffer now. We can never become just Netherlanders, or just English, or representatives of any country for that matter; we will always remain Jews, but we want to, too.

Be brave! Let us remain aware of our task and not grumble, solution will come. God has never deserted our people. Right through the ages there have been Jews, through all the ages they have to suffer, but it has made them strong too; the weak fall, but the strong will remain and never go under!

During the night I really felt that I had to die. I waited for the police, I was prepared, as the soldier is on the battlefield. I was eager to lay down my life for the country, but now, now I've been saved again, now my first wish after the war is that I may become Dutch! I love the Dutch, I love this country, I love the language and want to work here. And even if I have to write to the Queen myself, I will not give up until I have reached my goal. I am becoming still more independent of my parents; young as I am, I face life with more courage than Mummy; my feeling for justice is immovable, and truer than hers. I know what, I have a goal, an opinion. I have a religion and love. Let me be myself and then I am satisfied. I know that I'm a woman, a woman with inward strength and plenty of courage.

If God lets me live, I shall attain more than Mummy has ever done, I shall not remain insignificant, I shall work in the world and for mankind and now I know that first and foremost I shall require courage and cheerfulness!

WHAT DO YOU THINK?

1. *Why did Anne love the Dutch people?*
2. *What gave Anne Frank her courage?*
3. *According to Anne, what was the difference between her and her mother?*
4. *Were youngsters during the Holocaust psychologically stronger than their parents? What was the difference?*
5. *Are there differences between you and your parents?*
6. *Who do you think is better equipped to face adverse problems?*

Where Did the German Jews Go?

Shipload of Jews pleading for entrance to any country that would accept them.

Tens of thousands of frightened German Jews fled Germany. Albert Einstein was one of refugees who found safety in America. The painting shows Einstein with a violin in hand entering the U.S.A.

ALBERT EINSTEIN

Albert Einstein, mathematician and Jew, fled Germany in 1933 and found refuge in the United States. Six years later he sent President Franklin Roosevelt a letter informing him that atomic research in Germany created the possibility that the enemy was making a new kind of super-bomb. Roosevelt took the warning serious-ly and set up a committee of scientists to develop the atomic bomb. Many Jewish refugee scientists worked on the Manhattan Project. The atomic bomb shortened the war with Japan and saved thousands of American lives. The bomb ushered in the Atomic Age and has been both a blessing and a plague to humanity.

In a speech delivered on January 30, 1934, Adolf Hitler declared, "If a World War breaks out, the Jewish race in Europe will be eliminated." Thousands of frightened Jews fled from Germany to seek refuge in other countries. Thousands more would have done so but could not, because it was difficult to find a country that would allow them in.

The countries of Europe and the Americas admitted only a small number of Jews. The immigration process was often controlled by anti-Semitic officials. Some officials would only cooperate if given a bribe.

The voyage of the *St. Louis* illustrates the indifference of the Western nations.

The St. Louis

On May 13, 1939, the passenger ship *St. Louis* left Hamburg with 930 German Jewish refugees aboard, all carrying landing certificates for Cuba. When the ship arrived in Havana, the Cuban government would not allow them to land. For nine days the *St. Louis* circled off Havana and Florida. On June 5, Cuba said the refugees could go ashore if they posted a $500,000 bond within 24 hours, but it was impossible to accumulate so large a sum in so short a time.

The United States, too, refused to admit the passengers. On June 6, the ship headed back to Europe. On June 11, the captain threatened to beach it on the English coast in order to delay its return to Germany. The British allowed 280 "enemy aliens" to enter.

On June 17, the *St. Louis* docked in the Belgian port of Antwerp and the Jews were allowed to land. Within 12 months, the German blitzkrieg had overrun Europe and they were sent to the concentration camps where many ultimately were murdered.

Not just the passengers on the *St. Louis,* but millions of Jews could have been saved from the Nazis, but the U.S. State Department chose to ignore the signs of their impending doom.

Some Jews however were able to escape from Nazi Germany. Some went to European countries, others to the United States. Many German Jews who had formerly ignored or opposed Zionism now emigrated to Palestine. Many German Jews, however, hesitated to leave the land where their ancestors had lived for hundreds of years. Like many other Germans, they still believed that Hitler's regime would soon come to an end.

The Fourth Aliyah / 1924–1928

The Fourth Aliyah brought shopkeepers and artisans, mostly from Poland, where economic restrictions were being applied. The majority of the new arrivals settled in the cities of Tel Aviv, Haifa, and Jerusalem.

During the years 1924 to 1929, some 50,000 Jews came on aliyah to Israel. At the end of this period, the Jewish population of Israel was about 170,000.

The Fifth Aliyah / 1929–1939

Although German Jews had often been ambivalent about Zionism, many of them now turned to the land of their ancestors. As a result, the Fifth Aliyah, which extended from 1929 to 1939, was made up mostly of settlers from Germany and adjoining areas. The olim included students expelled from school by the Nazis, musicians, actors, artists, and writers, professionals, and manufacturers, and businessmen.

Henrietta Szold

One of the most important American Zionist activists was Henrietta Szold (1860–1945). In 1912, she founded Hadassah, an organization of American Zionist women. Over the years since, Hadassah has devoted itself to establishing hospitals and health and welfare services in Israel. The Hadassah Hospital and Medical Center in Jerusalem is widely regarded as the finest and most up-to-date medical facility in the entire Middle East.

Youth Aliyah

During the years preceding World War II, Henrietta Szold organized Youth Aliyah to rescue as many children and adolescents as possible from Nazi Germany.

Once the youngsters arrived in Palestine, Youth

June 7, 1936 edition of the *Palestine Post* detailing the beginning of the widespread terror and destruction that Arab uprisings were to inflict upon Jewish settlements during the next three years.

The *S. S. Max Nordau*, which left the Rumanian port of Constanza with 1,800 immigrants on May 7, 1946 was captured by the British six days later.

Henrietta Szold (1860–1945), humanitarian and Zionist leader. After a distinguished career as educator and editor, she founded Hadassah and settled in Jerusalem, where she supervised Hadassah's social services and headed Youth Aliyah.

Henrietta Szold with the first graduates of the Hadassah Nursing School, Jerusalem, 1921.

A painting by Leopold Pilichowski (1869–1933) illustrates the formal opening of the Hebrew University in Jerusalem, on April 1, 1925:
Lord Balfour is speaking, and seated behind him on the rostrum are the Sephardi and Ashkenazi chief rabbis of Palestine, General Allenby, the High Commissioner Sir Herbert Samuel, Dr. Chaim Weizmann, and the Chief Rabbi of the British Empire, Dr. Joseph Hertz.

Aliyah placed them in homes and helped them to obtain schooling and vocational training. Youth Aliyah saved thousands of children. Many fathers and mothers did not succeed in leaving Germany, but they were glad that at least their children would be safe.

The Growth of the Yishuv

The Jewish community of Palestine in the years before the State of Israel was founded was known as the Yishuv. Throughout the 1920s and 1930s, it steadily grew larger and more diversified.

New industrial centers and kibbutzim were founded. Tel Aviv, founded in 1909 as a garden suburb of Jaffa, became a beautiful modern city. Stockade-and-tower settlements, designed with an eye to defense against Arab marauders, sprang up throughout the land, especially in the undeveloped Negev area.

The Hebrew University

On the outskirts of the Old City of Jerusalem, a new Jerusalem was coming into existence. In 1925, the Hebrew University was founded on Mount Scopus. Its first lecture was given by the great physicist Albert Einstein (1879–1955), and its first chancellor was Judah Magnes (1877–1948), a prominent American Reform rabbi.

Today, the Hebrew University has two main campuses, the original one on Mount Scopus and a new one at Givat Ram. Its facilities include medical and professional schools, an agricultural institute, and Israel's National and University Library, with over 2 million books.

THE WAR REFUGEE BOARD

As the war fever in Europe increased, tens of thousands of Jews applied for refuge in the United States. Breckenridge Long, Assistant Secretary of State in charge of visas, did his best to halt the admission of refugees. Long hated the Jews and with the aid of like-minded officials in the State Department managed to reduce the admission of refugees to a trickle. Henry Morgenthau Jr., the Secretary of theTreasury, presented a personal report to President Roosevelt detailing the deliberate restrictions by Long and his aides halting the issuing of visas especially to Jews. On January 22, 1944, Roosevelt signed Executive Order 9417 officially creating the War Refugee Board and eliminating Breckenridge Long and his anti-Semitic cronies from the process.

NOW, THEREFORE, by virtue of the authority vested in me by the Constitution and the statutes of the United States, as President of the United States and as Commander in Chief of the Army and Navy, and in order to effectuate with all speed the rescue and relief of victims of enemy oppression, it is hereby ordered as follows:

1. There is established in the Executive Office of the President a War Refugee board (hereinafter referred to as the Board). The Board shall consist of the Secretary of State, the Secretary of the Treasury and the Secretary of War.

2. The Board shall be charged with the responsibility for seeing that the policy of the Government, as stated in the Preamble, is carried out. The functions of the Board shall include the development of effective measures for (a) the rescue, transportation, maintenance and relief of the victims of enemy oppression, and (b) the establishment of havens of temporary refuge for such victims. To this end the Board shall take the necessary steps to enlist the cooperation of foreign governments.

3. It shall be the duty of the State, Treasury and War Departments, to execute at the request of the Board, the plans and programs so developed. It shall be the duty of the heads of all agencies and departments to supply or obtain for the Board such information and to extend to the Board such supplies, shipping and other specified assistance and facilities as the Board may require. The State Department shall appoint special attachés with diplomatic status, selected by the Board, to be stationed abroad in places where it is likely that assistance can be rendered to war refuges.

4. The Board and the State, Treasury and War Departments are authorized to accept the services or contributions of any private persons, private organizations, State agencies, or agencies of foreign goverments in carrying out the purposes of this order.

5. To the extent possible the Board shall utilize the personnel, supplies, facilities and services of the State, Treasury and War Departments. In addition the Board, within the limits of funds which may be made available, may employ necessary personnel without regard for the Civil Service laws and regulations.

6. The Board shall be directly responsible to the President in carrying out the policy of this Government, as stated in the Preamble, and the Board shall report to him at frequent intervals concerning the steps taken for the rescue and relief of war refugees and shall make such recommendations as the Board may deem appropriate for further action to overcome any difficulties encountered in the rescue and relief of war refugees.

WHAT DO YOU THINK?

1. *Roosevelt was the President. Could he have bypassed Long and saved many Jewish lives?*
2. *Cordell Hull was Long's superior and was aware of what was happening. Why did he not relieve Long from his position?*
3. *Why did the President and his Secretary of State allow Long to hold up the issuing of visas?*

The Holocaust

The three leaders of the war against the Nazis with their advisors. *From left to right*, Winston Churchill of England, Franklin Delano Roosevelt of the United States, and Stalin of Russia.

The German commander's first announcement: "The German soldiers have come to free the population from Communist bondage. The Jews must wear armbands with a Star of David, they must not leave their quarters; they must carry out their required work and yield their radios."

SS Colonel Adolf Otto Eichmann was chief of operations in the scheme to exterminate all of European Jewry. At the end of the war, he escaped to Argentina, but in 1960 was kidnapped by the Israelis. Eichmann was tried before the Jerusalem District Court and was sentenced to death by hanging. Eichmann was the only criminal ever put to death in Israel. His body was cremated and his ashes were scattered over the Mediterranean.

The Western democracies feared another conflict on the scale of World War I and did everything possible to appease Hitler. His appetite for aggression was endless. After swallowing up Austria and Czechoslovakia without having to strike a blow, he attacked Poland in September 1939. The Poles fought back; Britain and France, aware that appeasement did not work, declared war on Germany.

The Second World War Begins

On April 9, 1940 the Germans attacked and overran Norway and Denmark. Soon after, Holland, Belgium, Luxembourg, and France were attacked. None of the armies could withstand the fast-moving German armor and their deadly air strikes.

By June 22, France sued for peace and 330,000 British and French troops were evacuated from the beaches of Dunkirk to England.

Millions of Jews were now under German control. Hitler felt that he was now in a position to solve the "Jewish Question." As Hitler saw it, the Jewish Question was simply the fact that Jews existed. He and his criminal cohorts devised a "Final Solution" as a way to eliminate the Jews. In all countries under Nazi control, Jews were rounded up, confined to ghettos, or shipped to concentration camps.

The Blitzkrieg

At first, Hitler had everything his own way, and his armed forces were victorious on every front. By 1941 his troops had conquered most of Europe: Norway, Denmark, Holland, Belgium, France, Yugoslavia, and Greece. Britain stood alone and was hard-pressed, despite Lend-Lease aid from the United States. Then Hitler attacked the Soviet Union. His winning streak continued for a while, but by 1943, with both the Soviet Union and the United States allied against him, the tide finally turned.

The Final Solution

Germany's victories brought millions of Jews under Nazi control. The Final Solution was now put into effect to kill all of Europe's Jews. The details of the program were worked out by a group of Nazi officials at the Wannsee Conference in January 1942.

In every occupied country, Jews would be rounded up, confined to ghettos, then shipped to concentration camps. Most would be killed outright. Some would be used as slave laborers until they were too worn out, from starvation and harsh treatment, to be useful. Among the most notorious of the death camps were Chelmo, Sobibor, Treblinka, and Auschwitz. The treatment of the inmates was almost beyond rational description. By the end of the war, somewhere between 3 million and 4 million Jewish inmates had been gassed and their bodies incinerated. Overall about 6 million Jews were killed. Many thousands of non-Jews, opponents of the Nazis, were also killed in the camps.

Auschwitz

Auschwitz, the largest extermination complex, was located at a railroad junction in southern Poland. It consisted of three camps. Auschwitz I was a labor camp and administration center. Within this camp were armament plants belonging to Siemens and Krupp.

Auschwitz II had a special extermination area called Birkenau where at least 1 million Jews were murdered. Its four gas chambers, using Zyklon-B, exterminated over 12,000 victims each day.

Auschwitz III had a huge I. G. Farben plant in which Jewish slaves labored to manufacture synthetic rubber from coal. The life expectancy of a Jewish worker in the rubber plant was three months; those in the coal mines that supplied the plant lasted 30 days.

The process of mass extermination was carried out with the full knowledge and cooperation of many business executives.

Raoul Wallenberg, "a righteous gentile" Wallenberg was a Swedish diplomat who saved thousands of Hungarian Jews. His chief operation was the distribution of Swedish certificates of protection which became known as "Wallenberg Passports." In November 1944, thousands of Hungarian Jews were on a death march to an extermination camp. He bravely followed them with a convoy of trucks and distributed medicines and food and managed to smuggle in 500 passports. After the war, the Soviets arrested Wallenberg, and in 1952, the Russians announced that Raoul had died in 1947 in a labor camp. The truth is still not known.

A heap of concentration camp victims.

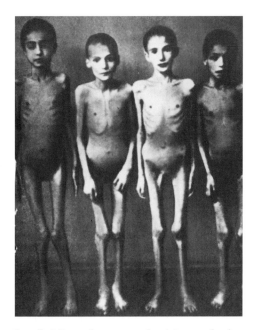

Josef Mengele was physician of the Auschwitz camp, where he conducted cruel medical experiments on Jewish inmates. After the war, Mengele was traced to Argentina, but he escaped. These are some of Mengele's victims.

The Nazi death camp of Auschwitz. Thousands of Jews were gassed, shot, and burned to death there.

Concentration camp photo.

The victims were assembled and packed in special sealed trains. On arriving in the camps they were forced into undressing rooms where they were shaved by barbers and stripped of their possessions. They were then packed into chambers and gassed. This highly efficient killing process could kill 2,000 Jews in the space of five minutes.

The Nazis mobilized Jewish slaves called Sonderkommandos to "process" the bodies. They removed gold fillings from teeth, shaved off the hair, then piled the bodies into crematoria where they were burned. In the meantime the clothing, hair, and other possessions were packed and sent to Germany for use in the war effort. Even the ashes of the victims were used as fertilizer for German farms.

To minimize the possibility of a revolt in the camp, the Sonderkommandos were periodically exterminated and replaced with fresh slaves. Many of them, driven mad by their macabre duties and the fate of their fellow Jews, willingly joined the victims in the gas chambers rather than continue to do the bidding of the Nazis.

Why Auschwitz Was Not Bombed

Although the Allies knew about Auschwitz, they made no attempt to interfere with the killings. The Jewish Agency pressed the Allies to bomb the gas chambers and the railroad tracks leading to the camp. All such requests were turned down with the excuse that the operation would endanger the lives of the pilots and had no clear military purpose.

British Prime Minister Winston Churchill, who advocated the bombing, wrote to Anthony Eden, his Foreign Secretary, "There is no doubt that this is the most horrible crime ever committed in the history of the world."

Why the Allies failed to bomb Auschwitz has never been fully explained. Had they done so, it is possible that many lives might have been saved.

MODECHAI CHAIM RUMKOWSKI (1877-1944)

The Nazis occupied the Polish city of Lodz, and established a Jewish Council called a Judenrat. On October 1939 they appointed Rumkowski, chairman of the Judanrat. He was responsible for organizing life for the 160,000 Jews in the ghetto. In his position he and his staff were forced to organize the deportation of Jews to the death camps. On September 11, 1942, Rumkowski deliveried this speech. A day later, the Nazis stormed the ghetto and rounded up 16,000 Jews for the death camps. Towards the end of the war, Rumkowski himself was sent to Auschwitz and killed.

RUMKOWSKI'S ADDRESS AT THE TIME OF THE DEPORTATION OF THE CHILDREN FROM THE GHETTO.

...The ghetto has been struck a hard blow. They demand what is most dear to it -children and old people. I was not privileged to have a child of my own and therefore devoted my best years to children. I lived and breathed together with children. I never imagined that my own hands would be forced to make this sacrifice on the altar. In my old age I am forced to stretch out my hands and to beg: "Brothers and sisters, give them to me! - Fathers and mothers, give me your children. . ." (Bitter weeping shakes the assembled public)... Yesterday, in the course of the day, I was given the order to send away more than 20,000 Jews from the ghetto, and if I did not - "we will do it ourselves." The question arose: "Should we have accepted this and carried it out ourselves, or left it to others?" But as we were guided not by the thought: "how many will be lost?" but "how many can be saved?" we arrived at the conclusion -those closest to me at work, that is, and myself -that however difficult it was going to be, we must take upon ourselves the carrying out of this decree. I must carry out this difficult and bloody operation, I must cut off limbs in order to save the body! I must take away children, and if I do not, others too will be taken, God forbid... (terrible wailing).

I cannot give you comfort today. Nor did I come to calm you today, but to reveal all your pain and all your sorrow. I have come like a robber, to take from you what is dearest to your heart. I tried everything I knew to get the bitter sentence cancelled. When it could not be cancelled, I tried to lessen the sentence. Only yesterday I ordered the registration of nine year-old children. I wanted to save at least one year-children from nine to ten. But they would not yield. I succeeded in one thing-to save the children over ten. Let that be our consolation in our great sorrow.

There are many people in this ghetto who suffer from tuberculosis, whose days or perhaps weeks are numbered. I do not know, perhaps this is a satanic plan, and perhaps not, but I cannot stop myself from proposing it: "Give me these sick people, and perhaps it will be possible to save the healthy in their place.- I know how precious each one of the sick is in his home, and particularly among Jews. But at a time of such decrees one must weigh up and measure who should he saved. who can be saved and who may be saved.

Common sense requires us to know that those must be saved who can be saved and who have a chance of being saved and not those whom there is no chance to save in any case....   *Documents of the Holocaust*

WHAT DO YOU THINK?

1. What would have happened if Rumkowski had not cooperated with the Nazis?
2. Who would have made the selection for the death camps if the Judenrat refused?
3. Rumkowski decided to give the Nazis the sick people. Was there another solution?
4. Did his decisions really matter?
5. Rumkowski was accused of collaboration. Was he guilty?

To Fight and Die with Honor

Jewish partisian group, operating in and near Vilna. Abba Kovner *(center)*, the poet, an active member was of the group.

Israeli stamp issued to commemorate the liberation of the Nazi concentration camps by the Allies at the end of World War II.

The execution of two Jewish partisans in Minsk, Russia. The 17 year old heroine was Masha Brushkina.

Unlike other conquered people in Europe, who could choose between cooperation or passive resistance, the Jews had no options or freedom of choice. Even those who collaborated, such as the members of the Judenrat (Jewish Councils) and their Jewish enforcers, were destined for annihilation. Any armed action could expect no help from outside groups. In fact, some Poles took great delight in helping recapture escapees from the death camps. Even some Polish partisans, who fought the Nazis, hunted and murdered Jewish escapees. They hated both the Nazis and the Jews. Even after the Allies defeated the Nazis, Poles continued murdering Jews. The Jews incarcerated in ghettos were under constant armed supervision and had no opportunity of obtaining weapons. Jewish rebels were aware that any uprising represented choosing certain death over the saving of lives. Most of the Judenrat despite the certainty of early death cooperated with the rebel groups. Often members of the Judenrat commited suicide upon realizing that they could do nothing to prevent the transportation to the death camps. Despite the certainty of death, many Jewish inmates decided to die with honor and inflict punishment on their murderers. Jews staged armed rebellions in many ghettos.

The Warsaw Ghetto

When the Germans captured Warsaw, in 1939, there were 400,000 Jews living there. The Nazis confined them to a ghetto about one mile square and set up a Judenrat, headed by Adam Czernaikow, (1880–1942), to govern the ghetto and carry out their orders. In 1942, deportations to Treblinka, the extermination center, began on a mass scale. Three days later, Czerniokow committed suicide rather than cooperate with the deportations. Within six weeks, 300,000 Jews were deported from Warsaw.

The Ghetto Uprising

In the next few months, the great majority of the ghetto residents were deported and murdered. On April

18, 1943, the underground learned that the Germans intended to wipe out the remaining 50,000 Jews. Everyone took shelter in carefully designed bunkers, and fewer than 1,000 members of the ghetto's fighting organization, armed with homemade bombs and a few guns, prepared for the hopeless battle.

Like the heroes of Masada, every man, woman and child in the ghetto became a warrior. On Passover morning, April 19, 1943, a heavily armed SS brigade moved into the ghetto. The surprised Nazi troops came under fire and suffered many losses and dead or wounded. To avoid street fighting, the Germans used artillery and flame throwers. It took four weeks of heavy fighting to obliterate the ghetto. When all the buildings were destroyed, the SS moved in with poison gas to kill the Jews who remained alive. A few survivors escaped through the sewers to other parts of Warsaw and lived to fight again.

Sobibor

There were several uprisings in the camps. Sobibor was one of the six Nazi extermination centers based in Poland. It is estimated that more than 250,000 Jews were liquidated there. In the beginning of October 1943, some 300 Jewish laborers were employed at the camp. They decided to revolt when they learned that they, too, were to be exterminated. Poorly armed, they managed to kill several German supervisors, but were prevented from escaping the camp by barbed wire fences and a large mine field. More than 200 Jews were killed, yet 30 managed to escape and some eventually reached Israel.

Auschwitz

Auschwitz was Germany's largest extermination camp. It is estimated that more than 1,000,000 Jews were gassed to death with Zyklon B, manufactured by I. G. Farben. In spite of the hopelessness, a resistance movement was organized. On October 7, 1944, the Jewish "special squad" was forced to assist in rounding up Jewish inmates. Instead, they set fire to a crematorium, killed several SS soldiers, and managed to cut through a barbed wire fence and escape. Just a handful survived the escape.

Misha Gildenman, kown as "Uncle Misha," commander of a Jewish partisan unit in Volhynia, Russia.

Mordecai Anielewicz helped organize the revolt against the Nazis in the Warsaw ghetto. He died fighting the Germans. This statue in memory of Mordecai Anielewicz is at Kibbutz Yad Mordecai in Israel.

Jewish partisan unit commanded by Captain Grynszpan.

The train station at Treblinka where thousands of Jews were brought to the extermination chambers.

NAZIS IN ARGENTINA

A book by Uki Goni an Argentinian journalist entitled *The Real Odessa: Smuggling the Nazis into Peron's Argentine* documents how Peron smuggled Nazi war criminals into Argentina. According to the records that have been uncovered in Europe, Peron's government brought more than 300 Nazis and dozens of French, Belgian, Italian, and Slovak fascists who were hunted by their countries into Argentina. The documents indicate that the network was run from the presidential palace by Rodolfo Freude, one of Peron's closest advisers.

The documents also show that the Catholic Church was deeply involved in the smuggling operation. Many of the fake immigration documents were signed by priests attached to the Pontifical Commission of Assisstance.

Juan Peron, *left*, his wife Eva, and Rodolfo Freude.

Vilna

In 1941, after two years of Soviet occupation, Vilna numbered 65,000 Jews. The Germans established two ghettos there and the deportations to extermination camps began in 1943. The unified fighting organization in Vilna revolted and about 200 prisoners managed to escape and join the Jewish partisan groups hiding in the forest.

Treblinka

Treblinka, a small Polish village, was the site of one of the largest Nazi extermination camps. Starting from 1942 until the end of the war, about 800,000 Jews were murdered there. About 600 prisoners revolted, armed only with homemade knives, but just a handful managed to escape.

On November 1943, the Germans murdered the inmates and destroyed the camp to hide their guilt when they realized that they were going to be defeated.

The Rat Line

Under the leadership of Bishop Stepanac, a Nazi escape route called the "rat line" operated from a Catholic college in Rome to save Nazi war criminals. A series of hiding places were set up in churches, seminaries, and convents where wanted Nazi criminals, disguised and with false identity papers, were shepherded to ports in the boot of Italy. From there, the "rats" enlisted the aid of smugglers who evaded Allied naval patrols and brought them to Argentina, where they were welcomed by the fascist dictator Juan Peron. Argentina had a large, cooperative German colony, and it was easy, using false identities, to blend into the population and lead a normal life.

Gestapo Chief Klaus Barbi, the "Butcher of Lyons," escaped by the rat line to South America. In 1980, he was captured, deported to France, and convicted for war crimes and imprisoned. He died a natural death in 1991.

MORDECAI ANIELEWICZ (1939–1943) GHETTO REVOLT COMMANDER

Mordecai Anielewicz was the commander–in–chief of the Underground Jewish Fighting Organization. He led the Warsaw Ghetto uprising, which began on April 19, 1943. He fell on May 8, 1943, together with scores of his fellow fighters, in the command bunker at 18 Mila Street. Soon after his death, Hashomer Hazair, of which he was a member, founded a kibbutz, Yad Mordecai, in Palestine in his memory. The kibbutz maintains a museum of the ghetto resistance.

His Last Communication as Ghetto Revolt Commander (April 23, 1943)

It is impossible to put into words what we have been through. One thing is clear, what happened exceeded our boldest dreams. The Germans ran twice from the Ghetto. One of our companies held out for 40 minutes and another for more than 6 hours. The mines set in the "brushmakers" are exploded. Several of our companies attacked the dispersing Germans. Our losses in manpower are minimal.That is also an achievement. Y (Yechiel) fell. He fell a hero, at the machinegun. I feel that great things are happening and what we dared to do is of great, enormous importance. Beginning from today we shall shift over to the partisan tactic. Three battle companies will move out tonight, with two tasks reconnaissance and obtaining arms. Do remember, short-range weapons are of no use to us. We use such weapons only rarely. What we need urgently: grenades, rifles, machineguns and explosives. It is impossible to describe the conditions under which the Jews of the Ghetto are now living. Only a few will be able to hold out. The remainder will die sooner or later. Their fate is decided. In almost all the hiding places in which thousands are concealing themselves it is not possible to light a candle for lack of air. With the aid of our transmitter we heard a marvelous report on our fighting by the "Swit" radio station. The fact that we are remembered beyond the ghetto walls encourages us in our struggle. Peace go with you, my friend! Perhaps we may still meet again. The dream of my life has risen to become fact. Self–defense in the ghetto will have to have been a reality. Jewish armed resistance and revenge are fact. I have been a witness to the magnificent heroic fighting of Jewish men and women of battle.

WHAT DO YOU THINK?

1. *Did the Jews realize that they were fighting a losing battle?*
2. *What type of weapons did the Jews need? Why did they need such weapons?*
3. *Were there any outside sources from which to obtain weapons?*
4. *What was Mordecai's dream? Did he realize his dream?*
5. *Did the Warsaw ghetto revolt encourage other revolts?*
6. *Were the German surprised at the resistance?*
7. *Why did the Nazis locate the extermination camps in Poland?*
8. *Why did the Poles hate the Jews?*
9. *Did the Polish Catholic Church try to help the Jews during the Nazi period?*

The British White Paper / 1939

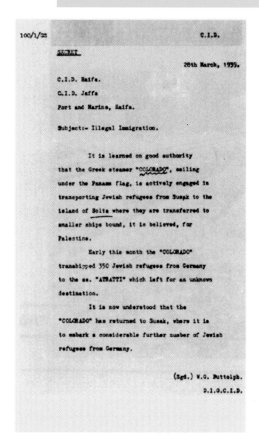

Secret message from a British spy warning of the activities of two "underground" ships, the *Colorado* and the *Atratti*. In 1939, these two ships, crammed with desperate Polish-Jewish refugees escaping Hitler's Holocaust, were intercepted by British warships and turned back. There is evidence that some of the spies were Jewish traitors who sold out to the British.

The White Paper

The British White Paper of 1939 declared that in 10 years, Palestine would be partitioned, and in the meantime, Jewish immigration would be severely restricted. This document was a complete and utter disavowal of the Balfour Declaration and of Great Britain's international obligations under the Mandate. The British appeasement of the Arabs was motivated by fear that the Arabs would support Germany, and threaten England's hold on the Middle East, if war broke out in Europe.

The publication of the White Paper in 1939 brought consternation to Jews everywhere. What would happen now to the Jews in the lands under Nazi domination? Where would they go? Restrictions on immigration were increasing in every country; even the gates of America were closing, for so many Jews had emigrated there that the German, Polish, Czech, and Austrian quotas were now filled.

The Jews of Europe went wherever they could. However, it became increasingly difficult to find a place of refuge. Some fled to South America, to Africa, and even to war-torn Shanghai. But even so, only a few could manage to escape at this late date. President Franklin D. Roosevelt had called an international conference at Evian-les-Bains, France, in 1938 to discuss ways and means of saving European Jewry. The conference was a dismal failure. The results of other endeavors were equally meager.

Aliyah Bet

In these dark days, a desperate new kind of aliyah was started. Operating illegally and in secret, it was called Aliyah Bet—Immigration Wave B. Agents of the Haganah, the Yishuv's underground defense force, secretly began transporting refugees from Europe to Palestine. Some of their ships were intercepted by the

British, but many others got through, Their human cargo would be landed on deserted beaches, late at night, and quickly spirited away to hiding places on the kibbutzim.

Displaced Persons

In the liberated concentration camps, there were hundreds of thousands of displaced persons (DPs), former prisoners or slave laborers who had nothing to return to and no place to go. The war and the Nazis had uprooted them and destroyed their lives.

The problem of the Jewish displaced persons was particularly acute. Most of the few Jews who had managed to survive no longer had homes or families.

Illegal Immigration

Unfortunately, the British White Paper of 1939 was still in effect, a pitiless barrier to further Jewish immigration to Palestine.

The Haganah, which had aided illegal immigration during the war in spite of the White Paper, again went into action. "Underground railroads" were again organized. The survivors of Hitler's death camps waiting in detention centers had cause for new hope.

Again, the Haganah took on the perilous task of landing illegal immigrants in secret, under cover of night. Often the passengers, scarred by years of camp life, had to wade through a stormy surf or row in small boats to elude the British guards.

The Irgun Zvai Leumi, a Palestinian underground movement founded in 1937 by members of the Betar youth organization and the Zionist Revisionist movement, was also very active in the "illegal" immigration of Jewish displaced persons.

The Internment Camps

The British showed little sympathy for the plight of the Jews. Their main concern was to maintain good relations with the Arab nations and avoid trouble in the Middle East. They used their military forces

Refugees in a detention camp strain at the barbed wire that keeps them from freedom and their homeland.

A boatload of "illegal" immigrants landing in Palestine under cover of darkness

Bewildered children in DP camps yearning for normalcy in their new homes in Eretz Israel. "When will we be allowed to go to our new home"?

The *Exodus*, a Haganah ship, carried 4,500 Jewish refugees to Palestine from the camps in Europe at the end of World War II. The British, still holding the mandate over Palestine, refused to allow the ship to dock and returned it to Hamburg, Germany. This brutal act helped swing world opinion against Britain and toward the creation of a Jewish state.

to prevent Jewish immigration and succeeded in intercepting most of the ships. The passengers were arrested and sent to internment camps on the island of Cyprus. There, behind barbed wire, they awaited the moment when they would be able to ascend to the homeland.

The *S.S. Exodus*

In 1947, the British policy became even more harsh. To set an example, they sent back to Germany the S.S. *Exodus,* a Haganah boat crammed full of immigrants, men, women, and children, who had survived the Nazi death camps. These refugees had risked their lives to come to Palestine. Now they were sent back to Germany, where there was no room for them except in DP camps, where they might languish forever without home or hope.

The fate of the *Exodus* stirred the Jews of Palestine to open revolt. Haganah and Irgun units destroyed British radar stations, bridges, and other military installations, and attacked British patrols. Arms were manufactured in secret factories and smuggled in from abroad.

The Palestine Problem

As the situation deteriorated, the British closed-door policy became a matter of world concern. Britain was unable to solve the Palestine problem, so the United Nations took up the question. In 1947, it sent a Committee of Inquiry to Palestine. The committee returned with a proposal to partition Palestine into two states—one Arab and one Jewish.

The Kielce Pogrom

At the end of the war, homeless, uprooted Jews began looking for refuge. About 200,000 of them, encouraged by the Polish government, returned, hoping to rebuild their shattered lives. However, on July 4 1946, 43 Jews were murdered in a pogrom. Immediately, thousands of Jews left the country. Some went to the DP camps in Germany and Austria. Others departed for Palestine through the escape routes in southern France.

July 1946. Funeral for the victims of the Kielce pogrom.

THE JEWISH AGENCY FOR PALESTINE

Statement on the MacDonald White Paper of 1939
The feeble British government, in 1939, yielded to terror by Germany in Europe and the Arabs in Palestine. The White Paper of 1939 declared that the building of a Jewish homeland in Palestine was completed, and for the next five years, only 75,000 Jews will be admitted. The restrictions condemned millions of desperate European Jews to Nazi destruction by restricting immigration into Palestine, the only country willing and able to accept them.

1. The effect of the new policy for Palestine laid down by the Mandatory Government in the White Paper of May 17, 1939, is to deny to the Jewish people the right to reconstitute their National Home in their ancestral country. It is a policy which transfers authority over Palestine to the present Arab majority, puts the Jewish population at the mercy of that majority, decrees the stoppage of Jewish immigration as soon as the Jewish inhabitants increase from one third of the total [population], and sets up a territorial ghetto for the Jews in their own homeland.

2. The Jewish people regard this breach of faith as a surrender to Arab terrorism. It delivers Great Britain's friends into the hands of those who are fighting her. It must widen the breach between Jews and Arabs, and undermine the hope of peace in Palestine. It is a policy in which the Jewish people will not acquiesce. The new regime announced in the White Paper will be devoid of any moral basis and contrary to international law.

Such a regime can only be set up and maintained by force…

5. It is in the darkest hours of Jewish history that the British Government proposes to deprive the Jews of their last hope, and to close the road back to their homeland. It is a cruel blow; doubly cruel because it comes from the Government of a great nation which has extended a helping hand to Jews, and whose postion in the word rests upon foundations of moral authority and international good faith. This blow will not subdue the Jewish people. The historic bond between the people and the Land of Israel will not be broken. The Jews will never accept the closing against them of the gates of Palestine, nor let their national home be converted into a ghetto. Jewish pioneers, who in the past three generations have shown their strength in the upbuilding of a derelict country, will from now on display the same strength in defending Jewish immigration, the Jewish home, and Jewish freedom.

The McDonald White Paper

WHAT DO YOU THINK?

1. *What did the Balfour Declaration guarantee the Jews?*
2. *Why did the British yield to Arab pressure and nullify the Balfour Declaration?*
3. *Did the Jews want a National Home or a State of their own?*
4. *What is the difference?*
5. *How did restriction on immigration condemn Jewish refugees to death?*
6. *In World War II, Palestinian Jews fought side-by-side with the British. How did the Arabs repay the British for siding with them against the Jews? Did any Arab nation participate in World War II in the fight against the Nazis?*

Holocaust Punishment

A session of the International Military Tribunal, Nuremberg, 1945–1946. In the dock are: (1) Hermann Goering, (2) Rudolf Hess, (3) Joachim von Ribbentrop, (4) Wilhelm Keitel, (5) Ernst Kaltenbrunner, (6) Alfred Rosenberg, (7) Hans Frank (8), Wilhelm Frick, (9) Julius Streicher, (10) Walther Funk, (11) Hjalmar Schacht, (12) Karl Doenitz, (13) Erich Raeder, (14) Baldur von Schirach, (15) Fritz Sauckel, (16) Alfred Jodl, (17) Franz von Papen, (18) Arthur Seyss-Inquart, (19) Albert Speer, (20) Konstantine von Neurath, (21) Hans Fritzsche.

Several thousand Germans were tried and convicted in Poland and by Soviet Russia.

The death of Hitler and the German surrender (May 8, 1945) arrived too late for 12 million human beings, 6 million of whom were Jews. One-third of the entire Jewish people had been destroyed; barely 30 percent of the Jews of Europe remained alive.

The International Military Tribunal

Of the thousands who had perpetrated war crimes and the Holocaust, only a small fraction were brought to justice. In 1945, an International Military Tribunal was set up to prosecute Nazi war criminals. Meeting in Nuremberg, the tribunal tried a number of Nazi leaders: 12 were sentenced to death, and were given life imprisonment. Hitler and Himmler had committed suicide just before the war ended, and Goering, who was sentenced to death by the tribunal, cheated the hangman by taking poison.

A few dozen minor war criminals were also tried by the Allies or by the Russians, but most were never caught or brought to trial, and an uncertain number escaped from Germany to South America or the Middle East, or even to the United States. Some former war criminals were protected by the American government, either working for the CIA in the Cold War struggle against Communism or, like Dr. Werner von Braun, helping to develop the space program.

Switzerland and the Holocaust

Switzerland was "neutral" during World War II. Many Jews, anticipating problems, deposited their assets in Swiss banks. High-ranking Nazis hid jewels, cash, and gold that they stole from their Jewish victims in numbered Swiss bank accounts.

Until 1997, the Swiss officially denied the existence of these Jewish and Nazi assets. However, under pressure of the World Jewish Congress, the Swiss reluctantly opened their accounts and agreed to return hundreds of millions of deposited and looted Jewish assets to Holocaust survivors.

The WJC also has documentary evidence regarding Nazi gold transfers and Jewish assets in other "neutral" countries such as Sweden, Turkey, Spain, and Portugal. As a consequence, the French government has appointed a committee to identify property stolen from French Jews. Over 2,000 works of art in French museums have been identified as stolen from Jews.

Austria and Anti-Semitism

Austria had an anti-Semitic tradition which preceded Hitler's takeover. The Catholic press, for generations, was filled with articles denouncing Jews. Anti-Jewish articles claimed that Austria was ruled by a tiny percentage of Jews who belonged to a different nation and race. A favorite topic was the *Protocols of the Elders of Zion*, which predicted Jewish mastery of the world.

In 1998, the Austrian government set up a Historical Commission to investigate the actions of the Austrian people during the Nazi occuption. In a 16,000–page report, the commission documented the plundering of Jewish property between 1938 and 1945. The report noted that the country resisted restitution to victims of the Nazis. Austria helped the Nazis drive Jews out of 60,000 apartments. Companies also reduced competition by taking over Jewish enterprises. "The looting of 200,000 Jews in Austria was the first step in their annihilation by the Nazis," said historian Clemon Jobolner.

The report accused Austria of resisting compensation. Finally, in 1993, after most of the victims had died, the Austrian government admitted complicity in the Holocaust. After more foot-dragging, the Austrian government, in 2001, set up a compensation fund for Holocaust victims.

A Viennese election poster of 1920 calls on German Christians to save Austria from the Jews.

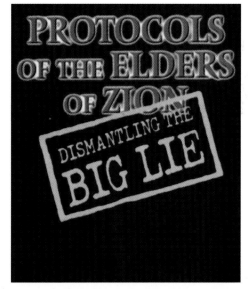

The legend of the *Protocols of the Elders of Zion* was fabricated in Paris by a forger working for the Russian *Okhrana* (secret police). The anti-Semitic fake pretended to prove the existance of a international Jewish conspiracy to seize world power. In the 1930's the *Protocals* found the greatest number of disciples in Germany. The theory of a Jewish conspiracy became a justification for Jewish genocide.

Since the establishment of the State of Israel, the *Protocols* have become popular in many Arab and European countries. In 2003, Egyptian prime time television aired a forty part anti-Semitic program called "Horsemen Without a Horse". The series was based on the Protocols of Elders of Zion.

The book *Dismantling the Big Lie* analyzes and disproves the deliberate lies and distortions.

Eichmann on trial in Israel.

Eichmann the Butcher

Jews have long memories, and sometimes many years pass before a wrong against them is avenged. After World War II, many of the monsters who murdered Jews during the Holocaust escaped. Some found a safe haven in Arab countries. Many escaped to South America, where they lived under new identities. In many instances, they were protected by anti-Semitic government officials.

Israel organized a special group of secret Nazi hunters whose job it was to find and expose these criminals.

In 1941, Adolf Eichmann had become head of the Department of Jewish Affairs at Nazi police headquarters in Berlin. Eichmann organized the deportation of Jews to the death camps and was responsible for stealing their property. He personally supervised the effort to destroy Hungarian Jewry.

After the war Eichmann was captured by the Allies, but in 1950, he managed to escape to Argentina. Friendly officials furnished him with false identity papers, and he lived there till 1960, when he was discovered by the Israeli Nazi hunters. Eichmann was kidnapped and secretly flown to Israel. After a long trial, he was found guilty and sentenced to death. His body was cremated, just as he had cremated 6 million Jews, and his ashes were scattered over the Mediterranean Sea.

His was the first and only judical execution ever carried out by the State of Israel.

The Yad Vashem Memorial: Ohel Yizkor–Hall of Remembrance. The walls are built of large, unhewn black lava rocks. On the mosaic floor are inscribed the names of the 21 largest concentration camps, and near the wall in the west burns a light.

EICHMANN THE BUTCHER

On February 21, 1961, Adolph Eichmann was on trial in Jerusalem. He was accused of "crimes against the Jewish people." The accused, during the period from 1939 to 1945, was responsible for the killing of millions of Jews.

Eichmann was found guilty and was executed on May 31, 1962. His body was cremated and the ashes were thrown into the Mediterranean.

The following is the abbreviated indictment by Gideon Hausner, the Attorney General of the government of Israel.

Six Million Accusers

When I stand before you here, Judges of Israel, to lead the prosecution of Adolf Eichmann, I am not standing alone. With me are six million accusers. But they cannot rise to their feet and point an accusing finger towards him who sits in the dock and cry: "I accuse." For their ashes are piled up on the hills of Auschwitz and the fields of Treblinka, and are strewn in the forests of Poland. Their graves are scattered throughout the length and breadth of Europe. Their blood cries out, but their voice is not heard. Therefore I will be their spokesman.

A New Kind of Killer

In this trial, we shall also encounter a new kind of killer, the kind that exercises his bloody craft behind a desk, and only occasionally does the deed with his own hands. Indeed, we know of only one incident in which Adolf Eichmann actually beat to death a Jewish boy, who had dared to steal fruit from a peach tree in the yard of his Budapest home. But it was his word that put gas chambers into action; he lifted the telephone, and railway trains left for the extermination centers; his signature it was that sealed the doom of thousands and tens of thousands. Finally, after torture and pillage, after everything had been wrung out of them, when even their hair had been taken, they were transported en masse to the slaughter. Even the corpses were still of value: the gold teeth were extracted and the wedding rings removed.

To him, the decree of extermination was just another written order to be executed; yet he was the one who planned, initiated and organized, who instructed others to spill this ocean of blood.

Eichmann's Guilt

Adolf Eichmann's guilt lies in the planning, initiation, organization and execution of the crimes specified in the indictment. We shall prove his guilt as planner, initiator, organizer and executor of the crime known as "the final solution of the Jewish problem." He was the pivot of the criminal conspiracy to exterminate the Jewish people, wholly or in part, and he was partner in the crimes committed by the S.S., the S.D., the Gestapo, including the members of the Einsatzgruppen, the Security Police commanders, senior S.S. and police officers, their emissaries and branch offices, and all those who were under their command and carried out their instructions in respect of all the acts of murder, plunder, torture and persecution specified in the indictment.

WHAT DO YOU THINK?

1. Who was the spokeman of the 6 million murdered Jews?

2. What was the Final Solution?

3. Is a soldier guilty if he obeys his commander and kills an innocent person?

4. What would you do if you were a soldier and were ordered to shoot an innocent prisoner?

The State of Israel Is Born / 1948

Rabbi Meir Berlin *(left)*, American president of the Mizrachi World Organization, talking with Jewish Agency leader David Ben-Gurion

David Ben-Gurion

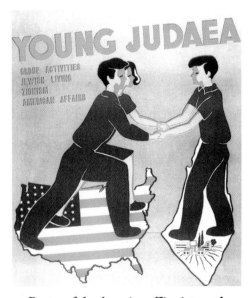

Poster of the American Zionist youth movement.

Before World War I, there were about 20,000 active Zionists in the United States. Most of them were affiliated with the Federation of American Zionists, which in 1917, was renamed the Zionist Organization of America. Associated with the ZOA were Hadassah, the women's Zionist organization, the Sons of Zion, a fraternal order; and Young Judaea, a youth group. There were also American branches of the Labor Zionist Party (Poale Zion) and the Orthodox Mizrachi Party.

The ZOA was largest in size and put forth major spokesmen who fought for the formation of a Jewish state. The dynamic oratory of Louis Lipsky, Stephen S. Wise, and Abba Hillel Silver moved thousands of Jews at national Zionist conventions and helped persuade American public to support the Zionist cause.

By 1930, the number of active Zionists in the United States rose to 150,000. The growth of the Nazi movement in Europe aroused many American Jews. By 1940, there were 400,000 enrolled Zionists.

America Speaks

In 1943, the American Jewish Conference made it clear that most American Jews favored statehood. During the United Nations deliberations on the partition of Palestine in 1947, American Jewry spoke out almost unanimously for this cause. The UN's decision to establish separate Jewish and Arab states in the mandated territory of Palestine was hailed with joy by American and world Jewry.

American public opinion, a series of resolutions passed by Congress, and the favorable attitude of President Truman all carried weight in persuading the nations of the world to vote for a Jewish state.

Despite Arab protests, the United Nations passed a resolution in favor of partition on November 29, 1947. Although the plan gave the Jews of the Yishuv only part of Palestine, the Jewish state of which generations had dreamed had become a reality. In Palestine Jews danced in the streets.

On May 14, 1948, the British gave up their mandate and left Palestine. The Jews at once set up a provisional government headed by David Ben-Gurion, and proclaimed the establishment of the State of Israel.

War of Independence

The Arabs bitterly opposed the Partition Plan and refused to accept the United Nations vote. On May 15, 1948, the day the State of Israel came into existence, the armies of Lebanon, Syria, Saudi Arabia, Jordan, Iraq, and Egypt jointly attacked, vowing to drive the Jews into the sea. The Israelis fought valiantly, holding out against ferocious attacks by Arab artillery, armored cars, and aircraft. In January 1949, after months of fighting and thousands of casualties on both sides, a truce was declared. Twenty months after the first attack, the severely beaten Arab governments agreed to end the war.

Israel's stunning victory came at great human cost. More than 4,000 of its bravest soldiers and 3,000 civilians lost their lives defending the homeland.

In January 1949, an armistice was declared. The State of Israel held elections and formed its first government. Dr. Chaim Weizmann, the revered Zionist leader, became its first President and David Ben-Gurion its first Prime Minister. In May 1949, Israel was admitted to the United Nations.

Ben–Gurion

David Ben-Gurion was born in the Polish village of Ploshi in 1886. His original name was David Green. Influenced by his father's Zionist activities, David moved to Palestine in 1906.

The emblem of Israel tells us a lot about the history and ideals of the Jewish people. The Temple menorah reminds us of the glory of the city of Jerusalem and also its sad destruction. The olive tree branches are symbols of peace. They tell the world that Israel wishes to live in peace with its neighbors.

A banner headline announces the birth of the new state. Although the State of Israel was proclaimed on Friday afternoon, May 14, 1948, the paper is dated Sunday, May 16, because the *Palestine Post* in Israel was not printed on the Jewish Sabbath.

Israeli civilians digging trenches and preparing for the expected invasion.

An Israeli stamp showing part of the Declaration of Independence

At that time, the Turks ruled Palestine and were strongly opposed to Jewish settlement. Laws were passed restricting Jews from purchasing land and constructing buildings and settlements.

Turkey fought on the German side during World War I and was stripped of the land of Palestine. The League of Nations gave the British a Mandate to rule the area. In 1939, giving in to Arab pressure, the British restricted Jewish immigration.

Arab terrorists began raiding Jewish settlements in an attempt to force the Zionists to leave the land. The terrorists attacked Jewish homes, ambushed cars and buses, and murdered young Jewish pioneers. In 1929, Arabs murdered 60 Jews in the city of Hebron.

Ben-Gurion called for active Jewish resistance. He helped to organize the Haganah, a Jewish self-defense militia. Armed Haganah members protected Jewish settlements as well as major cities in Israel against Arab terrorism. In 1947, the United Nations ended the British Mandate.

The Declaration of Independence

On the 5th of Iyar, 5708 (May 14, 1948), Jewish representatives from all over Palestine met in Tel Aviv. David Ben-Gurion proudly read the Declaration of Independence, proclaiming Israel an independent state and the homeland of the Jewish people.

In December 1949, Ben-Gurion declared Jerusalem the capital of Israel. At long last, after 2,000 years, the dream of the return to Zion had become a miraculous reality. After 50 years of leadership, David Ben-Gurion resigned in December 1963 and retired to the pioneering kibbutz of S'de Boker in the heart of the Negev.

Today, Ben-Gurion University in Beersheba stands in the Negev in tribute to the great Zionist leader who was Israel's first Prime Minister.

THE LAW OF RETURN

The establishment of the State of Israel destabilized the Jewish communities in the Arab countries. Waves of anti-Jewish violence struck almost every Jewish community from Libya to Iraq. In most Arab countries, Jews had roots going back thousands of years.

After the war began, and it became clear that Israel was winning its battle for survival, mobs began attacking Jewish homes, businesses, and synagogues.

There were significant Jewish departures from all Arab countries. Some were organized by Jewish organizations, some paid to be smuggled out, and some at great personal risk just disappeared.

The Law of Return was passed unanimously by the Knesset, the Israeli parliament, on July 5, 1950 and written into the law of the country.

1. Every Jew has the right to immigrate to the country.

2. Immigration shall be on the basis of immigration visas.

3. Immigration visas shall be issued to any Jew expressing a desire to settle in Israel, except if the Minister of Immigration is satisfied that the applicant:

(i) acts against the Jewish nation; or

(ii) may threaten the public health or State security.

3. (a) A Jew who comes to Israel and after his arrival expresses a desire to settle there may, while in Israel, obtain an irnmigration certificate.

4. Every Jew who migrated to the country before this law goes into effect and every Jew who was born in the country either before or after the law is effective enjoys the same status as any person who migrated on the basis of this law.

5. The Minister of Immigration is delegated to enforce this law and he may enact regulations to control the issue of immigrant visas and immigrant certificates.

WHAT DO YOU THINK?

1. Why did the establishment of the State of Israel alarm the Jews in Arabs countries?

2. Today, are there any significant Jewish communities in Arab countries?

3. Was it a good idea to give every Jew a right to settle in Israel? Why?

4. Were there any restrictions to the Law of Return?

5. How has the Law of Return saved the lives of many Jews?

6. Do you know of any Jewish communities that have returned to Israel?

The First Years of the New State

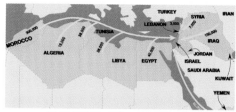

IMMIGRATION (Aliyah)
From Arab Countries

Israeli independence had a tremendous effect on Jewish communities in Arab lands. Most of the Arab countries instituted severe restrictions on their Jewish citizens. The hostile governments deprived them of their properties, their homes, and their businesses. These repressive measures initiated a huge exodus of Jews. Most of them arrived penniless, with only the clothes on their backs. In 1949, Operation Magic Carpet evacuated 50,000 Jews from Yemen.

In 1945 there wrere close to a million Jews living in the Arab world. Following the establishment of Israel, waves of persecution drove most of them to seek safety in Israel.

ANATOLE (NATAN) SHARANSKY
(b. 1948–) Scientist, activist, refusenik. Anatole Sharansky is a Jewish computer scientist who helped organize the Jewish refusenik movement in the USSR. In 1973, because of his activities, he was arrested and kept in solitary confinement for 18 months. He was finally placed on trial on the trumped-up charge of espionage. Despite worldwide protests, Anatole was sentenced to 13 years of imprisonment. After 11 years in prison and labor camps, he was released and immediately left for Israel. Anatole Sharansky, activist and refusenik, now leads the fight for the rights and welfare of new Soviet immigrants in Israel. Sharansky has become a member of the Knesset.

In January 1949, an armistice was declared. The State of Israel held elections and formed its first government. Dr. Chaim Weizmann, the revered Zionist leader, became its first President and David Ben-Gurion its first Prime Minister. In May 1949, Israel was admitted to the United Nations.

To many who witnessed the birth of Israel, it seemed like a miracle. After pain and hopelessness, after the deaths of 6 million martyred Jews, the day of liberation had dawned for the survivors.

The State of Israel had many problems. It was a small country, and most of the holy places of Jewish tradition were in Arab territory. Hebron, with the cave of Machpelah and the graves of the Patriarchs, was outside of Israel. Even the Old City of Jerusalem, and the Western Wall area, where once the Temple stood, were not in Israeli territory.

Exodus and Absorption

To compound Israel's difficulties, the Arab states remained hostile after the armistice, so defense was a major concern. In addition, there were vast numbers of newcomers to be absorbed—DPs from Europe and internment camps, as well as hundreds of thousands of refugees from Arab countries where Jews were no longer welcome. All of them had to be provided with food, medical care, shelter, jobs, and homes. Almost immediately after the establishment of the State of Israel, a campaign was organized to rescue the Jews of Yemen, Iraq, and Iran. They were evacuated by plane and brought safely to Israel. This project was known as Operation Magic Carpet.

The War of Independence in 1948 was followed by a short period of quiet. For Israel it was the best of times; for eight years there was no large-scale shooting war.

The Suez Canal

In 1956, President Gamal Abdel Nasser of Egypt closed the Suez Canal to Israeli shipping and ships trading with Israel. The Arabs applied pressure against Israel on all sides, slowly choking its economy.

On October 29, 1956, Israel attacked Egypt, operating in coordination with France and Britain, which hoped to regain control of the Suez Canal. In an eight-day campaign, the Israeli forces, under the command of General Moshe Dayan (1915–1981), captured the Gaza Strip and the entire Sinai Peninsula.

The United States and the Soviet Union then stepped in, forcing the British and French to withdraw from the Canal. Israel withdrew from Sinai, but only after a United Nations peacekeeping force was stationed along the Egypt-Israel border. The United Nations guaranteed that Israeli shipping would have access to the Suez Canal. Israel now had an open port, Eilat, for importing oil from the Persian Gulf.

Israeli soldiers shout in triumph as they reach the Suez Canal.

Kibbutz Galuyot

On May 14, 1948, the day Israel gained its independence, David Ben-Gurion announced, as if an answer to the familiar Hebrew prayer, that the new state would be open for *Kibbutz Galuyot*, the Ingathering of the Exiles.

In the years that followed, hundreds of thousands of Jews of different cultures, different languages, different worlds streamed into the Jewish homeland. Never before in the history of the world had so many people from so many different lands descended so quickly upon so small an area.

Today, Israel's population is close to 6 million Jews, and the diversity of its people makes the country almost like a miniature United Nations.

In addition to its Jewish citizens, Israel also has more than a million non-Jewish citizens, mainly Muslims, but also including Christian Arabs and Druze. Under Israel's democratic system, all citizens have full political and civil rights.

Israeli armored column waiting its turn to cross the Suez Canal.

Newly arrived Russian Jewish immigrants to Israel. More than 500,000 Russians have found new homes in Israel. As the political situation in Russia deteriorates, many new arriving families are welcomed.

153

Ethiopian immigrants on an Israeli air force plane from Addis Ababa to Israel during Operation Solomon.

The Falashas or Beta Israel of Ethiopia were traditionally an agricultural people, living in scattered villages. Their liturgical language is Ge'ez (ancient Ethiopic), and their religion combines biblical and African elements. They lived for centuries in isolation from the Jewish world; recently many Falashas have emigrated to Israel.

The thorny sabra plant and its sweet and juicy fruits. Native Israelis are called sabras because they are thorny on the outside, but friendly when you get to know them.

Ashkenazim

About half of Israel's Jews are the children and grandchildren of German and Eastern European Jews. They are called Ashkenazim, from the Hebrew word *Ashkenaz,* the name for the area that is now northern France and Germany. Most of the Zionist settlers who built up Palestine were from Eastern Europe. Many other Ashkenazim found freedom in Israel after the sickness of the Nazi Holocaust in Eastern Europe.

The Sephardim

Sephardim and Oriental Jews make up the other half of Israel's Jewish population. Sephardim are descendants of the Jews expelled from Spain in 1492 by King Ferdinand and Queen Isabella. These Jews scattered to many countries, but since they were originally from Spain they were called Sephardim, which in Hebrew means "Spaniards."

Eastern Jews

Many of Israel's Jews are immigrants from Asian and North African countries like Iraq, Yemen, Kurdistan, Persia, Afghanistan, Morocco, Libya, Tunisia, and Algeria. Sometimes Oriental Jews are called Sephardic Jews, although in actuality their backgrounds differ, since unlike the Sephardim they are not descended from ancestors who once lived in Spain and Portugal.

As the distinctions between the groups blur, Jews born in Israel no longer identify strongly as Ashkenazic, Sephardic, or Oriental; instead, they are sabras, native-born Israelis with their own Israeli culture—an amalgam of all three immigrant groups, plus a touch of something uniquely Israeli.

The term *sabra* is a nickname for Jews born in Israel. The sabra is a desert fruit that grows on cactus; it is hard and prickly on the outside but soft and juicy on the inside.

OPERATION MAGIC CARPET

In September 1950, Operation Magic Carpet began. The Jewish Agency and Israeli government secretly transported more than 50,000 Yemenites to Israel. Most of the Yemenite Jews walked hundreds of miles and tortuously made their way to Aden, where they were flown to Israel. Operation Magic Carpet began in 1949 and lasted a full year.

They did not proceed from these places all at the same time. From some—cities like San'a, Haulan, Sharab, Sa'da, Ibb, Dhamar—they went on the road in fairly continuous groups of forty or fifty or a hundred persons. Of the smaller localities, many were emptied of their Jews at one stroke, overnight. From dozens of villages, they proceeded in small detachments.

They descended mostly from the densely populated central and southern highlands, whence they had to traverse the mountain line from the Saudi Arabian border and for three hundred miles across the whole length of the Yemen. They came from the humid lowlands and the hot, sandy desert stretches along the Red Sea in the West. Some made the journey in ten or twelve days. These were the lucky ones. For most of them, it took four or six weeks; for some, a harrowing three months. We were instructed by the rabbi of our village to transfer all we had to the Arabs and whatever they agreed to pay we should accept, for the Miracle of the Redemption was at hand. We did as we were instructed and made ready for the journey. The orders were that no one in the village travel alone, but the whole village together. The money must be divided equally among rich and poor so that all might reach the Land together. This we did before we made our way to the city of San'a. The flour and the bread we transported on the camels together with the oil and the coffee. I don't really know how to describe the mass of humanity pouring in. They were hungry and sick, and most of them had terrible sores. Soon there were so many they covered every inch of the ground. Then came a time when there were nearly fourteen thousand people here, and you can imagine what it meant to wash, feed and clothe them. There would be a day-long queue only for food. There were still too few tents, and more people to lie about in the open, with little water to go round, no shade, no sanitary facilities; those toilets were not enough; they would urinate in the sand. They ate and slept in the sand.

WHAT DO YOU THINK?

1. *Why was the project called Magic Carpet?*
2. *What was the Miracle of Redemption?*
3. *Why were the refugees advised to travel in groups?*
4. *What do you think about the idea of pooling resources?*
5. *Why do Jews today pool resources to help their co-religionists?*
6. *Why did the rabbis advise the Yemenites to sell their belongings at any price?*
7. *Have the Yemenites been compensated for their properties and goods, which were confiscated by the government of Yemen?*
8. *How can Jews speaking a variety of languages, living in various lands with different customs, maintain a basic unity?*

Military Heroes of Israel

Lieutenant Colonel Yonatan Netanyahu.

The C-130 Hercules transport plane in which the Israel commando forces were flown to Entebbe.

Rescue at Entebbe / 1976

On June 27, 1976, an Air France plane carrying 300 people was hijacked by terrorists. The plane, with its 300 passengers, was forced to land at Entebbe, the capital of the African nation of Uganda. The hijackers demanded that Israel release terrorists in exchange for the passengers. This hijacking took place with the cooperation of the Ugandan government, headed by Idi Amin. He was known as the butcher of Uganda because of his savage cruelty. All non-Jewish prisoners were released, but more than 100 Jews were kept and threatened with death.

Col. Yonatan (Yoni) Netanyahu

The Israel Defense Forces set up a plan called Operation Yonatan, named for its leader, Col. Yonatan (Yoni) Netanyahu. He had distinguished himself as an officer with the paratroopers. In 1967, he fought in the Six-Day War and was wounded. In 1973, he fought in the Yom Kippur War. Now Yoni was entrusted with the job of freeing the Jewish prisoners in Entebbe.

Under cover of darkness, transport planes carried 100 highly trained Israeli commandos to Entebbe, more than 2,500 miles from Israel.

The Israeli troops silently deplaned and in a short fight quickly eliminated the Ugandan troops and the terrorists. Within 90 minutes, the hostages were on the plane and on the way back to safety.

There was one tragic death. Col. Yoni Netanyahu, the leader of the raiding party, was killed. Several years later, Idi Amin, the butcher of Uganda, was overthrown. He found refuge in Saudi Arabia.

In 1996, Yoni's brother, Benjamin Netanyahu, defeated Shimon Peres and became Prime Minister of Israel.

David "Mickey" Marcus

In 1948, thousands of volunteers flooded into the newborn State of Israel to save it. Professional soldiers, pilots. seamen, doctors, and fresh-faced teenage boys and girls hurried to save the tender life of the new state. An American named David Marcus (1902-1948) played an important role in Israel's battle for survival. David "Mickey" Marcus was born in Brooklyn and attended the U.S. Military Academy at West Point. During World War II, Marcus fought bravely and advanced to the rank of colonel. After the war, Marcus left the army and returned to New York to open a law office. Sometime later, he was approached by a member of the Haganah, who said, "You have studied military tactics at West Point and can help us to build an army in Palestine. Please help us train our settlers to protect our Jewish land." Marcus, given the code name of Michael Stone, was smuggled into Tel Aviv through the British blockade. In 1948, two weeks after Israel declared its independence, Prime Minister Ben-Gurion appointed David Marcus commander of the Jerusalem front. Thanks to Marcus's military tactics, the Jewish forces successfully opened the road to Jerusalem, saving the city from starvation and capture. Before dawn on June 11, 1948, David Marcus was accidentally shot and killed by a Jewish sentry. David Marcus is buried in the cemetery of the U.S. Military Academy at West Point.

Colonel Micky Marcus with Major Alex Broido during the Jerusalem campaing.

Eli Cohen, Israeli master spy.

Eli Cohen: Master Spy

Israel has satellites that fly over enemy countries and photograph troop movements, air fields, and army camps. Spying is another way of gathering information about the enemy. The Mossad is in charge of training spies and assembling information about enemy countries.

Eli Cohen was Israel's most famous spy. He was born in Egypt, where he learned the Arabic language and Arab customs. Later he moved to Israel and was trained as a spy. The Mossad sent him to Syria, where he used an Arabic name and pretended to be a rich Syrian citizen. He spoke the language so well that no one guessed he was really an Israeli.

Cohen became friendly with military officers who told him important secrets. He was taken on tours of secret army bases and air fields. This secret part fit so well that he began his own show on Syrian radio. He was a well-known personality throughout the Syrian nation. In 1964, Eli Cohen was discovered by Russian intelligence and sentenced to be hanged. The hanging was televised throughout the Arab world. Arabs cheered, but Israelis mourned the loss of a brave patriot who had given his life for his country.

Burned-out armored trucks on the road to Jerusalem. During the War of Independence in 1948, fierce battles were fought in this area between the Israelis and the British-trained Jordanian soldiers of the Arab Legion.

94. A GENERAL SPEAKS AFTER THE SIX-DAY WAR

On June 28,1967 the title of honorary doctor of philosophy was conferred by the Hebrew University of Jerusalem on Major General Yitzhak Rabin, then chief of staff of the Israel Defense Forces, who later became Israel's prime minister. He delivered the following address at a ceremony held in the amphitheater of the University on Mount Scopus.In 1995 Yitzhak Rabin was assassinated by Yigal Amir.

I regard myself here as the representative of the entire Israel Defence Forces, who brought victory to the State of Israel in the Six-Day War.

It may be asked why the University saw fit to award the title of Honorary Doctor of Philosophy to a soldier in recognition of his military activities. What do soldiers have in common with the academic world, which stands for civilisation and culture? What is there in common between those whose profession is violence and those who are concerned with spiritual values? I am, however, honoured that you have chosen through me to express your deep appreciation of my comrades-in-arms and of the uniqueness of the Israel Defence Forces.

Our educational work has been widely praised, and it received national recognition in 1966 when the Israel Prize for Education was awarded to the Israel Defence Forces. The Nahal, which combines military training and agricultural settlement, also provides teachers for border villages who contribute to their social and cultural development. These are only some examples of the Israel Defence Forces' uniqueness in this sphere.

Today, however, the University is conferring on us an honorary degree in recognition of our Army's spiritual and moral superiority, as revealed precisely in the heat of war. For we are all here in this virtue of the war which, though forced upon us, was forged into a victory which has astounded the world.

Anyone who has not seen a tank crew continue its attack though its commander has been killed and its track badly damaged, who has not watched sappers risking their lives to extricate wounded comrades from a minefield, who has not witnessed the concern and the extraordinary efforts made by the entire Air Force to rescue a pilot who has fallen in enemy territory, cannot know the meaning of devotion among comrades in arms.

The entire nation was exalted and many wept when they heard of the capture of the Old City. But the strain of battle, the anxiety which preceded it, and the sense of salvation and of direct confrontation with Jewish history itself cracked the shell of hardness and shyness and released well-springs of emotion and stirrings of the spirit. The paratroopers who conquered the Wailing Wall leaned on its stones and wept-in its symbolism an act so rare as to be almost unparalleled in human history. Rhetorical phrases and cliches are not common in our Army, but this scene on the Temple Mount, beyond the power of words to describe, revealed as though by a flash of lightning truths that were deeply hidden.

The units which penetrated the enemy lines and reached their objectives after hours of struggle, continuing on and on while their comrades fell to the right and left of them, were carried forward by great moral force and by deep spiritual resources far more than by their weapons or the techniques of warfare. We have always demanded the cream of our youth for the Israel Defence Forces.

Our armoured troops who stood their ground and defeated the enemy even when their equipment was inferior to his; our soldiers in all the various branches of the Israel Defence Forces who overcame our enemies everywhere, despite their superior numbers and fortifications-all of them revealed not only coolness and courage in battle but a burning faith in the justice of their cause, and sure knowledge that only their personal stand against the greatest of dangers could bring victory to their country and to their families, and that if the victory were not achieved the alternative was annihilation.

This Army, which I had the privilege of commanding through these battles, came from the people and returns to the people-to a people which rises to great heights in times of crisis and prevails over all enemies by virtue of its moral and spiritual strength. As the representative of the Israel Defence Forces, and on behalf of every one of its soldiers, I accept with pride this token of your appreciation.

WHAT DO YOU THINK?

1. What does the I. D. F. have in common with the academic world?

2. What motivated the Israeli soldiers to fight and defeat the superior enemy forces?

3. How did the Israeli soldiers and the civilians react to the capture of the Old City?

4. Who captured the Old City before the Six Day War.?

5. According to Rabin what could happened if the I.D.F. was defeated?

6. On whose behalf did Rabin accept the award?

The Six-Day War/1967

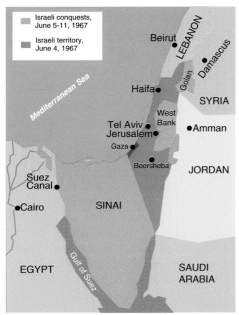

During the Six-Day War, Israel captured the Sinai, the Gaza Strip, the Golan Heights, and Judea and Samaria (West Bank).

Israeli tanks blast their way up the Golan Heights in Syria.

A Lebanese newspaper cartoon of May 31, 1967 shows the cannons of eight Arab states aimed at a shivering and frightened Israel.

June 1967 will be forever remembered as one of the most fateful periods in the history of Israel. For six fantastic days, the Middle East crossroads was torn by gunfire and screaming rockets. Then all was still. On the seventh day, when the smoke had cleared, the map of the world had been altered.

The tension was terrific on Sunday, June 4. Tel Aviv and Cairo buzzed with rumors. Tiny Israel, hemmed in by foes, listened to bulletins coming over the radio station Kol Yisrael: Syria had joined Egypt and Jordan in a military alliance. President Nasser of Egypt had proclaimed that Israel would be driven into the sea. Ahmed Shukairy, head of the Palestine Liberation Organization, arriving in Amman, stated: "When we take Israel, the surviving Jews will be helped to return to their native lands." Then he added: "But I think that none will survive."

The cities of Israel were empty of men—those 18 to 49 had left for the army. Yet spirits were high in this country of 2.5 million people, the size of Massachusetts, all included in one telephone book. Surrounded by 110 million Arab enemies, Israelis dug foxholes and trenches and marked time. And there was evening and there was morning . . . Monday, June 5.

A decade had passed, during which the Arabs had plotted revenge. In the spring of 1967, bolstered by a huge supply of Russian armaments, Nasser felt the time had come for action. He forced the 3,400-man UN force to withdraw from its position in the Sinai and then blockaded the Strait of Tiran, shutting off Israeli shipping from the East. This was an act of war.

Israel Strikes

On June 5, 1967, Israeli planes made a preemptive strike against Egyptian, Jordanian, and Syrian air bases and destroyed 450 enemy planes. With lightning speed, Israeli armored columns smashed through the

Egyptian army in the Sinai, not stopping until they reached the Suez Canal.

Before the war began, Israel had promised King Hussein of Jordan that no harm would come to his country if he stayed out of the fighting. Hussein ignored the peace overture and attacked Jerusalem. Israel counterattacked, and within a few days had defeated the Jordanians. Israeli forces were now in control of the West Bank (Judea and Samaria) and had captured the Old City of Jerusalem. The Temple Mount was under Jewish rule for the first time in almost 2,000 years.

By Thursday, Egypt and Jordan had been defeated. The Old City of Jerusalem, liberated at great sacrifice by the unbelievable bravery of paratroops under Colonel "Motke" Gur, was in Jewish hands.

Hardened soldiers, who had wrestled with death in the fight to free the city, rushed to the Western Wall. There they found an outlet for their emotions. Some kissed the ancient stones. Others wept for friends who had fallen in Jerusalem's streets.

Soldiers cheered as they saw the blue-and-white flag raised above the wall. Then a hush as the blast of a shofar pierced the air. Chief Chaplain Shlomo Goren, among the first to enter the Old City, lifted the ram's horn for the historic call. Rabbi Goren offered a Yizkor prayer for the dead, and then somebody raised his voice in the Israeli national anthem, Hatikvah, and the sound swelled in a thousand throats.

Israel Routs the Syrians

Now, only Syria remained on the field of battle. The entire Israeli air force—some 400 planes—flew non-stop raids against deeply-dug Syrian gun emplacements on the heights above the Sea of Galilee. The morning sun on Shabbat revealed Syrians running toward Damascus on roads littered with equipment and clothing. Israel's ground forces then conducted a mopping-up operation. At 6:30 P.M. a cease-fire was put into effect. Thus, by June 10, after only six

Rabbi Shlomo Goren, Chief Chaplain of the Israel Defense Forces, prays at the liberated Western Wall.

Entering the Old City of Jerusalem, *from left to right:* **Chief of Staff, Gen. Uzi Narkiss, Defense Minister Moshe Dayan, Gen. Yitzhak Rabin, commander of the Central Sector.**

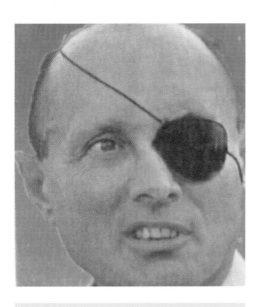

Moshe Dayan (1915–1981)
Israeli general and statesman: Moshe Dayan was born in Kibbutz Degania and at an early age was taken to live in Nahalal, the first moshav. As a teenager, he joined the Haganah. During the Arab terrorist attacks in 1936, Dayan served in an elite commando force headed by Orde Wingate, a Bible-reading British officer who supported Zionism even though he was a Christian.

During Israel's War of Independence, Dayan held the rank of lieutenant colonel and commanded various fronts. He became a major general in 1953 and led the Israeli army during the Sinai Campaign in 1956.

In 1957, Dayan left the army to enter politics. Just before the Six-Day War in June 1967, Dayan was appointed Minister of Defense. After the great Israeli victory, Dayan administered the area occupied by the Israeli army on the West Bank of the Jordan River.

days, victorious Israeli troops had defeated the combined Arab armies. Israel had control of the entire Sinai Peninsula, the Golan Heights, the West Bank, and the Old City of Jerusalem. Meantime President Lyndon Johnson and Premier Alexei Kosygin, using the famous hot line, had assured each other that both superpowers wished only peace in the Middle East, and the UN Security Council had met in New York to hammer out a ceasefire resolution.

The Western Wall Returns to Israel

The capitals of the world breathed a sigh of relief. What might have spread into a global conflict had been confined, and the flames of war were snuffed out. The Israeli Chief of Staff, Major General Yitzhak Rabin (1922–1995) solemnly declared: "All this has been done by us alone, with what we have, without anybody else." Said Moshe Dayan: "We have returned to our holiest of places, never to depart again."

A few days later, on a sunlit day, these two great leaders joined Prime Minister Levi Eshkol (1895–1965) in a visit to the Kotel Ma'aravi (Western Wall), the last remnant of the Second Temple.

Each one, following an old Jewish tradition, had written a prayer to place in a crevice in the wall. "What did you write?" reporters inquired. "Shema Yisrael," said Eshkol. "May peace be upon all Israel," said Dayan. "This is the Lord's doing; it is marvelous in our eyes," said Rabin, quoting the Book of Psalms.

Yom Yerushalayim

A week after the war ended, on Shavuot, 200,000 Jews prayed at the Western Wall. The 28th of the month of Iyar, the day the city was liberated, is now celebrated in Israel as Jerusalem Day (Yom Yerushalayim). Israelis rejoice at the unification of the holy city, but sadly mourn the brave soldiers who fell in battle.

Within a few days, the IDF had defeated the combined forces of Egypt, Syria, and Jordan. The map of the Middle East was changed forever

Headline of the Jerusalem Post on that momentous day.

JERUSALEM IS CAPTURED
Premier, Chief Rabbis pray at Western Wall

THE JERUSALEM POST

THURSDAY, JUNE 8, 1967 • EYAR 29, 5727 • RABIA AWAL 1, 1387
VOL. XXXVII, No. 11980 — PRICE : 35 AGORA

Mr. Levi Eshkol yesterday took part in afternoon prayers at the Western wall. He was the first leader of a Jewish government to visit the site of the Temple since its loss 1,897 years ago.

The Prime Minister, cheered by the tired men who had freed the Holy City, was accompanied by the two Chief Rabbis. It was approaching dusk and because the city's alley-ways still concealed last-ditch snipers, the official party's escort tried to speed their return to the newer city. But all lingered, not fully realizing that they have plenty of time to go again, and again.

A long file of prisoners was being led away across the square of the Temple Mount, in front of the Dome of the Rock. When Rabbi Yltahak Nissim approached, the file was broken to enable him to go by.

Earlier in the day, as soon as the road to the Wall was clear, the Chief Chaplain to the Forces, Aluf Shlomo Goren, came at a run, carrying a Sefer Torah. He recited the sheheheyanu blessing, and all Israel, both within the Land and without on having the privilege of establishing the age-old hope and without their right hand having lost its cunning.

Rabbi Goren sounded a blast on the shofar. He stayed there several hours, reciting the Hallel psalms of praise for the delivery, and also the prayer for the souls of those who gave their lives for Israel's victory.

The Defense Minister, Rav-Aluf Moshe Dayan, came soon after and there he made his declaration: "We will not give up this place."

During the day streams of soldiers came to the Wall, some to pray, others just to stare. Many put petitions in the spaces between the giant stones that Solomon had emplaced for the Glory of God. There were impromptu minyanim throughout the afternoon and even as dusk approached, some soldiers donned tefilin which they had not time to do at the normal morning hour. Then they were shooting their way in. Now they were still armed and still on watch, but they had a few minutes in which to voice their thanks to Him who had gone with them.

One chaplain brought to the wall a small sefer torah which had seen action on several occasions. It had accompanied the advance troops into Gaza 11 years ago.

As it was being ceremonially taken out of its ark, the men sang the line from the Psalms traditional at that point in the service: "Arise O Lord, let thine enemies be scattered, let those that hate Thee be driven before Thee."

West Bank Captured

After 60 hours of battle Israel forces yesterday controlled most of the West Bank of Jordan, including the Old City of Jerusalem, Nablus, Ramallah, Jericho and Bethlehem: in Sinai they cut through to the approaches of the Suez Canal and captured Sharm el-Sheikh, the Chief of staff, Rav Aluf Yitzhak Rabin, said yesterday.

WHAT DO YOU THINK?

1. *Why did Jordan ignore Israel's warning to stay out of the fighting?*
2. *Why did Nasser force the UN armed forces to withdraw?*
3. *Why did the Israeli air force launch a preemptive strike against the Arab air bases?*

The Yom Kippur War

An Arab poster depicts Israel as a snake. An Arab knife is severing its head from its body.

Daily between 1968 and 1973, Arab terrorists crossed Israel's borders to attack innocent people. Tel Aviv was shelled. A school bus was blown up in Eilat injuring 28 children. Russia encouraged the Arabs and sent them billions of dollars worth of arms.

At the 1972 Olympics, Arabs murdered 11 Israeli athletes. In reprisal, Israel hit terrorist bases in Syria and Lebanon.

The Sneak Attack Begins

On October 6, 1973—the holy day of Yom Kippur—the Arabs attacked Israel on two fronts at once. Syria attacked Israel's northern Golan front, and Egypt attacked across the Suez Canal into the Sinai.

Most soldiers were in the synagogues with their families. The Arab sneak attack succeeded and caught Israel off guard.

By the time Israel's troops assembled, the invading Arab armies had broken through the Israeli lines to both the north and the south. Massive Egyptian and Syrian armies penetrated Israel's defenses, the Egyptians pushing into Sinai and the Syrians moving into the Golan Heights.

The Israelis Counterattack

By the third day, Israel had started to take the offensive. With prayerbooks in one hand and machine guns in the other, Israeli soldiers left the synagogues and went straight to the battlefield. In nine days, the Israeli army pushed back all the invaders. The Egyptian army was surrounded in the Sinai and Israeli troops threatened Cairo, Egypt's capital. The Syrians were also forced back, and Israel was poised to attack Damascus, Syria's capital.

Once it had become clear that Israel was winning, the Egyptians urged their Soviet backers to force an end to the fighting.

The Israeli participants in the 1972 Summer Olympics in Munich, Germany, prepare to board an El Al flight home, taking with them the bodies of 11 comrades who were brutally massacred by Arab terrorists.

Russia and America Act

Meanwhile, a dangerous confrontation was brewing between the United States and Russia. The losses suffered by the Israelis made resupply by America a necessity. At first the United States hesitated, but when it learned that the Russians were resupplying Egypt and Syria, American planes began flying tons of equipment to Israel.

Henry Kissinger

Henry Kissinger (b. 1923) had come to America as a refugee from Hitler's Germany. As Secretary of State in the administration of President Richard Nixon, he reasoned that the war was ending in a draw: the Arabs had fought well enough to recover their "honor," but now knew that they could not defeat Israel. In the agreement that Kissinger worked out with the Russians, Israel was to refrain from completely destroying the Arab armies, and talks were to begin between Israel and Egypt aimed at a "just and durable peace" in the region.

The Ceasefire

By the time the ceasefire took effect, Israel had managed to trap over 20,000 men, Egypt's Third Army. An Egyptian defeat on such a scale was unacceptable to the Russian patrons of the Arabs, and would also have upset the battlefield stalemate Kissinger wanted in order to force the start of peace negotiations.

On October 24, the Russians threatened to take matters into their own hands if America did not force Israel to withdraw, thereby freeing the trapped Third Army. The United States could not allow Russia to intervene directly in the Middle East. Nixon ordered American nuclear forces to be put on alert.

For a few hours, a much more destructive type of war seemed to menace the world, but a compromise was reached. Instead of Russian or American troops, a neutral UN force was sent to patrol the ceasefire lines.

Secretary of State Henry Kissinger *(right)* talks to Abba Eban *(left)* and Yigal Allon *(center)* during his shuttle diplomacy which led to a settlement between Israel and Egypt in 1979.

Israeli soldiers on patrol near the Egyptian border.

Golda Meir

Israel allowed food and water to reach the Third Army but kept it trapped.

More than 11,000 Arabs died in the Yom Kippur War, but so did over 2,500 Israelis. Israel emerged victorious on the battlefield, but at a bloody price.

After the ceasefire, all Israel mourned the nation's loss of its soldiers. Prime Minister Golda Meir (1898–1979) said: "For the people of Israel, each human life is precious. Our dead soldiers are the sons of all of us. The pain we feel is felt by all of us."

As a result of the surprise attack, Golda Meir was forced to resign. Many voters had lost confidence in her. Yitzhak Rabin, of the Labor Party, became the new Prime Minister.

Golda Meir 1898 / 1978

Golda Meir was born in Kiev, Russia. There she witnessed the violent pogroms against the Jews. She said that her childhood memories of the pogroms influenced her to become a Zionist.

When Golda was eight years old, her family moved to the United States and settled in Milwaukee, where she became a schoolteacher. In 1921, she and her husband, Morris Meyerson, moved to Palestine, where they joined a kibbutz.

President and Mrs. Richard Nixon with Prime Minister Golda Meir at the White House in 1972.

Golda Meir became active in politics and was elected to head the Histadrut, Israel's central labor union. In 1948, before the War of Independence, she disguised herself as an Arab and secretly visited Emir Abdullah of Jordan in an effort to persuade him to keep his country out of the war.

Golda Meir's organizational abilities propelled her onto the international political stage, first as Foreign Minister and in 1969 as the first female Prime Minister of Israel. After serving as Israel's leader during the Yom Kippur War, she submitted her resignation. In 1974, because of ill health, she retired from all of her political posts. When she died on December 8, 1978, people all over the world mourned this great and courageous woman.

SOVIET JEWS GREET GOLDA MEIR

The Soviet Union tried to obliterate the Jewish religion. They closed Jewish schools, murdered Jewish leaders, and shut the synagogues. They could not wipe out the Jewish spirit. This Jewish identity showed itself during the visit to Moscow in the fall of 1948 by Israel's first ambassador to the Soviet Union, Golda Meir. Here is her description of that famous encounter.

As we had planned, we went to the synagogue on Rosh Hashanah. All of us—the men, women and children of the legation—dressed in our best clothes, as befitted Jews on a Jewish holiday. But the street in front of the synagogue had changed. Now it was filled with people, packed together like sardines, hundreds and hundreds of them, of all ages, including Red Army officers, soldiers, teenagers and babies carried in their parents' arms. Instead of the 2,000-odd Jews who usually came to the synagogue on the holidays, a crowd of close to 50,000 people was waiting for us. For a minute I couldn't grasp what had happened—or even who they were.

And then it dawned on me. They had come—those good, brave Jews—in order to be with us, to demonstrate their sense of kinship and to celebrate the establishment of the State of Israel. Within seconds they had surrounded me, almost lifting me bodily, almost crushing me, saying my name over and over again. Eventually, they parted ranks and let me enter the synagogue, but there, too, the demonstration went on. Every now and then, in the women's gallery, someone would come to me, touch my hand, stroke or even kiss my dress. Without speeches or parades, without any words at all really, the Jews of Moscow were proving their profound desire—and their need—to participate in the miracle of the establishment of the Jewish state, and I was the symbol of the state for them.

I couldn't talk, or smile, or wave my hand. I sat in that gallery like a stone, without moving, with those thousands of eyes fixed on me. The service ended, and I got up to leave; but I could hardly walk. I felt as though I had been caught up in a torrent of love so strong that it had literally taken my breath away and slowed down my heart. I was on the verge of fainting, I think. But the crowd still surged around me, stretching out its hands and saying Nasha Golda (our Golda) and Shalom, shalom, and crying.

Out of that ocean of people, I can still see two figures clearly: a little man who kept popping up in front of me and saying, "Goldele, leben zolst du. Shana Tova!" (Goldele, a long life to you and a Happy New Year), and a woman who just kept repeating, "Goldele! Goldele!" and smiling and blowing kisses at me.

All I could say, clumsily, and in a voice that didn't even sound like my own, was one sentence in Yiddish. I stuck my head out of the window of the cab and said, "A dank eich vos ihr seit geblieben Yidden" (Thank you for having remained Jews), and I heard that miserable, inadequate sentence being passed on through the enormous crowd as though it were some wonderful prophetic saying.

WHAT DO YOU THINK?

1. *Why did the Soviets try to obliterate the Jewish religion?*
2. *Why did tens of thousands of Jews, despite Soviet restrictions, come to meet Golda Meir?*
3. *How did the Russian Jews demonstrate their love for Israel?*
4. *Why was Golda overcome with emotion?*
5. *What did Golda mean when she thanked the Russians for remaining Jews?*

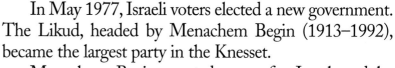

The Quest for Peace Continues

Left to right: **Begin, Carter, and Sadat after the peace treaty was signed in Washington on March 26, 1979.**

In May 1977, Israeli voters elected a new government. The Likud, headed by Menachem Begin (1913–1992), became the largest party in the Knesset.

Menachem Begin wanted peace for Israel, and he hoped that he and President Anwar Sadat of Egypt might reach an agreement. In November 1977, for the first time ever, an Arab leader, President Sadat, visited Jerusalem. Sadat addressed the Knesset on his wish for peace.

The Camp David Agreement

In 1979, Begin and Sadat met at Camp David in the United States. There, with the assistance of President Jimmy Carter, they hammered out their many differences. On March 26, 1979, they signed a peace treaty in Washington, D.C.

The other Arab states bitterly opposed the Camp David Agreement. They swore to take revenge on Sadat. In October 1981, he was killed by an assassin's bullet and was succeeded by Hosni Mubarak.

Hosni Mubarak: President of Egypt

Hosni Mubarak, the new President of Egypt, soon became the target of Islamic extremists, partly because he maintained diplomatic relations with Israel. His corrupt government offered little hope of a better life for the poor Egyptian people.

Mubarak is one of the most vocal defenders of the Palestinians. He has organized anti-Israel conferences and accused the Israelis of human rights violations. President Mubarak has urged the Arabs to resist Israel with violence.

Lebanon/Peace for Galilee / 1982

Lebanon is a pipeline terminus for oil coming from Saudi Arabia and Iraq. Before 1970, it was a very prosperous and modern country with a highly skilled and educated work force. Its capital, Beirut, was the banking, commercial, and resort center of the Middle East.

Hosni Mubarak

Things began to change in 1970 when the Palestine Liberation Organization, now headed by Yasir Arafat, was expelled from Jordan and set up a base in Lebanon. Israeli settlements along the Lebanese border came under frequent rocket and artillery attack.

In 1975, a brutal civil war broke out between Lebanon's Christians and Muslims. After many battles and thousands of casualties, the Syrians moved in and restored order. They became the power behind a new Lebanese government. The Syrians allowed the PLO to continue its attacks on northern Israel, which became more and more intense.

On July 6, 1982, The Israeli army launched Operation Peace for Galilee. Under the command of General Ariel Sharon, Israeli troops pushed into Lebanon and captured Beirut. Many of the PLO terrorists and their Syrian allies were killed or captured. Most of Lebanon's Christians were happy to see the Israelis. They had been robbed and beaten by the PLO and the Syrian troops. Thanks to the Israelis, they again had some security. Prime Minister Menachem Begin hoped that the PLO threat would be ended once and for all. But Operation Peace for Galilee caused much controversy. Many foreign governments objected, and thousands of Israelis protested as well.

In 1983 the Israeli troops were withdrawn and Begin resigned. Many of the Christians who cooperated with Israel had to leave Lebanon for safety.

As a result of the failure of Operation Peace for Galilee, Begin resigned and Yitzhak Shamir was elected Prime Minister.

Israel and Jordan

When Israel became independent in May 1948, Jordan's Arab Legion occupied East Jerusalem, Judea, and Samaria. Jordan gave citizenship to thousands of Arab refugees from Israel. After the Six-Day War in 1967, Jordan lost control of Jerusalem, Judea, and Samaria to Israel, but its population still included a huge number of Palestinians.

General Ariel Sharon commanded Operation Peace for Galilee.

Menachem Begin headed the Betar movement in Poland before he was 20 years old. Because of his Zionist activities, the Russians sentenced him to a Siberian labor camp. In 1942, he immigrated to Palestine, where he organized the armed Jewish underground struggle against the British. He evaded the police by disguising himself as a bearded rabbi. Begin founded the Herut (Freedom) Party and in 1977 became Prime Minister.

King Hussein

On March 13, 1997, a Jordanian soldier opened fire and killed seven girls from an Orthodox Jewish high school, and wounded eight. In a gesture of consolation, King Hussein visited the bereaved families and offered his heart-felt apologies and condolences.

Saddam Hussein, the President of Iraq, hates Israel and the United States. He has the will and the technical skill to manufacture and use weapons of mass destruction. In this photograph Hussein fires a rifle to greet his troops during a military parade.

Signing the peace treaty between Israel and Jordan. President Clinton (*front row, center*) and Secretary of State Warren Christopher (*rear row, second from left*) participated in and signed the agreement.

In September 1970—known in the PLO's annals as Black September—Yasir Arafat and his guerilla fighters tried to overthrow Hussein's government. Syria planned to invade Jordan at the same time, but was prevented by the threat of Israeli intervention. Thanks to Israel's support, the Arab Legion crushed the Palestinian revolt. The PLO, expelled from Jordan, found a new base of operations in Lebanon.

King Hussein Dies

After 46 years in power Jordan's King Hussein died. His elder son Abdullah became Jordan's new monarch. Despite the Palestinian problem, Abdullah has tried to remain at peace with Israel. He realizes that his only true friend and ally in the Middle East is Israel which saved his father's regime during the Black September uprising by the Palestinians.

Israeli-Jordanian Peace Agreements

On October 26, 1994, Prime Minister Yitzhak Rabin and Prime Minister Abdul Salam Majali of Jordan signed a peace agreement. Israel and Jordan have exchanged ambassadors. King Hussein reacted positively to the election of Prime Minister Benjamin Netanyahu in 1996, in part because of concern that a PLO state on the West Bank would be as much of a danger to Jordan as to Israel.

On September 2, 2002, Israel and Jordan announced that they would join forces to save the Dead Sea, the biblical body of water that is rapidly receding each year. Israel and Jordan plan to build a 186-mile pipeline at the cost of $1 billion dollars to pump water from the Mediteranean to the Dead Sea. Officials say that the project will preserve the unique wildlife and the tourist industry will flourish around it. The biggest dividend is the signal that peace and cooperation between Jews and Arabs is possible.

HEROES ALSO CRY

The following is an essay by an Israeli soldier under fire. The essay appeared in the **Jerusalem Post.** *The essay vividly describes the feelings of all combat soldiers who have lost buddies to enemy fire. Despite the bombs, shells, and booby traps, the soldiers have no alternative but to keep on fighting–to defend their country, their family, and their own life. Crying is a sound of relief at just remaining alive.*

We lay curled up in a shallow foxhole in the soft sand, Uriel and I. It was an ugly dawn hour, sky and earth were aflame. Uriel talked about Milan, from whence he had landed the day before yesterday and I told him about New York which I had left four days before. Uriel was saying he just had to fix me up with this gorgeous girl, Iris, because we were simply made for each other.

He was inserting sparkling new bullets into his clip, and I was sucking a mint to freshen my mouth after the night's sleep. Before the order came to leave the foxholes, we made a quick decision to have a big party at his house after the war.

Uriel promised to send me a gilded invitation. At noon, his body was lying under a blanket in the field hospital. Funny that we had thought of a party. I want to send you an invitation to weeping.

The date and the hour don't matter, but the program, I guarantee you, will be a rich one: weeping. We'll cry for hours, and together—because I just can't do it alone. All through the war I wanted to cry but couldn't. This time it will work; it must. Nothing can stop us. I'll cry for my dead: Avremele, Ilan, Amitai, Dudu, Uzi, Yair, Uriel—and you'll cry for yours.

And we'll cry together for the dreams which have been shaken, for the grand things turned trivial, for the gods that failed, for the meaninglessness, the lack of will, the impotence, the present devoid of even a single ray of light....

We'll cry for the friendships that have been cut off, the illusions . . . the plans that will never be carried out, the dark cloud that will now hang forever over every celebration.

And we'll feel sorry for ourselves, because we deserve pity—a lost generation of a tormented people in "a land that consumes its inhabitants."

The big deciders, the oh-so-sober ones, won't be allowed in. This isn't for them. Oh, will we cry. Bitterly we'll cry. Heartrendingly. Hugely. We'll cry cupfuls. Kettlefuls. Rivers.

Anyone feeling that he's had it, that he's all dried up, that he hasn't a tear left In him—will sneak out. On tiptoe, so as not to spoil the evening. Most likely, I'll be the last one left.

But, anytime at all—next month, in two months, next year—you can come again. The door's open. It's a standing invitation: from now on, my place is always open for crying.

WHAT DO YOU THINK?

1. *What happened to Uriel? Why did the author cry?*
2. *Young men, teenagers who are not even old enough to shave, make the best soldiers. They are strong, have stamina, and can easily be trained. These young men are the future of a nation. Yet, in war they are first to die. Is war the only way to settle a problem?*
3. *Do you think the United Nations can stop wars?*
4. *The UN tries, but has it ever succeeded? Why has it failed?*

The Oslo Peace Agreement 1993

Yitzhak Rabin
(1922–1995) served his country both as a soldier and as a diplomat. Born in Jerusalem, he graduated from the Kadoori agricultural school. In 1940, he enlisted in the Palmach and participated in numerous underground actions against the British Mandate. In 1946, he was arrested by the British and imprisoned for six months. During the War of Independence, Rabin commanded the Harel Brigade, which was active in the battle for Jerusalem. Appointed Chief of Staff in 1964, he led Israel's forces to victory in the Six-Day War of 1967. After serving as Israel's ambassador to the United States, Rabin became Prime Minister in 1974–77 and was reelected in 1992. On November 4, 1995, he was assassinated by Yigal Amir.

Rabin, Clinton, and Arafat triumphantly display shirts of victory on the lawn of the White House after they signed the peace agreement. After the agreement, terrorist attacks became more frequent and brutal.

The Middle East Peace Conference convened in Madrid, Spain, in 1991. While further meetings were taking place in Washington in 1992, a tiny group of PLO and Israeli delegates met secretly in Norway. Their discussions continued for 15 months. On September 13, 1993, Prime Minister Yitzhak Rabin of Israel and Yasir Arafat, head of the PLO, signed a peace agreement in Washington.

The Terms of the Agreement

1. The PLO would have jurisdiction over the city of Jericho and the Gaza Strip.
2. The PLO would have jurisdiction over police, fire, health, water, and education.
3. Israel would have jurisdiction over borders, roads, and the protection of Jewish settlements in the PLO enclaves.
4. A phased Israeli troop withdrawal would begin on December 13, 1993. Within nine months, Israel would withdraw from all West Bank cities. Soon after that, it would transfer all remaining land except the Jewish settlements to the Palestinian National Authority.
5. The final status of the territories would be settled at the end of five years.

On September 3, 1993, the Israeli Knesset, which has 120 members, approved the peace agreement by a vote of 61 to 50. Although all Israelis yearn for peace, many did not trust Arafat and the PLO, and felt that Israel was giving up too much too soon. Victory came, as expected, from the 44 members of Rabin's own party, 12 votes from the leftist Meretz party, and 5 votes from the Israeli Arab Knesset members. Without the Arab votes, the agreement would not have been ratified.

As part of the agreement, Israel agreed to withdraw its troops from six major Arab cities in Judea and

Samaria: Qalqilya, Ramallah, Jenin, Bethlehem, Tulkarm, and Hebron. Israel kept its part of the agreement and withdrew from all cities. As part of the agreement, it left a small detachment of Israeli troops to protect the 450 Jews who lived in Hebron.

Rabin Is Assassinated

Saturday night, November 4, 1995, was one of the most fateful times in the history of modern Israel. On that darkest of nights, Yitzhak Rabin, Israeli's Prime Minister and one of its great military heroes, was assassinated.

That evening 100,000 Israelis had assembled in Tel Aviv to participate in a political rally. Rabin delivered a speech and joined in singing the "Song of Peace." After the rally, Rabin and Shimon Peres began to walk to their cars.

Lurking in the dark shadows of the night, a young assassin named Yigal Amir was waiting. As Rabin approached his limousine, Amir quietly stepped out of the shadows and from about a yard away pumped three bullets point blank into the Prime Minister.

Rabin was rushed to a nearby hospital, where he died on the operating table. The shocked nation went into mourning, and the spot where Rabin was shot became a shrine filled with memorial candles, flowers, and posters.

Rabin's funeral was attended by President Bill Clinton, former Presidents Bush, Carter, and Ford, and the leaders of many other countries, including President Mubarak of Egypt and King Hussein of Jordan. Rabin was succeeded as Prime Minister by Shimon Peres, who vowed to continue his policies.

Benjamin Netanyahu Becomes Prime Minister

On June 2, 1996 Benjamin Netanyahu (b. 1949), of the Likud Party, defeated Shimon Peres and became Israel's new Prime Minister. His victory was in large part due to public disquiet about the way the peace agreement with the PLO was proceeding. While Israel

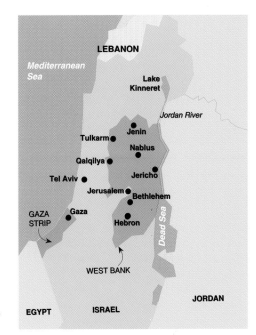

The Oslo accords stipulated that Israeli troops would withdraw from all West Bank cities. Israeli troops did not withdraw from Hebron because of the danger from the hostile Arab population.

Benjamin Netanyahu addresses the U.S. Congress. In the background is Vice President Al Gore. Newt Gingrich, Speaker of the House, congratulates him.

Among the foreign dignitaries paying their last respects to Yitzhak Rabin were *(from left to right)* President Bill Clinton, former Presidents Jimmy Carter and George Bush, Queen Beatrice of the Netherlands, Mrs. Peres and Prime Minister Shimon Peres, Queen Nur and King Hussein of Jordan.

had been carrying out all of its commitments, the PLO was not. It had not modified its covenant to eliminate language calling for the destruction of the Jewish state. Even worse, terrorist attacks had become increasingly more frequent and brutal. While Israelis desperately wanted peace, a majority of voters agreed with Netanyahu that it was necessary to proceed cautiously and slowly, and with more concern for security than Peres had shown.

Netanyahu was the first sabra Prime Minister of Israel. Although born in Israel, he lived for several years in the United States and earned degrees in business and architecture from the Massachusetts Institute of Technology. In 1967 he returned to Israel to serve in the army. As an officer in an elite commando unit, he played an important part in the team that rescued hostages from a hijacked Belgian plane in 1972. He served as Israel's United Nations ambassador in the 1980s and was also Deputy Foreign Minister.

Shimon Peres

Shimon Peres has had a varied and distinguished political career. At the age of 24, he became the manpower chief of the Haganah. After the formation of the State of Israel he was appointed Director General of the Defense Ministry. In 1981, he became Deputy Defense Minister under Prime Minister David Ben-Gurion and then under Levi Eshkol, and was responsible for setting up Israel's nuclear capabilities. In 1977, he ran against Menachem Begin and lost. He became Prime Minister in 1984, but in 1988 he ran against Yitzhak Shamir, and also lost.

As Foreign Minister in Yitzhak Rabin's cabinet, Peres conducted peace talks with the PLO, which ushered in the Oslo accords for Palestinian self-rule. Prime Minister Rabin and Peres shared the Nobel Prize for their peace efforts.

In 1995, after the assassination of Rabin, Peres became Prime Minister and Defence Minister. The following year he ran against Benjamin Netanyahu but was defeated. In March 2001, Peres became Foreign Minister and Deputy Prime Minister in the government of Ariel Sharon.

ILAN RAMON-ISRAELI ASTRONAUT

It was a happy group of families, friends, and officials waiting for the return of the space shuttle Columbia at the Kennedy Space Center in Florida. Soon Columbia would dock and shuttle would come to a stop and the reunions would start. That's the way it happened at 111 previous flights. But just minutes before touchdown the 22-year-old ship developed a problem and the shuttle had not arrived. People in Texas heard an explossion and saw flaming meteors racing through the sky as a rain of broken shuttle pieces fell to the ground.

On Sunday, February 1, 2003, the space shuttle *Columbia* disintegrated as it returned from its sixteen–day mission, and all seven astronauts lost their lives. The day brought great sadness to the families of the astronauts, sadness to the citizens of America, and sadness for a program that was a source of national pride. For Jews, the tragic disaster was magnified because of the loss of the first Israeli astronaut, Colonel Ilan Ramon.

Israel needed a hero to divert its attention from the devastating Palestinian conflict. In towns across Israel proud families gathered around their television set to watch the return of Israel's first astronaut, Colonel Ilan Ramon. Instead a day of joy turned into a day of mourning.

Ilan Ramon was born in Israel in 1954, and after graduating high school enlisted in the Israeli air force. He became a fighter pilot and fought in the Yom Kippur and Lebanon wars. In addition Ramon took part in the bombing of the Iraqi nuclear reactor at Osirak in 1981.

Ilan was the son and grandson of Holocaust survivors. He was aware that his flight was meaningful to Israelis and to all Jews around the world. In the shuttle Colonel Ramon carried two special keepsakes.

Dr. Joachim was in charge of an Israeli project to collect images of dust storms and to gauge their effect on the climate and weather. He presented Alon with a small Torah. This scroll had been given to Joachim at his Bar Mitzvah in a Nazi concentration camp. The rabbi who presided at the ceremony gave the Torah to Alon and asked him to tell the world of the atrocities that had occurred there.

Colonel Ramon's mother survived the Holocaust, and before the space journey they went to Yad Vashem to find a symbol to take into space. He chose a pencil sketch by a 14–year–old boy named Peter Ganz in a concentration camp. It was a drawing of Earth as Peter imagined it would look from the moon. Peter died in Auschwitz, 1944.

In space Ramon monitored the movement of dust clouds over the Mediterranean and he also carried a science project for Israeli children on growing crystals in space. In space Ilan ate specially prepared kosher meals. He also celebrated Shabbat by reciting the Kiddush in specially designed zero-gravity-proof Kiddush cup.

Ilan spent four years at the Johnson Space Center in Houston, training for his flight. Ramon and his wife Rona and their four children were members of the Shaar Hashalom Synagogue in Houston.

Everyone of the seven astronauts were fantastic people, and Ramon was proud to be a member of this illustrious group of brave people.

May their memory and deeds be a blessing for all of mankind.

WHAT DO YOU THINK?

1. Why did Ramon take Holocaust keepsakes into space with him?

Middle East Summit

Benjamin Netanyahu

Arafat and Benjamin Netanyahu, on September 28, 1998, cleared the way for summit negotiations during a meeting with President Clinton in Washington. On October 23, 1998, in Washington, D.C., they signed an agreement on conditions for an Israeli military withdrawal from parts of the West Bank.

The accord, known as the Wye River Memorandum, was intended to implement the second of three Israeli pullbacks from the West Bank. President Clinton intervened in the talks to move them toward completion. On November 7, 1998, the PLO, in accordance with the terms of the Memorandum, confirmed that all articles in the PLO charter calling for the destruction of Israel were null and void.

Highlights of the Accord

The Wye River Accord, expanding Palestinian self-rule on the West Bank, was signed by Israeli Prime Minister Netanyahu and President Yasir Arafat, on October 23, 1998 in Washington, D. C. The agreement called for

• Israeli military withdrawal from 13.1 percent of the West Bank;
• Reduction of the Palestinian Authority police force;
• Arrest of terrorist suspects;
• Release of 750 Palestinian prisoners;
• Opening of a corridor to allow Palestinians to travel between the West Bank and the Gaza Strip.

On December 14, 1998 the Palestinian authority voted to cancel all articles in the 1964 Palestinian Charter that called for the destruction of Israel.

Netanyahu Under Attack

The Wye River Accord came under attack from all corners of the Israeli political spectrum. Netanyahu's acceptance of the Wye Memorandum, which outlined a further stage of Israeli military withdrawals from the West Bank, caused his coalition to unravel. Following the Knesset's rejection of this peace program, the Prime Minister attempted to establish a national unity government. Despite the defections, Netanyahu expressed confidence that he would win re-election.

Netanyahu ran against General Ehud Barak, Israel's most decorated soldier and leader of the Labor Party. Barak won the election.

A Time of Transition

In his first two weeks as Prime Minister, Barak re-energized the peace process. He embarked on an ambitious agenda to make peace not only with the Palestinians, but also with Syria and Lebanon. His idea was to set in place a series of treaties that would end the wars between Israel and its Arab neighbors.

The Agreement

On September 5, 1999, in Sharm El-Sheikh, Prime Minister Barak of Israel and Yasir Arafat, the Palestinian leader, signed an agreement. The agreement represented a step that everyone hoped would usher in a new era of peace across the region. Starting on September 13, 1999, the Israelis would, in three stages, transfer control of 40 percent of the West Bank to the Palestinians. On September 8, 1999, the first pullback by Israeli forces took place.

On October 1, 1999 Israel opened a passage connecting Gaza with the West Bank. Israel also released 350 Arab prisoners. The Palestinians agreed to collect weapons and to submit a list of security officers and to accept a date for the "final status" negotiations.

Less than 24 hours after the new Israeli-Palestinian peace accord was signed, two cars packed with explosives blew up in in Haifa and Tiberias. The latest agreement obligated Israel to release prisoners who had committed terrorist acts. Two terror attacks within 24 hours after the agreement called that policy into question.

EHUD BARAK

Ehud was the heroic biblical judge who defeated the Moabites and ended several generations of their rule over Israel. Barak (which means "lightning" in Hebrew) was the bold military commander who joined forces with the prophetess Deborah and defeated the Canaanites under Sisera. Two very descriptive names for Israel's most decorated soldier.

On May 18, 1999 Ehud Barak was elected Prime Minister of Israel.

Barak is the child of Zionist pioneers who fled from Lithuania after Cossacks murdered their parents. He was born on February 12, 1942 on a kibbutz in the Heffer Valley near the Lebanese border. Ehud spent a 36-year career in the Israel defense forces, and served as a platoon leader, a tank battalion commander, an intelligence analyst, and from 1991 to 1995 he was chief of the general staff. Barak is the most decorated soldier in Israel's history.

Lt. General Ehud Barak left the military in 1995 and was appointed Interior Minister in Yitzhak Rabin's government. After the assassination of Rabin in 1995, Shimon Peres appointed him to the post of Foreign Minister. In 1997, after Netanyahu defeated Shimon Peres, Barak became the leader of the Labor Party.

In addition to his military career, Ehud Barak's credentials include a degree in physics and mathematics from the Hebrew University in Jerusalem. He also has a master's degree from Stanford University in economic engineering systems.

Ehud Barak and President Bill Clinton

A collection of hundreds of deadly Arab terrorist arms seized by the Israelis.

The Summit

On July 11, 2000, President Clinton, Prime Minister Barak, and Chairman Arafat met at Camp David for a summit conference to resolve the Arab-Israeli conflict. On the third day, the summit nearly collapsed after Clinton submitted a draft proposal that described Jerusalem as the united and eternal capital of Israel.

Barak's Strategy

Barak's effort to end the 50-year conflict failed. In the hopeof obtaining peace, he offered more far-reaching concessions than Israel had ever before put on the table. He was willing to divide Jerusalem and surrender military control of much of the West Bank. However much Israel offered, the PLO responded by demanding more.

The Clinton Peace Plan

Israel's voters rejected the Barak peace plan, which would have divided Jerusalem allowed many Palestinian refugees to return to Israel, and released all Palestinian prisoners. The opposition to the peace plan was led by the religious parties, the settlers, and the Russian Immigrant Party. Moreover, the Israeli military said that giving up the Jordan Valley would impair Israel's ability to defend itself.

Another bone of contention concerned the Temple Mount in Jerusalem. The American formula visualized the Muslims controlling the plateau which contains the Al Aksa Mosque and the Dome of the Rock, while Israel would control the area beneath the plateau which contains the West Wall, the last remnant of the ancient Temple. This formula was unacceptable to many on both sides.

Unresolved Issues

The Palestinians demanded a "right of return" for refugees, but Israel rejected this because it would mean the end of Israel as a Jewish state. An even greater stumbling block was the status of Jerusalem. Both sides wanted the holy city to be their capital.

On July 25, 2000, President Clinton announced that the summit talks were deadlocked. The two sides were unable to reach an agreement.

THE WYE RIVER MEMORANDUM-OCTOBER 23, 1998

President Clinton used his political power to motivate Arafat and Netanyahu to sign the Wye River Memorandum. The following is a shortened version of the document.

The following are steps to facilitate implementation of the Interim Agreement on the West Bank and Gaza Strip of September 28, 1995 (the "Interim Agreement") and other related agreements including the Note for the Record of January 17, 1997 so that the Israeli and Palestinian sides can more effectively carry out their responsibilities.

FURTHER REPLOYMENT

1. Pursuant to the Interim Agreement and subsequent agreements, the Israeli side's implementation of the first and second F.R.D. will consist of the transfer to the Palestinian side of 13% from Area C as follows:

I % to Area (A), 12% to Area (B)

The Palestinian side has informed that it will allocate an area/areas amounting to 3% from the above Area (B) to be designated as Green Areas and/or Nature Reserves.

II SECURITY

The Palestinian side agreed to take all measures necessary in order to prevent acts of terrorism, crime and hostilities directed against the Israeli side. Israeli side's authority and against their property, just as the Israeli side agreed to take all measures necessary in order to prevent acts of terrorism, crime and hostilities directed against the Palestinian side.

The Palestinian side will make known its policy of zero tolerance for terror and violence against both sides.

A work plan developed by the Palestinian side will be shared with the U.S. and thereafter implementation will begin immediately to ensure the systematic and effective combat of terrorist organizations and their infrastructure.

SECURITY ACTIONS

The Palestinian side will apprehend the specific individuals suspected of perpetrating acts of violence and terror for the purpose of further investigation, and prosecution.

Drawing on relevant international practice and the Palestinian side will issue a decree prohibiting all forms of incitement to violence or terror, mechanisms for acting systematically against all expressions or threats of violence or terror. This decree will be comparable to the existing Israeli legislation.

The two sides agree that their security cooperation will be based on a spirit of partnership and will include, among other things, the following steps:

3. Trilateral Committee

In addition to the bilateral Israeli-Palestinian security cooperation, a high-ranking U.S.- Palestinian-Israeli committee will meet to assess current threats, deal with any impediments to effective security cooperation and coordination.

PROHIBITING ILLEGAL WEAPONS

The Palestinian side will provide a list of its policemen to the Israeli side in conformity with the prior agreements. The Executive Committee of the Palestine Liberation Organization and the Palestinian Central Council will reaffirm the letter of 22 January 1998 from PLO Chairman Yasir Arafat to President Clinton concerning the nullification of the Palestinian National Charter provisions that are inconsistent with the letters exchanged between the PLO and the Government of Israel on 9/10 September 1993.

III. INTERIM COMMITTEES AND ECONOMIC ISSUES

1. The Israeli and Palestinian sides reaffirm their commitment to enhancing their relationship and agree on the need actively to promote economic development in the West Bank and Gaza.

2. The Israeli and Palestinian sides have agreed on arrangements which will permit the timely opening of the Gaza Industrial Estate.

IV. PERMANENT STATUS NEGOTIATIONS
The two sides will immediately resume permanent status negotiations on an accelerated basis and will make a determined effort to achieve the mutual goal of reaching an agreement by May 4, 1999.

V. UNILATERAL ACTIONS
Recognizing the necessity to create a positive environment for the negotiations, neither side shall initiate or take any step that will change the status of the West Bank and the Gaza Strip in accordance with the Interim Agreement.

This Memorandum will enter into force ten days from the date of signature.

Done at Washington, D.C. 23rd day of October 1998.
For the Government of the State of Israel:
Benjamin Netanyahu
For the PLO: Yassir Arafat
Witnessed by: William J. Clinton. The U.S.A.

WHAT DO YOU THINK?

1. Did the Palestinians implement any provisions of the pact.?

2. The Palestinians have signed several pacts with Israel. Have they ever fulfilled the provisions of any pact?

3. The Palestinian politicians sign agreements and the terrorists break the agreements. Who do you think controls the Palestinian government.?

Jerusalem and the Arabs

The Dome of the Rock

The Dome of the Rock was built by Caliph Abd al-Malik on the Temple Mount in Jerusalem in 691 C.E.

   The Dome is situated on a platform of rocks and earth built by King Solomon and King Herod more than 1,000 years before the Muslim religion decided to make it holy.

The Dome of the Rock contains the *even shetiyah*, or foundation stone. Jewish and Muslim tradition regard this stone as the center of the world.

   The Holy of Holies in King Solomon's Temple in Jerusalem and the Holy Ark were placed upon this rock. The *even shetiyah* is presently enclosed in the Dome of the Rock built on the Temple Mount in Jerusalem.

One of the most important issues in the Arab-Israeli dispute is the control of Jerusalem. This holy city has always played a central religious and political role in Jewish life. King David recognized its importance and made it the capital of ancient Israel. King Solomon made Jerusalem the religious center of Judaism by erecting the Holy Temple there. According to rabbinic tradition, Jerusalem is the center of God's spiritual world.

During the 2,000 years of exile, Jews never lost their love for the holy city. As they were led into Babylonian captivity in 586 B.C.E., they tearfully sang:

If I forget thee, Jerusalem,
May my right hand lose its cunning,
May my tongue cleave to its palate.

There are many references to Jerusalem in the daily, Sabbath, and holiday prayers. Worshippers in the synagogue always face toward Jerusalem.

In every generation, there has been a Jewish presence in Jerusalem. Jews continued to worship at the ancient Western Wall. Because of the tears of exile, the Wall was often called the Wailing Wall.

As part of the 1949 armistice agreement, the United Nations split Jerusalem into two parts, the New City to be controlled by Israel, the Old City and its holy shrines, by Jordan. The agreement stated that Jews would have free access to worship at the Western Wall and the shrines in the Old City.

In spite of the agreement, the Jordanians did not allow Jews to worship at the Western Wall. To further aggravate the situation, they vandalized the Jewish cemetery on the Mount of Olives and destroyed many of the Old City's historic synagogues.

In 1967, during the Six-Day War, Israel captured the Old City and reunited Jerusalem.

Jerusalem is sacred to three religions: Judaism, Christianity, and Islam. The Israeli government guarantees all religions freedom of access to their holy places and shrines. Everyone is free to worship God in complete freedom.

The Muslim View of Jerusalem

The two holiest cities of Islam are Mecca and Medina. Mecca is where Muhammad, the founder of Islam, was born. Medina is where he preached and developed the Muslim religion. Jerusalem is also considered a holy city by Muslims, although its role in the earliest years of Islam was comparatively minor.

Muslims believe that Muhammad, in a dream, was transported up to heaven from the Temple Mount in Jerusalem. In the 7th century, several decades after the Muslim conquest of Jerusalem, Caliph Abd Malik ibn Marwan built the Mosque of Omar on the site where Muhammad's dream was said to have occurred—the exact spot where the First and Second Temples had stood some 1,600 years earlier.

The capitulation of Jerusalem, written in Arabic for the conquering Caliph Omar.

Jerusalem: The Religious Claim

The Muslims base their claims to Jerusalem on two hadiths, or traditions, one religious, the other territorial. The religious claim is based on sura 17:1, of the Koran, also called "The Night Journey" because the first sentence reads, "Glory be to him who carried his servants from the sacred temple of Mecca to the temple that is more remote." The hadith explains that Allah sent the angel Gabriel to guide Muhammad from the temple in Mecca to the throne of Allah to the "more remote temple," which Muslims interpret as Jerusalem. While in heaven, Muhammad met Abraham, Moses, and Jesus. Interestingly the Koran contains no mention of Jerusalem.

Jerusalem: the Territorial Claim

The territorial claim is based on the legal theory that the world is divided into two regions. Areas under Muslim control are called *dar al-Islam,* "House

The Ascension
The angel Gabriel is guiding Muhammad to heaven on the back of a magical horse named Borak.

Relatives mourn over the bodies of three children who were murdered by Arab terrorists in a Christmas Day attack on a church in Daska, Pakistan.

The Knesset building in Jerusalem. The Knesset is the legislative body of the State of Israel. Its 120 members are elected by a secret ballot.

Throughout the ages, worshippers in the Diaspora have faced east toward Jerusalem, the City of God. The *mizrah* in synagogues and homes indicates the direction of Jerusalem.

The Old City of Jerusalem is divided into four sections or quarters: Jewish, Arab, Christian, and Armenian. The Christian quarter contains many churches, schools, and historical and religious sites.

of Submission," and those *not yet* under Muslim control are called *dar al-harv*, "House of Destruction," meaning land of the infidels. The concept teaches that territory once under Muslim control, such as Israel, must never be yielded to infidels.

Due to this religious concept, Muslims are required to go on a *jihad* and defeat the infidels (Israelis and Christians). He who dies for Allah is praised as a martyr and assured entrance into Paradise.

The fundamentalists have raised the duty of *jihad* to the sixth pillar of Islam. Thousands of young Arab men and women have been influenced by the *jihad* and have sacrificed their lives for this religious concept.

Jerusalem and the Palestinian Authority

The Palestinians insist that East Jerusalem must be the capital of the state they hope to establish on the West Bank. Israel maintains that Jerusalem is and will always be Israel's capital—to quote Yitzhak Rabin, "Jerusalem is the ancient and eternal capital of the Jewish people."

Because of these seemingly irreconcilable positions, the peace treaty with the PLO refers to Jerusalem in deliberately vague language. Israeli and Arab diplomats hope to solve the questions pertaining to the holy city before the treaty goes into full effect.

Jerusalem and the United States

Despite the bonds of friendship between Israel and the United States, the U.S. government continues to locate its embassy in Tel Aviv. The State Department refuses to recognize Jerusalem as the capital of Israel. In addition, it maintains a separate American consulate in East Jerusalem for Palestinians.

The U.S. Senate has passed a resolution that requires the the State Department to move the American embassy to Jerusalem, but no steps in this direction have been taken.

MUSLIMS ADOPT THE JEWISH SANCTITY OF THE TEMPLE MOUNT

Sovereignty over the Temple Mount in Jerusalem is one of the most difficult problems in the Israeli-Palestinian conflict. The roots go back into the past. Israelites, Christians, and Muslims have fought over this holy site, and built on it a succession of shrines.

The Muslim conquerors, whose religion was influenced by the Judaism and Christianity then practiced in Arabia, were aware of the sanctity of Jerusalem to both Jews and Christians, and they adopted it, thus adding a third contender to the holiness of the place. Their main competitors over the specific holiness of the Temple Mount were the Jews, who maintained its sanctity despite many generations of destruction and never gave up their hope for the rebuilding of the Temple on that very space. To the Christians, on the other hand, the significance of the compound was only in its desolate state, a visible sign of the victory of Christianity over Judaism.

Two biblical personalities related to the Temple Mount had meaning for Muslims. One was King Solomon, of the Old Testament personalities adopted by the Muslims, and the other was Abraham, father of Isaac and also of Ishmael, ancestor of the Arab people. Muslims substituted Ishmael for Isaac in the story of the Binding of Isaac, which was connected with the Temple Mount, believed to be Mount Moriah.

Judaism was one of the main influences on Islam in its early stages. This influence is clearly witnessed in the fact that when Muhammad was still in Mecca, he used to turn toward the Temple Mount in Jerusalem while praying. Thus Jerusalem was the first Muslim *kibla* (direction of prayer). Only later, after he moved to Medina, and perhaps after realizing that the Jews of Arabia would not accept his teachings, did he change the direction of Muslim prayer toward Mecca. In addition to the Jewish associations, adopted by the Muslims as their own, Muslim reverence of the Temple Mount is based on chapter 17 verse 1 of the Koran. "I declare the glory of Him who transported His servant by night from the Masjid al-Haram [the mosque at Mecca] to the Masjid al-Aqsa [the Farthest Mosque], the surroundings of which We blessed, so that We could show him some of Our signs." Traditions, elaborating on the manner in which Muhammad was transported to this mosque atop the winged animal Burak, set it on the Temple Mount in Jerusalem, holy to the Jews. Several traditions relate to the way in which the Temple Mount, specifically, the place of the former Jewish Temple were rediscovered soon after the Muslim conquest.

At the time of the conquest, the Temple Mount was covered by heaps of garbage, piled there by the Byzantine Christians. Both Muslim and Jewish contemporary sources relate that members of these two communities participated in cleaning the Temple Mount. It is told that they did the work under the watchful eye of Caliph 'Omar ibn al-Khatab, and that whenever a piece of a rock was exposed, 'Omar asked the Jews whether it was the rock on which their Temples once stood. As the work continued one of the elders pointed out to 'Omar the edge of the rock they were looking for, and 'Omar stood by until it was all exposed.

The Christian pilgrim Arculf, who visited Jerusalem between 679 and 682, describes a large, mosque, seemingly on the Temple Mount, which could contain some 3,000 people. Tradition attributes the building of this mosque to Caliph 'Omar. The very act of building the mosque was a public declaration that Islam has adopted the sanctity of Jerusalem.

Contested Holiness by Rivka Gonen

WHAT DO YOU THINK?

1. Were the Muslim conquerors aware of the sanctity of Jerusalem to the Jews?

2. Why did the Muslims choose Jerusalem as a holy city?

The Intifada Starts

Major-General Moshe Dayan organized a paratrooper unit in the 1950s. Many of these soldiers reached senior military posts over the years. Moshe Dayan is the one with the eye patch. Second from the left is Ariel Sharon

Sharon Visits the Temple Mount

On September 28, 2000, with the official permission of the Muslim religious authorities, Ariel Sharon and some other Israelis visited the Jewish holy places on the Temple Mount. This provoked a riot by hundreds of Arab protestors who threw rocks and other objects at the police.

The next day, Palestinians on the Temple Mount began throwing stones at peaceful Jewish worshippers at the Western Wall. Soon the riots spread throughout the West Bank and the Gaza Strip. Fighting erupted in Israel in the Arab towns of Nazareth and Bethlehem. In the months that followed, the Intifada uprising left numerous Palestinians killed or wounded. Arafat and other Palestinian leaders encourage and support the Intifada because it makes Israel look bad in the eyes of the world.

The Intifada and Human Consequences

The Al Aksa Intifada has generated severe political unrest, resulting in hundreds of Palestinian deaths, and thousands of injuries. Israel, too, has suffered numerous casualties, especially from attacks on motorists and terrorist bombings in all its major cities.

In addition to the life-and-death consequences, the Intifada violence has had a devastating economic effect. As a security measure, Israel has restricted the passage of Palestinian workers into Israel. It has also clamped down on the movement of Palestinian farm products and manufactured goods. As a consequence, more than 200,000 Palestinians have lost almost $500 million in wages, which has caused a huge drop in their living conditions. Palestinian unemployment increased from 70,000 in October 2000, to 260,030 in January 2001. Overall the Palestinian economy has lost more than $3 billion, and half the population lives under the poverty line.

Israeli children mourn the death of one of their friends during a terrorist attack.

Because of the collapse of the economy, and the widespread damage to government buildings and other elements of the infrastructure due to the fighting, the Palestinian Authority, has become paralyzed. Politically, Chairman Arafat seems unwilling, and perhaps unable, to control organizations like Hamas that stirred up the Intifada and oppose peace with Israel. According to many observers, he, too, opposes peace and is really seeking an ultimate confrontation.

Israel

The Intifada has also had a severe impact on the Israeli economy. Tourism, one of its most profitable industries, is way down, idling thousands of workers. Building contractors who depend upon Arab workers are having difficulty meeting their schedules. Farmers have reduced their plantings. The loss of production and decrease in investments have caused a huge drop in private consumption.

After 17 months in office and trailing by a wide margin in the polls, Ehud Barak announced his resignation. This set the stage for a new election. Barak felt that a win would give him a mandate to push ahead with his peace agenda.

The Palestinian rejection of Barak's peace offer convinced many Israelis that the Palestinians would never be willing to live in peace with them. Barak was discredited by the Intifada. Ariel Sharon, one of Israel's foremost military heroes, aroused confidence. In the view of most Israelis, he would know how to deal with the Palestinians. but would be strong enough to make peace if possible.

Sharon Wins

On February 6, 2001, just before his 73rd birthday, Ariel Sharon the leader of the Likud Party, was elected Prime Minister. For most of his life, Sharon had been engaged in defending Israel. At 13, he had patrolled the fields of his kibbutz at night with a club and a knife. As a young officer in the 1950s, he was

The Hebrew word for Intifada is *hitan'arut*. The photo appeared in a special issue of the Hebrew paper *Ha'aretz* devoted to the Palestinian uprising.

Masked Palestinian youths in Jerusalem throwing stones at Israeli soldiers. In the background are Palestinian adults who are directing the young rioters.

The planners will call the event a success if at least one youngster is killed or seriously wounded. The media have been notified and their cameras are ready to record the confrontation and report Israel's ruthlessness.

Israeli soldiers hunting for hidden
Palestinian terrorists.

Terrorist attacks against Israel include the
bombing of passenger buses.

Israeli soldiers bury one of their comrades
killed in combat against the terrorists.

active in reprisal raids against the Arabs. Sharon was a legendary commander of Israel's anti-terrorist strike force, Unit 101 as well as a paratroop battalion. His brilliant crossing of the Suez Canal in 1973 turned the tide in the Yom Kippur War.

Sharon the Politician

As Menachem Begin's Defense Minister, Sharon established more than 64 new settlements in strategic heavily populated Arab areas in Judea and Samaria. Sharon resigned when he was accused of indirect responsibility for the massacre of hundreds of Palestinians by Christian Phalangists in Beirut during the Israeli occupation of the city.

The Violence Continues

The Arabs decided to check the resolve of the newly elected Prime Minister. Palestinian violence reached a new level of cruelty: the mob lynching of two Israeli soldiers, the bludgeoning to death on May 10, 2001 of two teenagers in Tekoa, the suicide bombing of an Israeli night club in Tel Aviv on June 2001, which resulted in 21 deaths and countless wounded.

Intafada Tactics

The favorite tactic is to set up mortars and gunmen in a highly populated area. After several volleys, the gunmen disappear as soon as the Israeli military response. If the Israeli response kills innocent Arab civilians, especially children, the attack is called a success-even more so if leads to a worldwide reaction against Israeli cruelty.

A television campaign was launched by the Palestinian Military Information, which called upon Arab children to become martyrs by putting down their dolls and bicycles to pick up rocks to throw at the Israelis.

THE AL-FATAH CHARTER

The Arabic name for the Palestine Liberation Movement is Al Fatah. The aim of this organization is the destruction of the State of Israel. The seven "Points" of its program were adopted by the Central Committe of Al Fatah in 1969.

The Al Aksa Military Brigade is the operational arm of Al Fatah. It is responsible for many of the killings and bombings.

1. Al Fatah, the Palestine National Liberation Movement, is the expression of the Palestinian people and of its will to free its land from Zionist colonization in order to recover its national identity.

2. Al Fatah, the Palestine National Liberation Movement, is not struggling against the Jews as an ethnic and religious community. It is struggling against Israel as the expression of colonization based on a theocratic, racist, and expansionist system of Zionism and colonialism.

3. Al Fatah, the Palestine National Liberation Movement, rejects any solution that does not take account of the existence of the Palestinian people and its right to dispose of itself.

4. Al Fatah, the Palestine National Liberation Movement, categorically rejects the Security Council Resolution of 22 November 1967 and the Jarring Mission to which it gave rise.

This resolution ignores the national rights of the Palestinian people—failing to mention its existence. Any solution claiming to be peaceful which ignores this basic factor, will thereby be doomed to failure.

In any event, the acceptance of the resolution of 22 November 1967, or any pseudo-political solution, by whatsoever party, is in no way binding upon the Palestinian people, which is determined to pursue mercilessly its struggle against foreign occupation and Zionist colonization.

5. Al Fatah, the Palestine National Liberation Movement, solemnly proclaims that the final objective of its struggle is the restoration of the independent, democratic State of Palestine, all of whose citizens will enjoy equal rights irrespective of their religion.

6. Since Palestine forms part of the Arab fatherland, Al Fatah, the Palestine National Liberation Movement, will work for the State of Palestine to contribute actively towards the establishment of a progressive and united Arab society.

WHAT DO YOU THINK?

1. What are the two aims of Al Fatah?

2. Why did Fatah reject the Security Council Resolution of November 22, 1967?

3. The Al Fatah charter declares that it will work toward the development of a democratic society. Is there any Arab country that has a democratic government?

4. Have the objectives of Al Fatah changed since 1969?

Islam: The Beginning

THE HAJJ TO MECCA

The Five Pillars of Islam are: Confession, Prayer, Fasting, Charity, and Hajj (Pilgrimage).

Every devoted religious Muslim must undertake a pilgrimage at least once in his life to the sacred mosque in Mecca. Groups of Muslims from all over the world gather in Mecca chanting, "O Allah, we are coming." Some sources estimate the annual numbers of pilgrims at 2 to 3 million. They dress in unseamed, white robes and from that moment on are prohibited from cutting their hair and having sex. In Mecca, they perform the rite of circling the Kaaba, the holiest shrine in Islam, seven times, with stops at the Black Stone. The stone is a meteorite, which forms part of the building.

When he reached the age of 25, Muhammad married a wealthy widow named Khadija (*at right*). She relieved him of financial worries, bore him children, and eventually became the first convert to the Prophet's new religion.

Muhammad was born in the city of Mecca in the Arabian peninsula. Arabia was the domain of nomadic Bedouins who traveled through the harsh desert seeking pasturage for their flocks. Mecca was ideally located along the heavily traveled caravan routes which ran between Palestine and Yemen. At the time of Muhammad's birth, Mecca was both a flourishing center for trade as well as a religious center.

The shrine at Mecca was called the Kaaba, which means "cube." Muslims believe that Abraham and Ishmael built it on the ruins of an ancient temple. Among the stones, they found a black meteorite, which still forms part of the building. Pilgrims who manage to touch it feel that they have shaken hands with Abraham. The Kaaba is an empty room which is entered only twice a year for a cleansing ceremony.

According to the Bible, Abraham, at his wife Sarah's insistence, exiled his concubine Hagar and their son Ishmael. The two wandered in the desert until they ran out of water. Then an angel appeared and led her to a well, and their lives were saved. Accorning to the Koran, it was Ishmael whom Abraham offered to slaughter for God, not Isaac.

Muhammad was born in 570 C.E. and orphaned at an early age. He became a merchant and travelled to Syria and Yemen, where he became acquainted with Jewish and Christian scholars. At the age of 25, he married the rich widow Khadija, and at the age of 40, he had his first vision. He claimed he was visited by the angel Gabriel and ordered to become Allah's messenger and founder of the Muslim religion.

As a result of the revelation, Muhammad taught that God's word had been revealed previously to Jewish and Christian prophets but they had corrupted the message.

The Meccan people disliked his monotheistic teachings because they threatened their prosperity from the annual pilgrimage to worship the idols in the Kaaba. In 622, Muhammad and his followers were driven out of Mecca and took refuge in the town of Medina. This event is know as the Hegira. It is the starting point of Islamic history.

The new movement gained followers, and in 630 C.E., Muhammad was able to reenter Mecca and establish it as the center of Islam. By the time of Muhammad's death in 632 C.E., Islam had conquered all of Arabia.

When Muhammad finally defeated his enemies and conquered Mecca, he massacred one of the three Jewish tribes in the area because they refused to convert to Islam. The men were decapitated and the women and children sold into slavery.

The Koran states, "You will see that the Believers' worst enemies are the Jews, the Idolaters."

The Jews of the Nadir tribe surrender to Muhammad. Illuminated manuscript of the *Universal History* by Rashid al-Din, 13th century.

A Muslim warrier in combat.

The Koran

Muslim theology is based on the Koran and the hadiths (traditions). The Koran is the Bible of Islam. Muslims believe that it is entirely the heavenly words of Allah, transmitted to Muhammad by the angel Gabriel. He received these mystical revelations for a period of 20 years.

In February 610 C.E., on what Muslims call the "night of power and glory," the angel Gabriel appeared with an awe-inspiring summons and transmitted to Muhammad the first sura of the Koran. Over a period of 20 years, Muhammad continued to receive more revelations. Many of the messages have a strong sense of social justice, rituals, prayers, pilgrimage, hygiene and human behavior and many negative messages.

During the night journey, Muhammad led patriarchs, Old Testament prophets, and angels in prayer in a celestial mosque. While in Paradise, Muhammad met Moses, Jesus, and Abraham.

A Turkish illumination, 1594-95, pictures Muhammad directing his army at the Battle of Badr.

Terrorists cite the example of the prophet Muhammad, who was a military commander in more than 50 battles which caused tens of thousands of deaths. Muslim terrorists who willingly sacrifice their lives and blow up innocent women and children cite the command of Allah to eliminate those who do not follow the "path straight", as decreed in the Koran.

Muslim warriors attacking the fortified walls of Jerusalem. After the death of Muhammad in 632 C.E., the Caliph Abu Bakr took political and religious control of the Muslim Arabs. Abu Bakr invaded Palestine in 634 C.E. in order to gain control from the Byzantines. After a siege of almost two years, Jerusalem surrendered to the Arab army. Caliph Omar accepted the surrender and imposed the state of *dhimmi*, second-class citizenship, upon the non-Muslim inhabitants.

The Torah and the Koran

The Torah preceded the Koran by 1,900 years. The Torah made its appearance around 1280 B.C.E., while the Koran was compiled in 650 C.E. Muhammad borrowed from Jewish sources: the Bible, Talmud, and Apocrypha. The religious obligations, the Five Pillars of Islam, and numerous names, events, and stories in the Koran are found in the Torah. Adam, Noah, and Abraham are each mentioned 70 times; Ishmael, Lot, Joseph, Saul, David, Solomon, Elijah, Job, and Jonah figure prominently in the Koran.

The books of the New Testament, the Christian Bible, were canonized in the 4th century C.E. Muhammad also borrowed personalities, customs, and rites from New Testament.

Muhammad died in 632 C.E. The Koran was edited in 650 C.E. by Caliph Uthman, and all of Muhammad's prophecies, consisting of 114 suras (chapters), were written down. Only passages validated by two witnesses were included in the Koran.

The Hadiths: The Islamic Oral Tradition

The hadith, or oral tradition, was based on the earthly doings and sayings of the prophet. Like the Midrash and Halachah, the hadiths explained, expanded, and interpreted the meaning of the Koran. According to tradition, the disciples of Muhammad refused to write down the hadiths during his lifetime because of concern that his own human sayings could be confused with the divine, Allah-given words of the Koran.

Some hadiths were accurate recollections, but as time passed thousands of hadiths were "discovered". At one point, there were some 600,000 hadiths. Eventually, the Islamic jurists eliminated the spurious hadiths and slimmed them down to about 2,700 proven rules.

THE JEWS AND ISLAM

Muhammad, the prophet of Islam, expected the Jews of the Arabian city of Medina to embrace his teachings, but, instead, they rejected him. In revenge, he drove out two Jewish tribes and exterminated the third tribe. He beheaded the men. The women and children of the tribes were sold into slavery. The land of the three tribes was divided among Muhammad's followers, and his share of the spoils formed the basis of the new Muslim treasury. The Jews and Christians of Arabia were forced to pay tribute to the new overlord in the form of an annual percentage of produce and goods called jizya. *The Koran (9:29) encourages Muslims to fight against the "People of the Book" (i.e., Jews and Christians) until they pay the* jizya *and have been humbled.*

Here are several paragraphs mentioning Jews in the Koran.

Wretchedness and baseness were stamped upon them (i.e., the Jews), and they were visited with wrath from Allah. That was because they disbelieved in Allah's revelations and slew the prophets wrongfully. That was for their disobedience. **Koran, Sura 2:61**.

Some of the Jews pervert words from their meanings, and say "We hear and we disobey," and "hear without hearing," and "Heed us!", twisting with their tongues and slandering religion. If they had said "We have heard and obey" or "Hear and observe us," it would have been better for them and more upright. But Allah has cursed them for their disbelief, so they believe not, except for a few. **Koran, Sura 4:41**

And for the evildoing of the Jews, we have forbidden them some good things that were previously permitted them, and because of their barring many from Allah's way, and for their taking usury, which was prohibited for them, and because of their consuming people's wealth under false pretense, we have prepared for the unbelievers among them a painful punishment. **Koran, Sura 4:160–61**

The Jews say, "Allah's hands are chained." Their hands are chained, and they are cursed for what they have said! On the contrary, His hands are spread open. He bestows as He wills. That which has been revealed to you from your Lord will surely increase the arrogance and unbelief of many among them. We have cast enmity and hatred among them until the Day of Resurrection. Every time they light the fire of war, Allah extinguishes it. They hasten to spread corruption throughout the earth, but Allah does not love corrupters! **Koran, Sura 5:64**

WHAT DO YOU THINK?

1. *What happened historically that turned Muhammad against the Jews?*
2. *Name some of the evils of which the Koran accuses the Jews.*
3. *The Torah contains no anti-Christian or anti-Muslim passages; the New Testament contains materials at variance with Judaism but no anti-Muslim statements; the Koran contains statements against both Jews and Christians. How do you explain this?*
4. *How has the Koran engendered animosity toward the modern State of Israel?*
5. *Are there any Arab groups which have the courage to tell the truth about the Arabs' lack of progress?*

This Is Your Enemy

Prayer and brainwashing of youngsters in a mud-brick madrasa

Painting of a 14th-century madrasa.

A madrasa in Malaysia. Note the girls in the background.

Israel's Response to Terror

The assault against Israel starts with the children. Palestinian textbooks, starting from kindergarten, demonize the Israelis and preach a genocidal curriculum against the State of Israel.

Arafat's strategy is to escalate terror inside of Israel to a point when Israelis are afraid to live normal lives, of taking buses or going to the malls.

Arab Anti-Jewish Terror Is Not New

From the very beginning of Islam, Arabs have been antagonistic to Jews. In 630 C.E., when the Prophet Muhammad rose to power, he destroyed the three Jewish tribes that lived in the Arabian peninsula. When Caliph Omar captured the city of Jerusalem from the Byzantines, he put the Jews and Christians into a second-class status called *dhimmi*. When passing a Muslim in the street, Jews had to stand aside. Special clothing, a forerunner of the infamous yellow badge, was meant to show Muslims who was a *dhimmi*. During the Turkish period, from 1516 to 1918, the Muslims restricted Jewish immigration and the construction of settlements. The Turkish government closed its eyes to Arab terrorists who murdered hundreds of Jews. The British mandatory power in Palestine also allowed Arab terrorists to run riot.

Murder in Hebron

In 1929, hundreds of organized Arab terrorists attacked the Jews of Hebron and murdered people, burned synagogues, and plundered Jewish homes and businesses. When the State of Israel was established in 1948, heavily armed Arab armies simultaneously attacked the newborn state. From 1948 until the present, the State of Israel has fought six wars against Arab armies. The Koran preaches that those who die fighting the infidels will receive special rewards in heaven. Today, special Arab religious schools called *madrasas* run by religious clerics called *mullahs*, with tens of thousands of students, some as young as four and five, are brainwashed to hate the infidels (Christians and Jews).

The Intolerant Faith

The Koran calls for *jihad*–Holy War against infidels (Jews and Christians) who do not follow the "right path" as called for in the Koran. When Muslims run into opposition, the Koran recommends, "Fight them (Jews and Christians) so that Allah may punish them at your hands." Verses such as this have inflamed Muslims against the West.

The preachers depict Jews as murderers who need Muslim blood to bake matzot. This hate campaign is carried on in all Arab countries as well as in Europe, Asia, and even America. Blaming Israel diverts the attention of the masses from the true causes of their problems. Golda Meir, a Prime Minister of Israel, said, "If there was no Israel, the Arab world would have to invent one."

The Arab press glorifies the murderers and praises them as "holy warriors." In recognition of their sacrifices, the Saudi Arabian government rewards the families of martyrs with large cash awards. The Al Qaida network operates openly in most Muslim countries. Most pay to rid themselves of the militants so that they can expend their energies and vent their anger away from home. Donors are aware that the militants, who have no other skills and are today terrorizing the West, will tomorrow turn against then if they do not continue to provide blackmail monies.

Twin Towers Disaster

It is these graduates who blew up the Twin Towers in New York. These graduates blew up the U.S. destroyer *Cole* and caused the death of many American sailors. Today, there are numerous conflicts taking place all over the world that involve Muslims

Arab suicide bombers are a constant threat. This bomber was intercepted and killed before he exploded his bomb.

Hamas describes the murder of Jews as a way to Islamic heaven. Titled "We shall knock on heaven's doors with skulls of Jews," the Web site shows an ax splitting the words "the Jews."

Israeli gunboats captured a shipment of deadly missiles shipped to the Palestinian Authority by the Iranians. The missiles were ordered and paid for by the terrorist group Hezbollah.

Osama bin Ladin, leader of the Al Qaida terrorists

against Christians in Chechniya, the Philipines, China, Russia, Indonesia, and Singapore. All of these countries have active Muslim guerillas supported by oil money. These revolts have nothing to do with the Israeli problem. These are brainwashed guerillas trained in camps run by Al Qaida terrorists in Syria, Libya, Iran, Iraq, and Somalia. These camps are supported by Saudi Arabian oil money. Fifteen of the 19 terrorists who blew up the Twin Towers were Saudi Arabians, and the funds were supplied by Saudi Arabian "charities." The supply of terrorists willing to die for Islam is endless. The graduates of the madrasas are taught to hate the United States, called the Grand Satan, and, of course, to hate Israel and the Jews.

Arab Human Development Report

In July 2002, the UN isssued a report entitled *Arab Human Development*, prepared by a team of Muslim sociologists, scientists, and experts on Arab culture. The report covered 280 million Muslims living in 22 Arab countries and asked the question, "Why is the Arab world lagging behind?" The report warns that Arab societies are being crippled by their lack of political freedom, repression of women, and isolation from the world of ideas, which stifles creativity. Per capita income is shrinking, growth and science and technology are dormant. In comparison, countries in Asia, South America, and a few in Africa have made amazing leaps in technology, education, political freedom, research, and freedom of expression. Of course, the report also includes an excuse and a rare admission of guilt, "The Israeli–Arab conflict has been both a cause and an excuse for delaying democratic change." The report does not directly criticize Islamic militancy and the effect of fundamentalist religious vigilantes.

DANIEL PEARL–THE TRUTH SEEKER

Reporters are alway on the lookout for scoops. Some reporters are muckrakers hunting for dirt without concern for the consequences. A few are "truth seekers," who devote their energy and talents to exploring different sides of contentious issues. The French Middle–Ages Talmudist Meiri, wrote, "The truth is burdensome, therefore its bearers are few."

Daniel Pearl, likeably called Danny by his admirers, was one of those few committed foreign correspondents who tried to understand and give voice to all parties in the Middle East quagmire. Danny was working from Bombay, India, as bureau chief for the Wall Street Journal, *when he was contacted and promised an exclusive interview with a terrorist leader. Despite warnings from his family and friends, the "truth seeker" flew to Karachi, Pakistan, for the scoop.*

Daniel Pearl was born on October 16, 1963, in Princeton, New Jersey to Judea and Ruth Pearl, Israeli citizens. When he was 3, his family moved to Southern California. He graduated with honors from Stanford University with a degree in communication. While at Stanford, he interned at several newspaper in Massachusets. In 1990, he joined the Wall Street Journal and in 1996 was promoted to foreign correspondent.

Daniel was a man with an infinite number of interests and talents. He was a bluegrass fiddler, a classical violinist, a deejay with his own radio show, and an excellent skier. But, more than that, he was a journalist who honestly devoted himself to exploring all sides of the issues.

As a young man, he traveled to Russia where he met with refuseniks in Leningrad and Moscow and offered them hope and support.

He was in Bombay, India working on a story about the Islamic militant underground when he was contacted by an Arab promising to arrange a interview with the Islamic militant Ahmed Omar Sheikh. He was met and escorted to a car in downtown Karachi to meet and interview the elusive Muslim. In the car he was blindfolded and driven around in circles for to a closed nursery school where he was imprisioned. During his first week in captivity Danny tried to escape but was caught and roughed by his captors. On the sixth day three heavily armed Arabs from Yemen arrived. The journalist with a knife at his throat was videotaped saying, "I am a Jew, my mother is a Jew." Then he was forced to read a statement criticizing the United States and Israel. After this they placed a blindfold over his face and stabbed him to death. The Arabs then dismembered Pearl's body and buried the parts in the school garden.

After an intense investigation by Pakistani authorities and the CIA, Ahmed Sheikh was caught and sentenced to death. The authorities believe that the murder was ordered by the Al Quaeda. The murder besides being anti-Israel and anti-Semitic also had a geopolitical aspect. The murder was intended as a warning to Pakistan's president who had aligned his country with U.S. polices. Danny was survived by his wife Mariane, whom he met in France, his parents Judea and Ruth, and his sisters Michelle and Tamara. A son, Adam, was born after Danny's death.

Danny is also survived by millions of people all over the world who deeply mourned his senseless and horrible murder.

WHAT DO YOU THINK?

1. Why did Danny ignore the advice of his friends and family.?
2. What would you do if you were a reporter and offered an interview with a terrorist?
3. What did the Arabs accomplish by murdering Danny Pearl?

Jews, Israel and Iraq

The largest Jewish communities are circled Alexandria in Egypt; the land of Israel; and Babylonia.

The Babylonian Jewish community had grown and prospered. By the 1st century C.E. there were more Jews in Babylon than in Judea. The Babylonian Jews maintained their own synagogues, their own houses of study, and their own courts where Jewish law was observed.

Jews have lived in Mesopotamia, the seat of the Assyrian and Babylonian Empires, since the first deportations of the "Ten Tribes" from the Northern Kingdom of Israel during the 8th century B.C.E.

Because Jews lived under more tolerable conditions in Babylonia than anywhere else, they flourished and at the time of the fall of the Second Temple numbered more than one millon. The Babylonian Talmud was created there and was taught in the famous academies of Sura, Pumbeditha, and Nehardea. Under the leadership of the exilarchs and the geonim, Babylonian Jewry dominated the Jewish world down to the middle of the 11th century, when it went into and eclipse.

From the beginning of the 18th century, Jews living in Baghdad were exposed to harassment by the Muslim rulers. Many Jews, at the start of the 18th century left to settle in India and China. Others emigrated to the Western Hemisphere.

At the end of World War I, Jews were the plurality of the population in multiethnic Baghdad. When the British entered Baghdad in March 1917 , there were 80,000 Jews out of a total population of 200,000. The Jews were the richest and best educated.

From 1948, when the State of Israel was proclaimed, the departure of Jews from Iraq was forbidden. Thousands of Jews were arrested, imprisoned and heavily fined. On March 9, 1950 the authorities changed their attitude and permitted Jews to leave if they would relinquish Iraqi nationality and their possessions.

The exodus from Iraq, called Operation Ezra and Nehemiah, was organized by the Jewish Agency. It ended in 1952, after the majority of Jews, numbering about 120,000, had left for Israel. Together with the refugees who fled through Iran, about 140,000 Iraqi-born Jews settled in Israel. Before the mass immigration to Israel started, there were some 170,000

A page from a hand printed 12th century Persian bible.

Arabic–speaking Jews in Iraq. The Jewish refugees have never been repaid for their properties and possessions which were stolen by Iraqi goverment officials. The value is estimated at several billions of dollars.

The handful of remaining Jews lived under conditions of fear and danger, which peaked on January 27, 1969, when nine Jews were hanged from lamp posts in Baghdad after being accused of spying for Israel and the C.I.A.

Mission to Iraq / 1981

Ever since the beginning of the conflict with Israel, the Arab countries have been able to obtain the most up-to-date weaponry—short of nuclear arms. In 1980 the Israeli government grew very anxious over reports that Iraq was developing nuclear, chemical, and biological weapons. Israel was especially concerned about the nuclear production facilities in Osirak, 10 miles from Baghdad.

On June 7, 1981 Israeli aircraft flew about 600 miles through enemy air space and bombed the Iraqi nuclear facility. The plant was destroyed and all the aircraft returned safely.

The whole world condemned Israel, but secretly most of Iraq's neighbors applauded the raid, since an Iraq armed with nuclear bombs would have been a threat to the whole region. The full benefit of the raid on Osirak was seen during the 1991 Persian Gulf War. Iraq used biological weapons against U.S. troops, and might have used nuclear weapons if they had been available, but fortunately, thanks to Israel, it had none.

Israel and the Gulf War / 1991

On August 2, 1990, 100,000 Iraqi troops invaded Kuwait and quickly took control of the country. Six hundred oil wells were set afire. Torture, killings, mass arrests, and looting of anything of value continued without a stop. On August 7, 1990 President George Bush set in motion Operation Desert Storm under the command of General Norman Schwarzkopf.

David Sassoon and three of his sons ca. 1850. David Sassoon understood that the Muslims would never allow the Jews to live in peace, so he moved his family and his business.

The Sassoon family, originally from Baghdad, relocated to Bombay, India. They were called the "Rothschilds of the East." They directed an enormous commercial empire which included factories, financial institutions, and trading companies in all major Far East countries.

Israel stamp issued commemorating the 29th aniversary of Operation Ezra and Nehemiah. The mass exodus of Iraqi Jews to Israel.

President Saddam Hussein of Iraq launched an ambitious program to modernize his arsenal of offensive weapons. He built chemical, gas, and biological weapons and used them against the Kurds and Iranians. In addition, he began building a nuclear weapons facility at Osirak. In 1981 an Israeli air attack destroyed the half-built reactor.

Israel, however, was not part of the coalition because the Arab members did not want to be seen fighting side-by-side with Israel against their Arab brothers. President Bush extracted a promise from Prime Minister Yitzhak Shamir not to take military action against Iraq even if Israel was attacked.

Saddam Hussein fired a total of 86 Scud missiles, 40 at Israel and 46 at Saudi Arabia. Some were intercepted by U.S. Patriot missiles. In Israel 250 people were wounded. In and around Tel Aviv about 9,000 apartments were damaged. The most lethal Scud attack was on a U.S. barracks in Saudi Arabia; 28 Americans were killed.

The U.S.–led Operation Desert Storm, defeated the Iraqis, but stopped short on the outskirts of Baghdad.

General Norman Schwarzkopf explains the aims and objectives of Operation Desert Storm.

MISSION TO IRAQ / 1981

In 1980, the Israeli government grew very anxious over reports that Iraq was developing nuclear, chemical, and biological weapons. Israel was especially concerned about the nuclear production facilities in Osirak, 10 miles from Baghdad.

On June 7, 1981 Israeli aircraft flew about 600 miles through enemy air space and bombed the Iraqi nuclear facility. The plant was destroyed and all the aircraft returned safely. The full benefit of the raid on Osirak was seen during the 1991 Persian Gulf War. Iraq used biological weapons against U.S. troops, and might have used nuclear weapons if they had been available, but fortunately, thanks to Israel, it had none.

The following is the report of the raid in the Jerusalem Post.

THE JERUSALEM POST

NYD
IS 5.50

EIGHT PAGES FROM SUNDAY'S
The New York Times
THE WEEK IN REVIEW
INSIDE TODAY

Tuesday, June 9, 1981

VOL. LI NO. 15246

Jets destroy Iraqi atomic Site

It was "now or never" Prime Minister Menahem Begin said last night, explaining his decision to bomb the Iraqi nuclear reactor.

By July the reactor would have been "hot already" Begin told a Kol Yisrael a radio interviewer. A bombing attack then would have "endangered the lives of thousands of innocent people in nearby Baghdad" exposing them to radiation. No Israeli government would have bombed under those conditions, he said.

Government sources told *The Jerusalem Post* last night that the decision had been taken by the cabinet last October.

At 5 P.M. on Sunday, with the planes already on their way to Iraq, Begin convened the cabinet and informed the ministers that the operation was under way.

In his interview last night, Begin said as "not credible" a French scientific report that the Iraqi reactor was being built for peaceful purposes. Israel's own information, Begin said, was the reactor was intended to manufacture atom bombs for use against Israel.

Iraq's President Saddam Hussein had butchered his own colleagues, would have had "no hesitation" in dropping "three or four or five" of those bombs on Israel, Begin declared. They would have pulverized Israel's population centers, and decimated its army.

Thus Sunday's air force action against the Iraqi reactor was a "life-saving operation."

"I've lived with this thing for two years", Begin continued. "Sometimes", he said, "when he would chat with children, I would be struck by the thought : My God, what's going to happen to these children in a few year's time, an atom bomb might fall on them."

Begin said Churchill's famous declaration after Dunkirk also expressed the Israeli nation's debt to its own air force "those wonderful young men. Never have so many owed so much to so few."

WHAT DO YOU THINK?

1. *What could have happened during the Gulf War in 1991 if Israel had not destroyed the Iraqi nuclear reactor in 1981?*
2. *Has any country ever given Israel credit for the destruction of the reactor?*
3. *President George W. Bush in 2003 faced the same problem as Begin. What did he do? What do you think of his decision?*
4. *President Saddam Hussein threatened to use bombs and missiles against Israel. If he did, how should the Israelis have reacted?*
5. *What would have been the consequences of waiting?*

Operation Iraqi Freedom and Israel

Saddam Hussein

After Desert Storm, the allies punished Iraq by imposing sanctions: limiting use of oil monies and weakening Hussein by limiting his ability to develop weapon systems of mass destruction. However, they failed because Saddam Hussein continually denied access to UNSCOM (United Nation Special Commission) inspectors to his laboratories.

Hussein, an egomaniac, portrayed himself as the *shaykh*, or defender of Muslim, and Palestinian rights, and the only Arab leader strong enough to stand up to the West. He evaded the sanctions with the aid of France, Russia and Germany. All three were owed billions of dollar for food and machinery. They all had negotiated lucrative oil concessions in Iraq. Moreover, they were eager to assemble a power bloc to counter America's growing political, military, and economic strength as the world's superpower.

After twelve years of evasions and negotiations, the Security Council, in 2003, under U.S. pressure, signed Resolution Number 1441 authorizing toughened inspections for weapons of mass destruction (WMDs) Once again Saddam Hussein denied that he maintained, possessed, or produced WMDs.

The United States wanted a second resolution authorizing the use of force, but the trio opposed the demand. As a result, the United States, Britain and their allies gave Hussein until March 17 to hand over any banned weapons he possessed. Saddam refused to comply, and on March 20, 2003 coalition forces stationed in Kuwait crossed into Iraq and Operation Iraqi Freedom began. In 26 days coalition forces defeated the Iraqi army and entered Baghdad.

Israel and Operation Iraqi Freedom
The war in Iraq triggered fears in Israel of attacks by weapons of mass destruction. The United States sent several Patriot missile batteries and thousands of sol-

diers to service them. The Israeli government issued hundreds of thousands of gas masks. Schoolchildren proudly carried their masks into their schoolrooms.

Israelis were urged to prepare for gas attacks by insulating a room with plastic and duct tape in case of a poison gas or biological attack.

Israel's Arrow anti-missile batteries and their crews were on high alert, glued to their radar consoles, and the planes of the Israel Defense Forces patroled the skies around the clock. Fortunately the swift coalition victory made all these preparations unnecessary.

The U.S. army has found a suspected mobile Iraqi chemical or biological weapons truck.

New Palestinian Leadership

After months of suicide bombings, in which hundreds of Israelis were killed, and thousands wounded, President George W. Bush, on June 24, 2002, publically disclosed the terms of a proposed settlement for the Israeli-Palestinian dispute. The terms were explicit, and he declared he believed in the principle of a Palestinian state living side by side with Israel in peace and security.

The price for the Palestinians was the removal of Yasir Arafat as their leader and the creation of a new leadership based on the rule of peace and an open economy free from corruption.

Mahmoud Abbas (Abu Mazen) and Yasir Arafat

Bush also urged Israel to cease settlement activity in the so-called occupied territories and to negotiate a settlement between the parties based on U.N. Resolutions 242 and 348, which call for border adjustments.

After months of European and U.S. pressure and sometimes violent discussion, the Palestinian Parliament voted for a reform leadership headed by the new Prime Minister, Abu Mazen. Yasir Arafat did his best to undermine Abu Mazen (also known as Mahmoud Abbas) He described Mazen as an American stooge and opposed the dismantling of the Aqsa Martyrs Brigade and the other military groups which took credit for numerous suicide bombings.

Palestinian Prime Minister Abbas, *second from right*, and Cabinet Affairs Minister Yasser Abed Rabbo, *right*, receive the "road map" peace plan from the United Nations, Middle East envoy Terje Roed-Larsen, *second from left*, and E.U. special envoy Miguel Angel Moratinos in Ramallah on April 30, 2003.

According to some political observers the new Prime Minister represents hope for a new beginning. He has declared the *intifada* a mistake and pledged to end terrorism by disarming Palestinian terror organizations.

Possibilities of Peace

The victory in Iraq has sent shock waves throughout the Middle East, opening an opportunity for regional peace. Russia, the European Union, the United Nations, and the United States accepted George W. Bush's "road map" for peace.

Unfortunately, the "Quartet" managing the so-called road map for peace includes three members known for their anti-Israel and anti-Semitic policies. Russia for the last 500 years has been a hotbed of anti Semitism and pogroms. The U.N. has passed hundreds of resolutions comdemning Israel, and only a few against the Arabs. The E.U. under the leadership of France, with about ten percent of Muslim population, is anti-Israel.

Despite all the misgivings, Israel has accepted the road map but with reservations. On the surface, the plan seems similar to the 1991 Madrid peace conference, and the 1993 Oslo Accords. The difference is in the details and the changes in the political climate.

The most obvious change is in the Palestinian leadership. Hopes are placed on the shoulder of Mahmoud Abbas, also known as Abu Mazen, who was confirmed on April 29, 2003 by the Palestinian Parliament as prime minister. Abbas, unlike Arafat, has declared his willingness to fight terrorism and work toward peace. Israel's Arab neighbors have also shown a willingness to formally acknowledge the Jewish state and make peace.

On April 30, 2003, Daniel Kurtzer, the U.S. ambassador to Israel, officially delivered the road map to Israel. On the same day, international officials gave the road map to Prime Minister Mahmoud Abbas.

Thousands of Israeli settlers protest the "road map" plan to demolish so called "unauthorized" settlements.

President George W. Bush met with Ariel Sharon and Mahmoud Abbas in Aqaba, Jordan. They both, with reservations, endorsed the "road map" to peace.

THE ROAD MAP TO PEACE?

The following is a shortened text of the peace plan for the Middle East by the Quartet which includes the United States, the European Union, Russia, and the United Nations, The Quartet released its "road map" for peace, which calls for a scheduled series of reciprocal measures and the creation of a Palestinian state in 2005.The road map detours around three roadblocks: Jerusalem, Palestinian refugees (not Jewish refugees), and settlements in the West Bank and the Gaza Strip.

Israel has accepted the road map with many reservations. Israel is concerned that the road map managers will push them to make concessions which could destroy its ability to defend itself. Politically, the Israeli government faces a revolt by so-called right-wingers if it accepts the creation of a Palestinian State.

The following is a performance-based and goal-driven road map, with clear phases, timelines, target dates and benchmarks aiming at progress through reciprocal steps by the two parties in the political, security, economic, humanitarian and institution building fields, under the auspices of the Quartet. The destination is a final and comprehensive settlement of the Israel-Palestinian conflict by 2005, as presented in President Bush's speech of June 24,

• A two-state solution to the Israeli-Palestinian conflict will only be achieved through an end to violence and terrorism, when the Palestinian people have a leadership acting decisively against terror and through Israel's readiness to do what is necessary for a democratic Palestinian state to be established.

• A settlement, negotiated between the parties, will result in the emergence of an independent, democratic and viable Palestinian state living side by side in peace and security with Israel and its other neighbors.

Phase 1:
Ending Terror and Violence, Normalizing Palestinian Life, and Building Palestinian Institutions, Present to May 2003

In Phase 1, the Palestinians immediately undertake an unconditional cessation of violence according to the steps outlined below; such action should be accompanied by supportive measures undertaken by.Israel. Palestinians and Israelis resume security cooperation end violence, terrorism, and incitement through restructured and effective Palestinian security services. Palestinians undertake comprehensive political reform in preparation for statehood.

• Israel takes all necessary steps to help normalize Palestinian life. Israel withdraws from Palestinian areas occupied from Sept. 28, 2000, and Palestinian leadership issues an unequivocal statement reiterating Israel's right to exist in peace and security and calling for an immediate and unconditional cease-fire to end armed activity and all acts of violence against Israelis. Israeli leadership issues an unequivocal statement affirming its commitments to the two-state vision of an independent, viable, sovereign Palestinian state living in peace and security alongside Israel.

SECURITY
• Palestinians declare an unequivocal end to violence and terrorism and undertake visible efforts on the ground to arrest, disrupt and restrain individuals and groups conducting and planning violent attacks on Israelis anywhere.

• Restructured and retrained Palestinian security forces and I.D.F. counterparts progressively resume security cooperation.

• Arab states cut off public and private funding and all other forms of support for groups supporting and engaging in violence and terror.

• As comprehensive security performance moves forward, I.D.F. withdraws progressively from areas occupied since Sept. 28, 2000 and the two sides restore the status quo that existed prior to Sept. 28, 2000.

• As early as possible Palestinians hold free, open, and fair elections

HUMANITARIAN RESPONSE
• Israel takes measures to improve the humanitarian situation.

SETTLEMENTS
•Israel immediately dismantles settlement outposts erected since March 2001.
Consistent with the Mitchell Report, Israel freezes all settlement activity (including natural growth of settlements).

Phase II: Transition – June 2003 to December 2003

• In the second phase, efforts are focused on the option of creating an independent Palestinian state with provisional borders.

As has been noted, this goal can be achieved when the Palestinian people have a leadership acting decisively against terror, willing and able to build a practicing democracy based on tolerance and liberty.

Progress into Phase II will be based upon the consensus judgment of the Quartet of whether conditions are appropriate to proceed, taking into account performance of parties.

• Phase II ends and starts after Palestinian elections and ends with posible creation of an independent Palestinian state with provisional borders in 2003. Its primary goals are continued comprehensive and effective security and normalization of Palestinian life.

• Convened by the Quartet, in consultation with the parties, immediately after the successful conclusion of Palestinian elections, to support Palestinian economic recovery and launch a process leading to the establishment of an indenpendent Palestinian state with provisional borders. Based on the principles described in this document. Arab States restore preintifada links to Israel. Revival of engagement on issues including regional water resources, environment, economic development, refugees and arms control issues.

•New constitution for a democratic Palestinian state is finalized and approved by appropriate Palestinian institutions.

• Creation of a indenpendent Palestinian state with provisional borders through a process of Israeli-Palestinian ingagement, launched by the International conference.

• Enhanced international role in monitoring transition, with the active, sustained, and operational support of the Quartet.

Quartet members promote international recognition of Palestinian state, including possible U.N. membership.

INTERNATIONAL CONFERENCE

• Convened by the Quartet, in consultation with the parties, immediately after the successful conclusion of Palestinian elections, to support Palestinian economic recovery and launch a process leading to the establishment of an independent Palestinian state with provisional borders. Based on the principles described in this document. Arab States restore preintifada links to Israel. Revival of engagement on issues including regional water resources, environment, economic development, refugees and arms control issues.

• New constitution for a democratic Palestinian state is finalized and approved by appropriate Palestinian institutions.

• Creation of a independent Palestinian state with provisional borders through a process of Israeli-Palestinian engagement, launched by the International conference.

• Enhanced international role in monitoring transition, with the active, sustained, and operational support of the Quartet.

Quartet members promote international recognition of Palestinian state, including possible U.N. membership.

Phase III: Permanent Status Agreement and End of the Israeli–Palestinian Conflict, 2004 to 2005

• Progress into Phase III, based on consensus judgment of Quartet, and taking into account actions of both parties and Quartet monitoring. Phase III objectives are consolidation of reform and stabilization of Palestinian institutions, sustained, effective Palestinian security performance, and Israeli-Palestinian negotiations aimed at a permanent status agreement in 2005.

SECOND INTERNATIONAL CONFERENCE

Convened by Quartet, in consultation with the parties, at beginning of 2004 to endorse agreement reached on an independent Palestinian state with provisional borders and formally launch a process with the active, sustained, and operational support of the Quartet, leading to a final, permanent status resolution in 2005, including borders, Jerusalem, refugees, settlements, and support progress toward a comprehensive Middle East settlement between Israel and Lebanon and Israel and Syria, to be achieved as soon as possible.

• Continued sustained and effective security performance, and sustained, effective security cooperation on the basis laid out in Phase I.

• Parties reach final and comprehensive permanent status agreement that ends the Israel-Palestinian conflict in 2005, fhrough a settlement negotiated between the Parties based on U.N. Security Council Resolutions 242, 338, and 1397, that ends the occupation that began in 1967, and includes an agreed, just, fair, and realistic solution to the refugee issue, and a negotiated resolution on the status of Jerusalem that takes into account the political and religious concerns of both sides, and protects the religious interests of Jews, Christians and Muslims worldwide, and fulfills the vision of two states, Israel and sovereign, independent, democratic and viable, in Palestine, living side-by-side in peace and security.

• Arab state acceptance of full normal relations with Israel and security for all the states of the region in the context of a comprehensive Arab-Israeli peace.

WHAT DO YOU THINK?

The road map is a momentous document which can if fairly administered can end the more than 50 year conflict between Israel and the Palestinians. It can also initiate a new political order in the Middle East.

1.   *Who will monitor the Palestinian movements towards peace?*
2.   *Notice that in the photograph on page 201, the representatives of the U.N. and the E.U. are delivering the road map to Abu Mazen. Why didn't they also delivered a copy to Israel? Why was it left to the U.S. embassador to Israel to delivery the map? What does the photograph tell you about the objectivity of the U.N. and the E.U.*
3.   *Should Israel continue following the road map if the violence continues?*
4.   *The road map asks Arab governments to stop funding Arab terror groups. Should Israel continue to travel the road map if the funding continues?*
5.   *Who will monitor the funding? Can Israel trust the Quartet to monitor the funding? The E.U. members have contributed billions of dollars to the P.A. How do the E.U. members know whether their funds were used by the terrorists.*
6.   *The road map asks Israel to freeze and dismantle settlements in advance of a peace settlement? Suppose their is no agreement? What happens to the dismantle settlements? Should they be rebuilt?*
7.   *Phase I asks the Palestinians to undertake political reform in preparation for state hood. Is there any Arab government on which it can model political reforms? Are there any Arabs governments which grant women equal rights? That practices democracy? That practices human rights?*
8.   *Phase III talks about a final status agreement in 2005, based upon a negotiated agreement between the parties. What happens if their is no agreement? Who will settle the differences between the parties? Can Israel rely upon the objectivity of Russia, the U.N. and the E.U.?*
9.   *What happens if Israel decides that most of the Quartet nembers are pro-Palestinian and the road map is a lynching party? What are Israel's options?*
10. *The Arabs demand the right of return. What would happen to Israel if 4 million Arabs returned?*

The Tragedy Continues

Sheik Ahmed Yassin is the spiritual leader of Hamas. He is violently anti-Israel and in his sermons he promotes terrorism. Israel has tried to remove him by bombing his Gaza City apartmet where he was meeting with Hamas members.

Sheik Yassin said that his movement will not take part in any Palestinian government which tries to make peace with Israel.

The Road Map

On June 1, 2003, President George W. Bush personally followed up his "Road Map to Peace" by flying to Sharm al-Sheikh, Egypt, where he met with Arab leaders and asked them to support the newly elected Palestinian prime minister, Mahmoud Abbas. President Bush was determined to support Abbas and help him fight terrror and achieve a political solution to the Israeli-Palestinian problem by 2005.

From Egypt, President Bush flew to Aqaba, Jordan, and met with Abbas and Prime Minister Sharon. Both of the leaders pledged, with reservations, to follow the Bush road map. Unfortunately both leaders face opposition at home by hard-liners. The difficulty of achieving peace was highlighted by events which took place several days after the summit.

The out-of-power Mr. Arafat belittled the achievments of the summit and became a very defiant and dangerous impediment to a peace settlement. On June 9, 2003, the three Palestinian terror groups, Hamas, Islamic Jihad, and the Al Aksa Martyrs Brigade, attacked Israeli troops in Gaza and killed five soldiers.

The attack was a clear and violent denunciation of the American peace plan and an attempt to torpedo the authority of Abbas.

Mahmoud Abbas Resigns

After 100 days in office, Mahmoud Abbas resigned because Arafat denied him the authority to fight or control the terrorists and reenergize the peace process.

For all his weaknesses Abbas was committed to a political solution. He angered Arafat and his Hamas cohorts by calling the intifada a failure that worsened the condition of the Palestinians and eroded international support.

Both the Bush administration and Prime Minister Sharon welcomed and praised Abbas, but

An Israeli soldier on the watch against Arabs suicide bombers.

lost their support because he was ineffective and could not
dismantle the terror network. Abbas tried, but he was continually sabotaged by Arafat, who has still not abandoned his primary goal of destroying Israel. Arafat was the man who rejected Prime Minister Barak's unprecedented offer at Camp David
and he still has given any indication that he has changed his
mind.

Arafat was also encouraged by the three quartet members, the European Union, Russia and the U.N., who continue
to support him financialy and politically. As a replacement,
Arafat has appointed his puppet, parlimentary speaker Ahmed
Qureia to succeed Abbas. Mr. Qureia immediately declared
that he would not disarm the terrorists.

But America and Israel have indicated that they will not
deal with a Palestinian government controlled by Arafat

Doctor David Applebaum

**David Applelebaum and daughter Nava .
She wanted to be a cancer researcher.**

On September 9, 2003 two suicide bombers detonated
themselves at a bus stop near Tel-Aviv killing eight soldiers.
Four hours later a second bomber exploded outside a cafe in
Jerusalem killing seven and wounding 30 others.
Responsibility, for the attacks was claimed by Hamas.
Among those killed in Jerusalem was David Applebaum and
his daughter Nava. As an ordained rabbi he decided to became
a doctor, Applebaum was a specialist in emergency response, to
terrorist attacks.

Applebaum's daughter, Nava, was to be married on
September 13, 2003. By Tuesday the Applebaum home in
Jerusalem was jumping with joy. As night came a proud father
and beautiful daughter Nava disappeared for a cup of coffee
and a pre-marriage talk. The pair lined up at a take-out counter
when the bomber ran in and blew himself up. Instead of laugh-
ing and dancing at a wedding, the guests wept at a funeral.
Instead of standing under a huppah father and daughter were
laid to rest on a hill outside Jerusalem. They were the 850th
and 851st Israeli Jews to be murdered. From September 2000
to September 2003, about 2500 Palestinians and 860 Israelis
have been killed in attacks and counter-attacks.

The Israeli Security Wall

The suicide bombers, despite heroic precautions of the IDF have managed to penetrate Israeli security and murder more than 850 Israelis since the intifada began in 2000. To deter the bombers, Israel decided to build a high-security fence with concrete walls, guard towers, and barbed wire fences to prevent bombers from entering its towns and cities.

The Palestinians call this wall a land grab, since the proposed route runs over the Green Line established after the 1967 war. The Palestinians claim that the wall will separate families and infringe on what they have decided is their territory.

The Bush administration is also protesting the route of the security fence in certain areas. Israeli and American officials have met to discuss ways of solving some of the problems created by the wall.

The Next Generation of Suicide Bombers

The next generation of suicide bombers are now being trained in Hamas madrassas, nurseries and high schools. World maps in all Arab countries carry no mention of Israel. Children on television programs, and in schools and summer camps are trained to shoot and enact suicide attacks. Toys stores sell miniature suicide belts as play toys. Homes, shops, and even hospitals proudly display photos of suicide bombers. Television and radios continually spout ridiculous anti-Semitic theories of Jewish world domination. By the time, these brainwashed children reach their teens, many are already primed to become assassins.

Who will purge the minds of these programmed Arabs? The next generation of suicide bombers are eagerly waiting to ascend to Islamic heaven.

As history has shown, the same Saudi Arabian princes who have funded these schools with hundreds of millions of dollars each year will eventually themselves become the victims of their own homegrown assassins.

> In the meantime bloodshed continues on both sides.

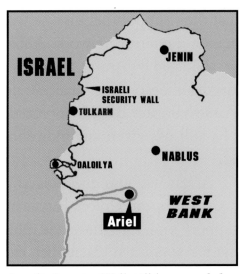

Israel's Security Wall will be expanded to protect the settlement of Ariel. The new fence will enclose the three sides of Ariel. The city of Ariel and three other Jewish settlements in the area, north of Jerusalem contain 18,000 Israelis.

As usual the Palestinian have never missed an opportunity to miss an opportunity.

If the Arabs once again continue to delay a peace agreement, then the Security Wall will become the new Israeli border.

SUICIDE BOMBER KILLS 20

HAIFA, Israel, Sunday, Oct.5
A bomber charged into a crowded seaside restaurant in this northern Israeli city on Saturday afternoon and detonated explosives that killed at least 19 people, besides herself. At least three of the dead were children and six were Arabs.

The attack was carried out by Hanadi Jaradat, a young woman from the West Bank town of Jenin. Islamic Jihad the group behind many bombings claimed credit for organizing the bloodbath

The restaurant is owned by Israeli Arabs and Jews. The wounded and dead included members of the Matar family, the Arab owners. Haifi is known for its harmonious relations between Jew and Israeli Arabs.

INDEX